To Love Is To Act

Victor Hugo Seated (Victor Hugo assis),
photo by Walery, 1876

To Love Is to Act

Les Misérables *and Victor Hugo's*
Vision for Leading Lives of Conscience

Marva A. Barnett

With a Foreword by
Alain Boublil and Claude-Michel Schönberg

SWAN
ISLE
PRESS

CHICAGO

MARVA A. BARNETT, professor emerita at University of Virginia, is an award-winning educator and life-long teacher of French language, literature, and culture. Marva Barnett holds a Ph.D. in Romance Languages and Literatures from Harvard University. Her other books include *Victor Hugo on Things That Matter* (Yale University Press, 2010) and, co-edited with Gérard Pouchain, a volume of letters to Victor Hugo from the woman who loved him for fifty years, Juliette Drouet: *Lettres inédites de Juliette Drouet à Victor Hugo* (Publications des Universités de Rouen et du Havre, 2012). Professor Barnett was named *Chevalier des Palmes académiques* in recognition of her contributions to Hugo studies.

Swan Isle Press, Chicago 60628
© 2020 by Swan Isle Press
All rights reserved. Published 2020.
Printed in the United States of America
First Edition

24 23 22 21 20   1 2 3 4 5

ISBN-13: 978-0-9972287-6-2 (paperback)

Swan Isle Press gratefully acknowledges that the publication of this book was made possible, in part, with generous support from the following:

THE UNIVERSITY OF VIRGINIA

THE GOLDEN MERCER CHARITABLE GIVING FUND

EUROPE BAY GIVING TRUST

AND OTHER KIND DONORS

Library of Congress Cataloging-in-Publication Data
Names: Barnett, Marva A., author.
Title: To Love Is to Act : Les Misérables and Victor Hugo's vision for
  leading lives of conscience / Marva A. Barnett.
Other titles: Misérables and Victor Hugo's vision for leading lives of
  conscience
Description: First edition. | Chicago : Swan Isle Press, [2020] | Includes
  bibliographical references. |
Identifiers: LCCN 2019057992 | ISBN 9780997228762 (paperback)
Subjects: LCSH: Hugo, Victor, 1802-1885. Misérables. | Hugo, Victor,
  1802-1885. Misérables--Film adaptations. | Hugo, Victor, 1802-1885.
  Misérables (Musical) | Love in literature. | Forgiveness in literature.
  | Conscience in literature. | Social justice in literature.
Classification: LCC PQ2287.M5 B37 2020 | DDC 843/.7--dc23
LC record available at https://lccn.loc.gov/2019057992

The paper used in this publication meets the minimum requirements of the American National Standard for Information Sciences— Permanence of Paper for Printed Library Materials

To Bob

No matter what you do, you will never destroy
that everlasting vestige of man's heart, love.

—VICTOR HUGO, *LES MISÉRABLES*

CONTENTS

List of Illustrations   *xi*

Foreword by Alain Boublil and Claude-Michel Schönberg   *xv*

Acknowledgments   *xvii*

Introduction   *xxi*

Chapter 1   Seeing Others   *1*

Chapter 2   Why Forgive?   *17*

Chapter 3   Love Is Action   *37*

Chapter 4   Seeking—and Finding—God   *59*

Chapter 5   Is Change Possible?   *81*

Chapter 6   Listening to Our Best Selves   *99*

Chapter 7   Either Valjean or Javert!   *119*

Chapter 8   Finding Strength to Carry On   *139*

Appendices

   A   Time Line of Hugo's Life, Works, French History,
and *Les Misérables* Events   *159*

   B   Titles of Hugo's Works in French and English   *173*

   C   Further Resources   *177*

Notes   *181*

Bibliography   *205*

LIST OF ILLUSTRATIONS

Victor Hugo in his Hauteville House study, by an anonymous photographer, 1859-61, Courtesy of the Maison de Victor Hugo (*cover, Chapter 4*)

Victor Hugo Seated (*Victor Hugo assis*), photo by Walery, detail, 1874, Musée Victor Hugo—Maison Vacquerie (*frontispiece*)

Alain Boublil, Photo © Daniela Beltran, Courtesy of Alain Boublil (*foreword*)

Claude-Michel Schönberg, Photo © Seamus Ryan, Courtesy of Claude-Michel Schönberg (*foreword*)

MISERIA (Latin for *Misery*), by Victor Hugo, July 10 (no year), Courtesy of the Maison de Victor Hugo

Les Misérables manuscript, Photo © Marva Barnett, Bibliothèque nationale de France

Quill pens with which Hugo wrote *Les Misérables*, Photo © Marva Barnett, Maison de Victor Hugo

Place des Vosges, Paris, Photo © Marva Barnett

Les Misérables epigraph from Hugo's manuscript, Photo © Marva Barnett, Bibliothèque nationale de France

Jean Valjean, by Gustave Brion, 1862, Courtesy of the Maison de Victor Hugo

Seine where Léopoldine died, Photo © Marva Barnett

Léopoldine and Charles Vacquerie's tombstone in Villequier, France, Photo © Marva Barnett

Jean Valjean (Hugh Jackman) accepts Bishop Myriel's candlesticks in the 2012 film production of *Les Misérables*, Courtesy of Universal Studios Licensing LLC, ©2012 Universal City Studios Productions, LLLP

Communards' wall in Père-Lachaise cemetery, Paris, Photo © Marva Barnett

Justicia (Latin for *Justice*), by Victor Hugo, 1857, Courtesy of the Maison de Victor Hugo

Hugo at one of his weekly lunches with poor children in the Hauteville House garden (detail), by Edmond Bacot, spring 1862, Courtesy of the Maison de Victor Hugo

Juju and Toto, by Victor Hugo, undated, Photo © Marva Barnett, Bibliothèque nationale de France

Marine Terrace, by Victor Hugo, May 21, 1855, Private collection

"Aimer, c'est agir" ("To love is to act") in Hugo's handwriting, May 19, 1885, Courtesy of the Maison Littéraire de Victor Hugo, Bièvres, France

Look-out at Hauteville House with view of ocean, Photo © Marva Barnett

The End of the Temporary Breakwater on Guernsey, as Seen from my Look-out (*L'extrémité du brise-lames provisoire à Guernesey, vue de mon look-out*), by Victor Hugo, January 13, 1865, Courtesy of the Maison de Victor Hugo

Jean Valjean with Petit Gervais, 1957, Film still from *Les Misérables* with Jean Gabin, Maison de Victor Hugo

Les Misérables chain drawing, Victor Hugo, undated, Photo © Marva Barnett, Bibliothèque nationale de France

The Dolmen Where the Mouth of The Shadow Spoke to Me (*Le Dolmen où m'a parlé la bouche d'ombre*), by Victor Hugo, ca. 1855, Courtesy of the Maison de Victor Hugo

Conscience before a Bad Action (*La Conscience devant une mauvaise action*), by Victor Hugo, [1866], Courtesy of the Maison de Victor Hugo

Exile (*Exil*), by Victor Hugo, 1854, Courtesy of the Maison de Victor Hugo

My Destiny (*Ma destinée*), by Victor Hugo, 1857, Courtesy of the Maison de Victor Hugo

Javert (Terence Mann) and Valjean (Colm Wilkinson) confront each other in the 1987 original Broadway production of *Les Misérables*, Photograph by Michael Le Poer Trench, © Cameron Mackintosh Ltd.

Ecce Lex (Latin for *Behold the Law*), 1854, by Victor Hugo, Courtesy of the Maison de Victor Hugo

Conciergerie prison, Paris, Photo © Marva Barnett

Gavroche Dreamer (*Gavroche rêveur*), by Victor Hugo, undated, Courtesy of the Maison de Victor Hugo

Gavroche and his brothers inside the Bastille elephant, by Gustave Brion, 1862, Courtesy of the Maison de Victor Hugo

PERGE & SURGE at Hauteville House, designed by Victor Hugo, 1859, Photo Courtesy of and © Jean Baptiste Hugo

AD AUGUSTA PER ANGUSTA at Hauteville House, designed by Victor Hugo, 1859, Photo Courtesy of and © Jean Baptiste Hugo

Marva Barnett, Photo Courtesy of and © Dan Addison (*back cover / rear flap*)

FOREWORD

When you write a musical based on Victor Hugo's masterpiece "Les Misérables," you believe you know every detail of the work you've been entrenched in for months. You're convinced that you know every character inside out, the chronology of events from every angle, as well as every major event of Victor Hugo's epic life story, which has permeated the novel.

Then we met Marva Barnett. Marva invited us to teach as artists in residence at the University of Virginia where she is Professor Emeritus. We were amazed to discover that someone, an American no less, knew even more than we thought we did about the great man. No small feat. Her vast encyclopedic knowledge extended not only to Hugo's life and work, but also to ours, inspired by his. As an eternal Hugo admirer, Marva devoted her life to analyzing and reanalyzing the why's and how's of the worldwide appeal of "Les Misérables" since 1862.

The concept of justice and the universal moral compass at the heart of the novel has been influential in every country, as "Les Misérables" has been translated into most languages for the past 157 years and counting. Marva has also deconstructed every layer of our own labors in order to explain both the universality of the book and the subsequent success of our musical.

She studied in detail every character in "Les Misérables," with each having come to epitomize a human quality or fault. We all know a Fantine, a Marius, a would-be Cosette, and we fear to meet a Thénardier or a Javert in real life. Jean Valjeans come more rarely.

After reading her new book, one could wonder whether Hugo wrote "Les Misérables" or if it was Jean Valjean and all the others who invented Victor Hugo. Over numerous discussions with Marva, as well as during our master classes at the University of Virginia, we appreciated and enjoyed her deep knowledge of French culture and her boundless passion for any form of artistic expression. For a work of art to exist you need a reader or a spectator, and Marva, in herself and in the words of this book, makes the message of "Les Misérables" fresh and new again for another generation of readers and spectators.

—Alain Boublil and Claude-Michel Schönberg

ACKNOWLEDGMENTS

One of the great pleasures of writing this book has been conversations with the friends and colleagues who contributed ideas, commented on drafts, offered support, and made connections.

I am immensely grateful to those who unfailingly encouraged me through this book's multiple iterations. My husband, Jon Guillot, cheers me on despite, as he puts it, "having seen my wife fall in love with someone who died over 130 years ago." Mary Esselman and Andrew Kaufman generously shared their writing and publishing expertise. Like them, LaVae Hoffman tirelessly listened as I explored my understanding of Hugo and his epic. With his smiling support and brilliant translation and editing skills, Robert F. Cook at once kept me enthused and improved the manuscript.

I owe an enormous debt to all the Hugo scholars whose work has informed mine, and I cannot possibly thank them all here. You will find them in the notes and bibliography and on the website of the Groupe Hugo at the Université Paris 7, which provides a rich trove of information. Still, I must express my particular gratitude to Jean-Marc Hovasse and Gérard Pouchain for their willingness to respond to my specific questions and share insights. Alain Lecompte's analysis of the power of Claude-Michel Schönberg's music enriched my interpretations.

Equally vital has been the help of dedicated museum directors and curators in Paris, Guernsey, Villequier, and Besançon. Hugo specialists all, they warmly welcomed my questions and shared their collections, including images that illustrate the book. *Milles mercis* to Gérard Audinet, Michèle Bertaux, Marie-Laurence Marco, Thomas Cazentre, Marie-Jean Mazurier, Odile Blanchette, Lise Lezennec, and Émilie Thivet.

A great joy associated with exploring *Les Misérables* has been getting to know the creators of the musical *Les Mis* and some of the artists who brought Hugo's story to life on stage and screen. I deeply appreciate Claude-Michel Schönberg, Alain Boublil, Cameron Mackintosh, Tom Hooper, Colm Wilkinson, and Hugh Jackman for their ideas and rich, ongoing conversations. A heartfelt thank you, as well, to Herbert Kretzmer, Sue Coombs, Jane Austin, Chloe Dorigan, Natasha Hannah, Roni Lubliner, and Peer Ebbighausen for their kind assistance.

Many other friends and colleagues graciously talked with me and shared their expertise in ways that helped make this book a reality. With pleasure, I offer my gratitude to Loretta Williams, Martha Woodroof, Janet Horne, R. G. Skinner, Suman Venkatesh, Jean Baptiste Hugo, Elsa Pereira, Deborah Murray, Alison Levine, Mehr Farooqi, Rob Kelly, Mary Jane Peluso, Emily Swallow, Judith Reagan, Richard Warner, Erica Arvold, Christian Greenwood, Steve Arata, John Nemec, Sherwood Frey, Claire Cronmiller, and Mary Ann Leeper.

As all teachers know, our students further our thinking and teach us more than they might realize. Discussions in my University of Virginia courses on Victor Hugo's works and the ongoing power of *Les Misérables* generated masses of new insights. I learned much from the hundreds of students who had the courage to tackle Hugo's genius with me, and I am especially grateful to these young women who also contributed research, comments on drafts, and logistical aid for Hugo-related events: Abby Deatherage, Katy Greiner, and Emily Umansky.

Writing books takes time and travel, and this project was enriched, too, by remarkable opportunities for artistic residencies, exhibitions, and talks associated with *Les Misérables*. For both financial and moral support I am indebted to these colleagues and offices at the University of Virginia: associate deans Christian McMillen and Brie Gertler of the College and Graduate School of Arts and Sciences, Vice Provost for the Arts Jody Kielbasa, former Chair of the Drama Department Colleen Kelly, the Center for International Studies, and the Office of the Vice President for Research.

I have been fortunate to have worked with two wonderfully knowledgeable, thoughtful, and generous editors, people crucial to a book's success. With honesty and clarity, my developmental editor,

Nina Ryan, patiently inspired and guided me to rediscover my personal writing voice. David Rade, my Swan Isle Press editor—who saw something in this project from its earliest glimmer in my mind—is a steadfast, astute collaborator and advocate. I cannot thank him enough for his encouragement and deep understanding of how to create books.

Clearly, *To Love Is to Act* grew from conversations of all sorts with a community of other writers, artists, students, friends, and Hugo scholars. My greatest hope is that readers will keep the conversation going.

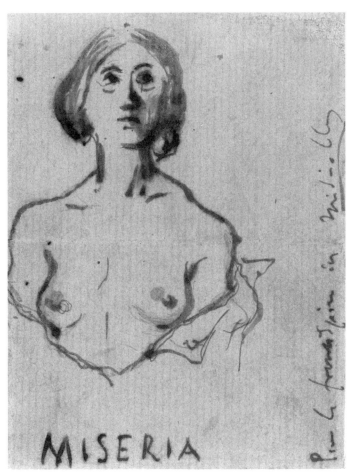

MISERIA (*Latin for* Misery). *Hugo's drawing, which he labeled as "*For the Les Misérables *frontispiece," dated July 10*

"Why would we listen to Victor Hugo today?" I asked actor and philanthropist Hugh Jackman. I'd found myself talking with Jackman as part of my search to understand the power of Hugo's *Les Misérables* and its progeny. I was delighted to find that Jackman marvels at Hugo's masterpiece as much as I do. One of the most famous novels ever written and a triumph of narrative art, *Les Misérables* speaks deeply to us both despite its daunting length. Hugo's language lifts me, and his loving characters unendingly inspire—especially his hero, the ex-convict Jean Valjean, whom Jackman played in the 2012 movie version and got to know intimately, as the insights he shared with me will show.

Victor Hugo's complete works inhabit forty-one inches of my bookshelves. In those poems, plays, novels, essays, speeches, letters, and graphic art, he aimed to create beauty but, more importantly, to prompt people to act through love and conscience to build a better world. In his epic *Les Misérables*, Hugo asks big questions about social justice and the daily decisions that define character. But he doesn't just leave us with questions. He helps us think them through alongside his iconic characters.

Hugo's experiences, excitement, and exhortations to action come through in "his" musical. And millions of people who haven't picked up the novel love his rousing story through the show widely called *Les Mis*. The artists who created that international stage and screen sensation knew Hugo's novel well and found it fascinating, so I wanted to hear from them. Hugh Jackman invested months in studying *Les Misérables* to get inside Jean Valjean's skin. Obviously appreciating Hugo's ability to convey human emotion with passion and without irony, Jackman expresses clearly how the novel's real-world dimension touched him:

> What Victor Hugo was seeing in his backyard, really, in
> his country—this *great* inequity and this *incredible* injustice
> going on—is exactly the same today, and sparking pretty
> much most of the conflicts in the world. I know some of
> them seem to be veiled in religion, but I'm sure most of
> them start with poverty. There's about a billion people on
> the planet hungry right now—all the time.

At this point, Jackman sped up and spoke with even more intensity:

> How can we carry on with our lives just because it's not
> in our backyard—even though some of it is—how can we
> just carry on? Even climate change, poverty's completely
> linked to that. So I do think that Les Misérables is
> definitely valid today. When I read it, it certainly touched
> me on a personal level, just in terms of what are you
> prepared to stand up for and what are you prepared to do?

My University of Virginia students and I ask ourselves similar questions while reading and discussing Les Misérables, and we find remarkable parallels between contemporary social issues and the ones Hugo confronted. In fact, isn't our world an even bigger challenge for people who care, for those who want to follow their conscience? With digital access and news 24/7, we're bombarded with tragedies at home and around the world. So many people in need, so many cultures battling each other, the very land we live on and water we drink in peril. How can we absorb the news of one more random shooting or terrorist attack—much less help the myriad earthquake or hurricane victims, or the single mom struggling to support her children? How can those of us who are not in the "1%" respond to today's economic inequities? It seems at times that our social systems are collapsing, and compassion fatigue can strike.

Closer to home, our private lives can be just as difficult. How can we stay focused on our jobs when someone we love is seriously ill? Even when life goes smoothly, how do we balance work and family? How much should I help others when people say that I must take care of myself first? When I see injustices around me, how can I make things better? Where do I find the resilience so highly touted for happiness and long life? We all face times when it would be easier to throw in the towel. How on earth can we get help from a French poet who died over 130 years ago?

Quite simply, Victor Hugo lived an extraordinary life, a life of broad experience, compassion, and conscience. "Live and learn" might have been Hugo's motto, as he evolved from a royalist into a liberal, moved forward after shattering family losses, and grew in spiritual understanding. His work encourages us to recognize the significance of our experiences and build on them, as he did. Despite many obstacles and setbacks—and despite his oh-so-human personal shortcomings—Hugo never considered giving up his tenacious fights for democratic ideals and social justice, for women's rights and children's education, for a united Europe and world peace. He spoke out because he cared. Practically the last words he wrote were "To love is to act" ("*Aimer, c'est agir*").

With *Les Misérables* Hugo explored what our human capacity for love can do for us, especially pointing out how love prompts conscientious living. For Hugo, love engenders hope and underpins our God-given conscience, which spurs us toward selflessness. Ultimately, through his characters' resplendent responses to misery, he shows how we, too, can grow individually *and* make the world a better place. Hugo grappled with social issues like the poet he was—by envisioning grand possibilities. Confronting some of his own flaws, he aimed in daily life to follow his conscience and put into action his love for humanity. In *To Love Is to Act*, we'll explore how crucial events in Hugo's life relate to his universal *Les Misérables* themes, beginning with his life-changing experiences just before he started his novel, and then turning to how his life and ideas can inspire us today.

Hugo couldn't have known early on how exciting and tragic his life would be, but from a young age he recognized that life can be tough. His incompatible parents mostly lived apart and formalized their separation when Victor was thirteen, in 1815. His brother Eugène, who loved their childhood friend Adèle Foucher probably as much as Victor did, had a mental breakdown on Victor and Adèle's wedding day. Eugène had to be committed to Bicêtre, a hospital also used as a prison (it was the same place from which Jean Valjean was fictitiously transported to hard labor). Only eight years later, in 1830, Victor was shocked to discover that Adèle and his best friend were in love. Throwing himself more deeply into his literary career, Victor met at rehearsal the beautiful actress Juliette Drouet, whose love sustained and sometimes distressed him for fifty years.

Working hard in order to support two households, Victor was devastated when his beloved elder daughter, Léopoldine, drowned at nineteen in a freak boating accident. He never truly stopped grieving but found temporary solace in the arms of a woman not much older than his daughter, the married Léonie d'Aunet Biard. Their affair brought them both public shame and ended only when Hugo was forced into exile. A price had been put on his head, dead or alive, because he had resisted President Louis-Napoléon Bonaparte's coup d'état in 1851. Hugo's resolute rejection of Bonaparte's rule then led next to his exile from Paris, and later from Brussels and the island of Jersey—for nineteen years altogether, the duration of the Second Empire.

Four of Hugo's children and his first grandson died before he did. The fifth, Adèle (named after her mother), lost her sense of reality after an ill-fated love affair.[1] Like her uncle Eugène, she was committed to an asylum, and the doctors told Hugo that he had better not visit her. Hugo lived through two successful revolutions (complete with barricades and blood in the streets) and through several failed insurrections. Soon after his long-delayed, triumphant return from exile, Hugo and his family faced the Prussians' siege of Paris in 1870-71 and witnessed up close its deadly famines. In old age, Hugo saw his wife, Adèle, and then Juliette die before he did—at the age of 83, a very long life in the nineteenth century.

Hugo's private trials and public stances fill *Les Misérables*. At times, Jean Valjean's emotions are Hugo's, as when Valjean's despair over losing his adored daughter to marriage echoes the author's. Broader themes from Hugo's life pervade the novel, too, ranging from a need for personal redemption in his love life, to his never-ending quest to understand God, to his unquenchable belief in human potential and optimism for the future even in the face of present tragedy. At times, Hugo puts himself literally in the novel, as when he makes clear that its narrator is indeed the author of the 1834 novella *Claude Gueux*—a real-life story about a man who had stolen a loaf of bread, just as Valjean did. Such references make the author come alive but, more importantly, show how keenly Hugo desired to connect with his readers. "My life is yours, yours is mine, you live what I live; there is only one destiny," he wrote in the preface to his autobiographical poetry collection *Les Contemplations*. "So take this mirror and see yourself in it."

Stories that bring to life human feelings, dilemmas, and challenges *do* confront us, prompting us to think about how we are living our lives. Like me, Hugh Jackman saw himself in *Les Misérables* when he read the novel before playing Valjean. And, on the film set, Jackman discovered that Hugo's human insights touched him perhaps as profoundly as the author's call to eliminate poverty. When we talked a few weeks before the movie premiered, Jackman explained how shooting the final scene had provoked questions about his own life. "I'm thinking of the lyric at the end," he began, "when Valjean's in the convent: 'Alone I wait in the shadows; I count the hours before I sleep; I dreamed a dream, Cosette stood by; it made her weep to know I die.'" Jackman had found himself wondering how *his* children might feel when he dies:

> Basically, at the end of Valjean's entire life—of everything he's given, of everything he's striven to do— at this point, the thing he loves and really cares about is Cosette. And he had to give her up because of who he was and his humility, and he's amazing to do that. But he sits there in that chapel dying and knowing he's alone, and he's not sure if Cosette even cares.
>
> As I was filming that [here Jackman gave an emotional laugh], it was near the end of being away from my family for four or five months. It was a very confronting song to sing because immediately—as a man with a twelve-year-old and a seven-year-old—I imagined: What would it be like if, in thirty years, my kids went, "Well, you know, Dad is dying, whatever. He was a good dad, whatever." That was a very confronting feeling. You never think, as a father, that it will be that way, but, hey, what if I'm away too much more? Who knows what will happen in life? . . . I haven't

told anybody else this, but the *whole* film for me felt very confronting.

In *Les Misérables*, Hugo invites us to pay attention to our personal conscience and to social ethics. If the hate-filled, dangerous ex-convict Jean Valjean can be so moved by the bishop that he dedicates himself to a life of conscience, why can't we? Valjean—and then Fantine, Éponine, Marius, Gavroche, Enjolras, and eventually Javert—grapple with complex life questions like those we all face. How can we follow our conscience when others don't and when desires tempt? If our conscience comes directly from God, as Hugo believes, how do we trust ourselves to be our own moral guides? In today's fast-paced world, how do we make time to really see other people? Can we connect to those different from us and act from a place of altruistic love? Why would we want to be forgiving? What is worth fighting for? Is it courageous or stupid to battle unjust laws? When tragedy strikes, where do we find the strength to go on? With so much poverty and misery in the world, how can we make a difference? Hugo wrestles with such big practical and spiritual questions in very human ways that make them accessible. A visionary, Hugo imagined a world where people care for each other, where their capacity for generous love leads to mercy, where everyone has a voice in society and a true chance to grow and thrive.

Les Misérables had been resonating with readers long before Hugh Jackman felt its magnetic pull. Inside and outside France, the first edition fascinated readers. "Never was a book devoured so furiously," wrote Hugo's Belgian publisher, Albert Lacroix, stunned by its worldwide success.[2] Copies flew off the shelves. The novel was released simultaneously in serial form in early April through June 1862 in Paris, Budapest, Brussels, Leipzig, London, Madrid, Milan, Naples, Rotterdam, Rio de Janeiro, St. Petersburg, and Warsaw. Hugo had driven a hard bargain for his manuscript: the dazzling sum of 300,000 francs, equal to over $1.5 million today. Yet Lacroix had made an excellent deal as well, netting over 500,000 francs

Hugo's bound final manuscript of Les Misérables

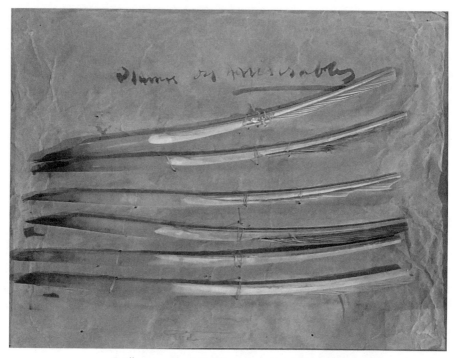

Quill pens with which Hugo wrote Les Misérables

profit.³ The first two volumes (of ten)—"Book I: Fantine"—sold out in Paris in only three days, even though Hugo had been exiled from France for over a decade. Journalist Gustave Simon recounted how people pressing against one bookstore's doors made it difficult to open them at 6:30 a.m., when the crowd dove for the 48,000 copies of Parts II and III, "Cosette" and "Marius."⁴

Managing the book's PR campaign in Paris, Hugo's wife wrote him that workers were pooling their disposable income of a few cents each to buy one copy together, read it in turn, and draw lots to see who would get to keep it. Adèle continued, addressing her husband in the third person, as she sometimes did in letters shared with the whole family:

> My great man, living at such a distance, doesn't really understand the effect of *Les Misérables*—the novel produces unparalleled emotion in people of all classes. The book is in everyone's hands; the characters have already become iconic; people talk about them all the time, at every opportunity. These characters' images appear in all the bookstores' display windows; monstrously large *Les Misérables* posters have gone up at every street corner. Victor Hugo's work and name are missiles that perturb and emotionally move Paris.⁵

Some famous French authors loved *Les Misérables*. Novelist George Sand declared it to be a work of poetic genius, and poet Arthur Rimbaud called it a "true poem." It struck a powerful chord with Russian novelist Fyodor Dostoevsky, who "devoured" it in 1862 and returned to it repeatedly over the next fifteen years. Dostoevsky saw Hugo as a prophet and a strong proponent of spiritual regeneration. Leo Tolstoy found *Les Misérables* both "powerful" and inspirational for his *War and Peace*. Decades later Tolstoy confirmed that he had been "a great admirer" of Hugo, a writer he predicted would outlive many generations.⁶ English social novelist Charles Dickens was impressed with Hugo as a person. After visiting him in his Place des Vosges home in January 1847, during the period when Hugo was drafting what would become *Les Misérables*, Dickens wrote that

Hugo looked like a "Genius, as he certainly is very interesting from head to foot." English poet, playwright, novelist, and critic Algernon Swinburne sent his positive review of *Les Misérables* to Hugo and called him "the greatest writer whom the world has seen since Shakespeare." American muckraker Upton Sinclair called *Les Misérables* "one of the half-dozen greatest novels of the world."[7]

Such a provocative novel did not find universal success, of course. Many critics' opinions differed radically from the public's. "I find neither truth nor grandeur in this book," wrote Gustave Flaubert, who had admired Hugo's poetry, but whose *Madame Bovary* differed significantly from Hugo's novels. Symbolist poet Charles Baudelaire in his youth had esteemed the poet Hugo, and he published a reasonably positive review of *Les Misérables*. In private, however, he wrote his mother that the novel was "squalid and inept." One of Hugo's most virulent critics, the novelist Barbey d'Aurevilly, praised Hugo's style but believed that Hugo planned "to bring down all social institutions, one after the other, a despicable idea, but an idea that his writing infuses with power."[8] In general, those interested in preserving the status quo feared Hugo's epic, a reaction that no doubt pleased him. *Les Misérables* triggered violent antagonism from the Catholic Church and from conservatives who supported the Second Empire. They assailed Hugo's intellectual integrity, his motives and ambitions, and his message that society carried some responsibility for human suffering. In fact, *Les Misérables* was on the Vatican's list of forbidden books from 1864 until 1959.[9]

Still, *Les Misérables* was quickly translated into most major languages.[10] When the U.S. editions went on sale, America was in the midst of its great civil war. The first translation, by journalist and Egyptologist Charles Wilbour, was published in the Union North the morning of June 7, 1862.[11] The following year, a bowdlerized translation that suppressed Hugo's antagonism toward slavery appeared in the Confederate South. A soldiers' edition of this "Richmond" or "Volunteers" translation was popular among General Robert E. Lee's troops, and they began to call themselves "Lee's miserables."[12] Around the campfire, they listened to the novel read aloud by the man deemed to have the greatest "elocutionary

Place des Vosges, where the Hugos lived from 1832 until 1848
(Hugo began Les Misérables *here in 1845)*

skill." Indeed, they sometimes renamed each other Marius, Enjolras, or Courfeyrac after Hugo's barricade defenders.[13] In the United
States, over the next 150 years, Hugo's novel went on to join other
fine French works in homes and libraries across the nation, taking
its place in American cultural history alongside his *Notre-Dame de
Paris* (retitled *The Hunchback of Notre-Dame*). And, of course, *Les
Misérables* has had a long life in popular media, inspiring since 1906
at least sixty filmmakers in nearly twenty countries as diverse as Tur-
key, Vietnam, and Lithuania, as well as dozens of animated movies,
television series, and radio broadcasts.[14]

In the early twentieth century, *Les Misérables* was much read in
societies struggling with oppression and in socialist and communist
countries, even though Hugo's work had temporarily fallen from
favor in France. French author André Malraux, who travelled and
lived around the world, found *Les Misérables* everywhere, from India
to Africa to Latin America. Talking with Indian independence leader
Jawaharlal Nehru, for example, Malraux learned in 1930 that Hugo's
novel was "one of the most celebrated books" in India.[15] In 1951, the
five-millionth copy of the 1902 Chinese translation was printed in
the People's Republic of China. More recently, the former president
of Venezuela, Hugo Chávez, attributed to *Les Misérables* his turn
toward socialism, as he recognized the reality of what Hugo por-
trayed: "You want to meet Jean Valjean?" he asked a crowd of reporters. "Go to Latin America. There are many Jean Valjeans in Latin
America. Many; I know some."[16]

Award-winning Claude-Michel Schönberg and Alain Boublil,
creators of the musical *Les Mis*, understood the characters' authen-
ticity. When I asked Schönberg why they had chosen to adapt that
particular novel for the theater, he credited Hugo's genius as a writer.
"But the most important thing is that it was a great subject for a
musical," he continued. "Because in the University of Virginia, where
you work, I am sure you know one Javert. There's Thénardiers, too,
and in the American administration, I am sure, you can give me the
name of two Thénardiers you know very well. We all know a few
Cosettes. These characters are archetypes of human society wherever you go, whether Japan, South America, North America, South

Africa, Europe." (Yes, I thought right away of a "Javert" I know.) Or, as the musical's producer Cameron Mackintosh put it, "The characters are not just good and evil. They reflect the shades of gray that make up humanity." These recognizable characters—together with Schönberg's moving music and many artists' innovative theatrical choices—have helped make the musical a huge popular success, much like Hugo's novel.

Boublil and Schönberg's original *Les Misérables* in French sold a quarter-million records as a concept album in 1980. Later that year, Robert Hossein staged it as a mix of musical theater and dramatic musical tableaux, entertaining a half-million people during its three-month run at a Parisian sports arena. Fifty thousand more were turned away when the show had to close for the next booked event.[17] Five years later, British theatergoers' demand for the show exploded after producer Cameron Mackintosh—working with Boublil, Schönberg, lyricist Herbert Kretzmer, and Royal Shakespeare Company directors Trevor Nunn and John Caird and their team— reimagined *Les Misérables* in English as a sung-through musical. Since that London opening, over seventy million people in forty-four countries have helped make what fans call *Les Mis*, or *Les Miz*, the world's longest-running musical.[18] Many patrons leave the theater inspired, sounding not unlike Hugh Jackman, who emailed me after his film's launch, "One question I am getting a lot is….does playing Valjean change you…and the answer is yes!!!!!!! It makes you want to be a better man….every day."[19]

What makes *Les Misérables*—whether the novel or the musical— so influential to so many? Seeing the story's positive impact on my students and other *Les Mis* fans, I embarked on a journey to explore Hugo's inspirational power. I dreamed of talking with the musical's creators. Mutual friends put me in touch with Hugh Jackman. He, in turn, introduced me to composer Claude-Michel Schönberg, to Alain Boublil (who had envisioned the musical and co-authored the *Les Mis* book, or libretto), and to Tom Hooper (who had directed Jackman as Valjean in his 2012 film version). Musical theater producer Cameron Mackintosh and singer/actor Colm Wilkinson (who originated the role of Valjean in London and New York and who played Bishop Myriel in Hooper's film) also generously spoke with me about how they see Hugo and his novel. Finally, British lyricist Herbert Kretzmer shared his thoughts through interviews he had previously given.

Les Mis expresses the heart of *Les Misérables* because these artists kept Hugo's novel central to their adaptations. In each conversation, whether in London or in the Colonnade Club of my own University of Virginia (UVA), I heard over and over again how they connected with Hugo's ideas in ways that parallel my affinity with the novel. "Honestly, the book has been the source, the book has been the key, the book has been everything," Alain Boublil told me during his UVA artistic residency. His colleague Claude-Michel Schönberg focused more on the author himself as we sat in his London garden, saying that he found Hugo to be "a universal mind," who had "a very modern process of thought." These two musical geniuses deeply respect Hugo's work, as does director Tom Hooper. "*Les Misérables* was my Bible when I made the film," Hooper said as we talked in a pub outside Regent's Park. "When you read the novel, well, Hugo is such a clear storyteller. Everything single thing is mapped out. I felt like this is a storyteller who wants you to follow him completely. So I wanted to honor that and use him to help me to guide the audience with the story." Like Hooper, Colm Wilkinson called the novel "my Bible," telling me that he had kept the Norman Denny translation in his dressing room: "In between shows—or even during a show—I'd just get into a page and read it, and it would bring me back to the piece again." Wilkinson found Hugo's work so potent that, as he sang Valjean's words with emotional impact, he found that he was "actually speaking the novel to a certain degree." Over twenty-five years later, Hugh Jackman similarly found the novel crucial: "Obviously, for an actor, Hugo's work is unbelievable. It's about the best bit of background preparation you can do. I read *Les Misérables* through twice, the first time very scientifically and breaking everything down and writing notes. Then I read it again before we started to film, just reading it to enjoy, really."

These artists appreciate the detail and realism of Hugo's characters and settings, but Hugo aimed to write something more: a story that would resonate around the world, as he told his Italian publisher:

> You're right, sir, when you say that *Les Misérables* is written
> for all peoples. I don't know whether it will be read by
> everyone, but it is meant for everyone. . . . The wounds of
> the human race, these large wounds that cover the globe,
> they don't stop at blue or red lines on the world's map. .
> . . Wherever men live in ignorance or despair, wherever
> women sell themselves for bread, wherever children
> lack a book to learn from or a hearth to warm them, *Les
> Misérables* knocks at the door and says, "Open up, I am
> here for you."[20]

Producer Cameron Mackintosh attributes some of the success of *Les Mis* to that very universality, as he told me: "The genius of Hugo's characters is that they exist everywhere and always. It has nothing to do with nineteenth-century France—it has everything to do with humanity." Herbert Kretzmer, who crafted the majority of the English lyrics, observed the story's broad appeal as he watched *Les Mis* performed in many languages: "*Les Misérables* audiences all over the world have responded to the musical in much the same way. I have seen people from Budapest to Boston laugh out loud or reach for their Kleenex at precisely the same moments in the plot."[21]

Beyond aiming to portray human, relatable characters, however, Hugo consciously wrote *Les Misérables* in order to help change society. The key points he laid out in the novel's famous epigraph resonate today when we see widespread poverty and hunger despite economic advances, lack of adequate schooling, and some wages so low that full-time workers struggle. Hugo's poetic summary—the novel's epigraph—invites readers from any culture to make the connection to their own situations:

As long as through the workings of laws and customs there exists a damnation-by-society which artificially creates hell in the very midst of civilization and complicates destiny, which is divine, with a man-made fate; as long as the three problems of the age are not resolved: the debasement of men through proletarianization, the moral degradation of women through hunger, and the blighting of children by keeping them in darkness; as long as in certain strata social suffocation is possible; in other words and from an even broader perspective, as long as ignorance and poverty exist in this world, books like this one cannot be useless.[22]

With *Les Misérables*, Victor Hugo steadfastly maintained his position as a committed writer, a social novelist. A century later, existentialist Jean-Paul Sartre (who would have not have agreed with Hugo on many fronts) saw him as a fellow écrivain engagé.[23] Hugo was one of the first French authors to put poverty front and center in his work, and he led the way in basing his fiction on serious research. For him, as for dozens of nineteenth-century authors, the act of witnessing, understanding, and portraying social/political forces and inequities was in itself an act of conscience, an action based on a belief in positive change. Seeing close connections between literary freedom and personal freedom—both targets of authoritarian governments—Hugo argued for free speech, even personally going to court over the censoring of his play *Le Roi s'amuse* in 1832.

In his forties, Hugo threw himself into public service and celebrated those who fought for liberty, including feminist anarchist Louise Michel and socialist Pauline Roland. In his fifties and sixties, rather than languishing through a nineteen-year exile, Hugo became a worldwide champion *for* democratically-elected governments and *against* the death penalty and slavery. Even in his seventies, he was making the case for radical clemency, the coming together of European nations, and peace throughout the world. More than his younger contemporaries such as Balzac, Flaubert, and Baudelaire—and even more than George Sand and Émile Zola—Hugo took public political and social stands and highlighted the motivating power

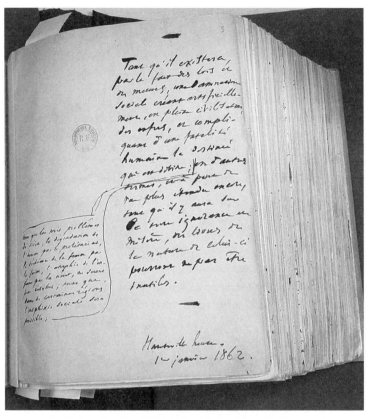

Epigraph to Les Misérables *in Hugo's handwriting,*
bound with the manuscript

of love. All his battles for a humane society are reflected in his epic *Les Misérables*.

To provide helpful background to the magnitude of Hugo's life and the scope of *Les Misérables*, I include these appendices:

Appendix A pinpoints major moments in Hugo's life and work alongside relevant historical details, together with a chronological summary of events in *Les Misérables* to help you follow the plot. (Alert: The *Les Misérables* chronology contains spoilers.)

Appendix B lists the French and English titles of Hugo's works so that you can easily find a translation of the titles I mention.

Appendix C offers further resources to help you pursue your interests in Victor Hugo's life and works.

For clarity, I refer to the novel as *Les Misérables* and to the staged musical and 2012 movie musical as *Les Mis*. Quotations from the novel and references to them are labeled by Part, Book, and Chapter: for example, "(I, 2, 12)" refers to Chapter 12 ("The Bishop at Work") in Book Two ("The Fall") of Part I ("Fantine"). For your convenience, I translate quotations from Hugo's work into English and cite his original French in the notes at the back of the book, together with other references. Translations result from collaborations with my friend and colleague Robert F. Cook. For *Les Misérables*, we worked from my current favorite translations: Christine Donougher's 2013 Penguin Books edition and Lee Fahnestock and Norman MacAfee's unabridged 1987 Signet Classics edition (which is based on Wilbour's 1862 translation). Excerpts from the musical's libretto generally come from Edward Behr's *The Complete Book of* Les Misérables, though some are edited to match the twenty-fifth anniversary edition of the musical.

Thank you for joining me in exploring *Les Misérables* with Victor Hugo and creative minds behind *Les Mis*. May you find the adventure exciting, thought-provoking, and invigorating!

Seeing Others

Jean Valjean, by Gustave Brion, 1862

*In the face of conscience, to be capable
is to be culpable.*[24]

"You know why Victor Hugo wrote the story, don't you?" said *Les Mis* composer Claude-Michel Schönberg when we met in the garden at his London home. "He saw Jean Valjean being arrested in the street." Schönberg was referring to this entry from Hugo's journal, dated February 22, 1846:

> It was a beautiful, very cold day, despite the midday sun. I
> saw coming down the rue de Tournon [in Paris] a man led
> by two soldiers. The man was blond, pale, thin, distraught;
> he was about thirty, wearing rough canvas pants; his naked,
> scraped feet in wooden clogs had bloody scraps of cloth
> wrapped around his ankles to make do as socks; his short
> peasant's smock, muddied down the back, showed that he
> regularly slept outdoors; he was hatless, with bristling hair.
> Under his arm he had a loaf of bread. People were saying
> that he had stolen the bread, and that was why they were
> taking him away.[25]

As he waited at the barracks door, Hugo watched the blond man and noticed what he was watching: a large, elegant carriage emblazoned with a ducal crown. Through its open window, they could both see a dazzlingly beautiful woman dressed in black velvet sitting on a seat upholstered in lovely buttercup-yellow damask. Laughing, she played with a charming toddler tucked up in ribbons, lace, and furs. Hugo wrote:

> This woman did not see this dreadful man, who was
> looking at her.
>   I stood there locked in thought.
>   For me, this man was no longer a man, he was the
> specter of wretchedness; he was, in full daylight, in
> sunlight, the deformed, dismal apparition of a revolution
> still plunged in shadows, but on its way. . . . Once this man

perceives that this woman exists, and the woman does not perceive that the man is there, catastrophe is inevitable.

The social catastrophe that Hugo foresaw erupted two years later to the day. The February 22-24 riots and barricades of the 1848 revolution forced King Louis-Philippe into exile and launched the Second Republic. But even if Hugo had his finger on the pulse of social unrest, why should he have noticed—or cared about—this thin, forlorn man? In the 1840s, Hugo was at the pinnacle of literary and social success. Without doubt a major French poet and the undisputed leader of the French Romantic movement at a time when writing great literature paid well, Hugo had been elected to the influential French Academy, the Académie Française. Hugo was also a viscount, a title inherited from his father, who had been a Napoleonic general. To top it off, in 1845 the king had named Hugo to the august Chamber of Peers, the upper house of the French legislature, thus confirming his elite social status. Hugo was, in fact, on his way to a Chamber meeting when he witnessed this incident.

But Hugo's upcoming meeting did not stop him from *seeing* what was in front of him.[26] Nor from *caring about* and *doing* something about any injustice he saw. For Hugo, conscience meant being aware and empathetic—and then acting for the good. An inveterate walker who loved to crisscross Paris, Hugo kept his eyes on people and happenings. His imagination turned them into characters, stories, poems. Hugo saw the one-way glass panel between this pitiful man and this privileged woman. In analyzing the scene, he put his finger on a universal reality—a highly problematic one. It can be hard for us to see the homeless, the poor, or the underprivileged as individuals. In *Les Misérables*, though, Hugo names these people: Gavroche, Éponine, Fantine, Jean Valjean. Hugo realized, moreover, how personal wretchedness can lead to social cataclysm. At the same time, he makes us care about both.

With his simple journal observation, Hugo shows us that conscience begins with seeing. And seeing should lead to caring. On that cold day, Hugo sees people's lives both as they are and as they *should be*. The desperate man, unhappily, sees, too. The wealthy woman does not even try. Each person presents a dilemma of conscience that is just as relevant to us today. If I were in this scene, I'd be one of the financially lucky ones: the woman in the carriage, most likely, parked in my car, engrossed in a National Public Radio story. What if we *are* that bystander? Are we paying attention to others' lives and caring about what we see? If not, what will open our eyes to the misery around us? Or what if we are the hungry man? Would we steal the bread? In either case, what does our conscience tell us to do?

Suppose, on the other hand, that we are just as observant as Hugo? Even without Hugo's insight and writing skill, I hope I'd be puzzling over what underlies the man's thinness and troubled demeanor. If that destitute, probably homeless man stole the bread, as everyone says, he made the wrong choice. No matter how hungry he is, he doesn't have the right to steal. But that makes me wonder: How can people who were born in poverty, or who lack education and personal connections, or who have just had a run of bad luck pull themselves back up? Can I do anything to help individuals before (even after) they've fallen so far? Or can I do something to move other people, or society, toward helping more?

That is Hugo's point in *Les Misérables*: we need to really see each other, and we must respond to what we see. Of course, Hugo does not have all the answers. Even though he understands this distraught man's plight, for instance, he cannot undo his crime, release him from the soldiers, or remake his life. What Hugo does, however, is raise our awareness of misery in the world and exhort us to do what we can. He brings *les misérables* to life in ways that encourage us to feel concern for these wretched people, even knowing that they are fictional. Caring about those characters, many readers and fans of the musical *Les Mis* are inspired to think about how they can respond to what they see around them.

How did Hugo come to write such a compelling novel? Because I knew how he had fought against poverty, prostitution, the death penalty, torturous imprisonment, slavery, and exploitative child labor (to name just a few of his social justice causes), I had, like Schön-berg, assumed that this February 1846 journal entry showed us what sparked his novel. Still, Hugo's quest in *Les Misérables*—exploring the power of conscience and love for individuals and societies—made me wonder whether the novel had grown from more than this street scene. And, given his lifelong interest in the poor and the out-cast, why did he begin composing it when he did?

Looking back at Hugo's life, I found that he started writing the novel on November 17, 1845. That was three months *before* he saw a real-life Jean Valjean arrested right in front of him, ignored by a woman who might have moved in Hugo's social circle. Clearly, that encounter, as grippingly relevant as it was, could not have prompted the novel. Did Hugo write this marathon work only because of his growing concern for the have-nots? Or did something in his life prompt a desire for personal improvement, or redemption? Hugo did, after all, call *Les Misérables* "the drama of conscience, the epic of the soul."[27]

Despite his scrupulous notes, his frequently autobiographi-cal literary writing, and his deep awareness of his own historical importance, Hugo left little explicit evidence about what prompted him to begin *Les Misérables* when he did, twenty years after he first made notes about its people and events.[28] But we do know that in the period immediately before he began this novel, two experiences made a profound mark on Hugo. The first was so tragic that it affected him forever, the other both publicly humiliating and pri-vately devastating.

On September 4, 1843, Hugo's daughter, Léopoldine, drowned in a boating accident on the Seine River. She had been, by all accounts, the most beloved of his four children, and Hugo doted on all of them. Talented, well-educated, beautiful like her mother, Léopol-dine brightened Hugo's life as "the soul of our life and our house."[29] Fondly called "Didine," she fell in love at sixteen with Charles Vac-querie. Hugo, far from ready to lose Léopoldine from the family cir-cle, dragged his feet over approving their engagement. In the end, he put on a good face for Léopoldine's wedding (on February 15, 1843) but privately called it "this distressing happiness of marrying off one's daughter."[30] He was saddened by the physical distance between them after she and Charles moved to the Vacquerie family home in tiny Villequier, a two days' stagecoach journey from Paris.

In July, Hugo visited the couple before leaving on his two-month-long annual vacation with his longtime friend, muse, and lover, Juliette Drouet (see Chapter 3 for more about Juliette). He delighted in strolling along the beach with Léopoldine on his arm. He even decided that he liked her husband well enough. Writing from Paris, Hugo expressed his tenderness for his daughter by calling her "my poor dear":

> The day we spent at Le Havre is a ray of light in my mind;
> I will never forget it as long as I live. . . . I went away sick
> at heart, and the next morning as I went by the harbor,
> I looked up at the windows where my poor dear Didine
> was sleeping. I sent you a blessing, and I called God down
> upon you from the very depths of my heart. Be happy, my
> daughter, always, and so I will be happy. In two months I
> will have you in my arms again. Until then, write to me.
> Your mother will tell you the address. Kisses, over and
> over. V.[31]

Hugo never held her in his arms again. Seven weeks later, Léopoldine drowned less than a mile from home. Instead of driving to meet with his notary in nearby Caudebec, Charles had decided to sail there with his Uncle Pierre and Pierre's ten-year-old son. Thinking the trip a bad idea despite the beautiful weather, Charles's mother urged her daughter-in-law to stay home. At the last minute, however, Léopoldine decided to go. After the meeting, they returned by boat, even though the notary had found it so unstable that he preferred to walk. Newspaper articles reported no witnesses but hypothesized that a sudden wind gust had capsized the boat (the actual cause of the accident was never determined). Everyone believed that Charles, a strong swimmer, had tried to save his wife. Later that day, officials dragging the river found the bodies of all four travelers.[32]

The bend in the Seine where Léopoldine and Charles Vacquerie drowned

*Léopoldine and Charles Vacquerie were buried in the
same grave in the Villequier cemetery.*

Tragedy enough, we would think, to lose your eldest child, barely nineteen years old, in such a pointless way. What made Léopoldine's death yet more horrific for Hugo was that he learned about it from a newspaper five days later, after the funeral even. He and Juliette were returning from Spain, traveling incognito in southwestern France, visiting historical sites, sightseeing as tourists do, and simply enjoying being together.

On September 9 they arrived midday in Rochefort, where they would catch the evening stagecoach for La Rochelle. Juliette suggested that they pass the time in the Café de l'Europe. The big room was empty, except for the woman at the counter and a young man smoking. Victor and Juliette settled at a table beneath a winding staircase and ordered a bottle of beer. Juliette opened *Le Charivari*. Victor flipped through *Le Siècle* and saw under "News in Brief" these words reported from the *Journal du Havre*: "The sinister news of a terrible event, one that will bring grief to a family dear to literary France, reached us this morning—painful news for our local population, which counts several fellow citizens among the victims."

Who the victims were, what the "terrible event" was, and how the victims died became clear only bit by bit. Victor Hugo's own name leapt out at him about a quarter way through the piece, as the father of Charles Vacquerie's wife. But not until the end would he have seen the key phrase: ". . . the net brought back the inanimate body of the unfortunate young woman, who was carried to the riverbank and laid out on a bed." Incapable of saying more than "What a horrible thing!", Victor handed Juliette the paper.[33]

We know what happened next because Victor asked Juliette to record the events for him. Her journal tells how he strode like a madman beyond the city's ramparts, tramping through the outlying districts and fields before he returned to wait, crushed, for the stagecoach. On the way to La Rochelle, Juliette wrote, Hugo's "courage and resignation" were "more poignant than the wildest grief."[34] In La Rochelle, they had to wait nearly twenty-four hours before they would make the cold, rainy overnight trip to Saumur in a coach with a broken window. And so went the agonizing three-day journey to Paris, where the couple arrived at 8:00 p.m. on September 12.

Victor went immediately to his wife and three remaining children. We can only imagine those scenes. But he tells us something of his feelings in a heartbroken letter to his wife. That letter to Adèle echoes with the same deep grief that he expressed to their great family friend, Louise Bertin, in this more detailed letter, where his sometimes confused verb tenses reveal his anguished state of mind:

September 10, 1843, from Saumur

Dear Miss Louise, I am suffering, my heart is broken; you see, it's my turn. I need to write to you. You loved her like a second mother; she loved you, too, you know.

Yesterday I had just taken a long walk in the sunlit marshes. I was tired and thirsty. I come to a village whose name, I think, is Subise [Soubise] and go into a café. They brought me a beer and a newspaper, le Siècle.

I began to read. That's how I learned that half of my life and heart was dead.

I loved that poor child more than words can say. You remember how charming she was. She was the sweetest, most gracious woman.

Oh God, what did I ever do to you? She was too happy. She had everything: beauty, wit, youth, love. Her total happiness shook me. I accepted the physical distance between us just so she would be lacking something. There always has to be a cloud. That one wasn't sufficient. God doesn't want us to have paradise on earth. He took her back. Oh, my poor angel, to think I won't see her again!

Pardon me, I am in despair as I write. But it comforts me. You are so good, you have such a fine soul, you will understand me, won't you? I love you from the bottom of my heart, and, when I am hurt, I go to you.

11

I'll be in Paris at the same time as this letter. My poor
wife and my poor children really need me.

I set all my respectful greetings at your feet.

Victor Hugo

All the best to my good Armand [Louise's brother]. May
God protect him and may he never go through what
I am going through.[35]

"Oh God, what did I ever do to you?" What a human reaction!
Why do bad things happen to good people? Isn't this somehow all
my fault? Haven't we all *felt*, at least, similar questions rise up inside
us when tragedy strikes? In anguish, Hugo is also in crisis and struggling with his conscience. He was, after all, traveling with his lover
when his daughter drowned. His world has been shaken to such a
point that, three years later, when he finally writes about Léopoldine's death (in poems published in *Les Contemplations*), he will
confess that he "cried bitterly for three days" and "wanted to break
his head on the pavement."[36] For the one time in his life, Hugo will
question God's existence. He was responsible for his daughter, he
loved her dearly, and she is gone. How can he go on without her?
How could he have been away at such a time? These are the kinds of
moments that change us, that make us see ourselves and the world
differently. Hugo had such moments—more than most.

After Léopoldine died, Hugo stopped publishing and could not
bring himself to visit her grave for about three years. He barely
involved himself with the French Academy or political discussions.
He needed a new reason to live, and Léonie d'Aunet Biard may have
helped revive his "dead" heart. Four years older than Léopoldine,
Léonie was twenty-three, and Hugo forty-one. Parallels between his
deep fatherly love for his daughter and his admiration for Léonie are
easy to draw. To both these "angels," for example, he wrote poems
seeking their prayers. In other ways, too, Hugo explicitly linked the
divine with these two young women and with others he cherished, as

Marius does in the letter in which he describes his love for Cosette as an "angelic sacred unity" (IV, 5, 4).[37]

Yet, at the same time, Victor's letters show that Léonie unleashed in him either a sensuality previously unknown or one he was now more comfortable expressing. In no other letters did he write so openly about physical pleasure: "I'm sending you the kind of kisses that will turn you all pink from head to toe," or "I was so happy in your arms today! What spiritual ecstasy there was mixed in with our pleasure! O my beloved, love is the meeting place of heaven and earth. At one point, the union of souls and the union of bodies become one single happiness, both ideal and real."[38]

Very much in love, Victor and Léonie did not consider their affair sordid. Their letters echo not only their mutual physical attraction, but also their cerebral connection, as Léonie was a young intellectual whom Victor and Adèle had met socially. A few years earlier, at nineteen, Léonie d'Aunet had been the first European woman to travel as far north as the Arctic Circle, when she had accompanied her fiancé, artist François-Auguste Biard, and a team of explorers to Spitsbergen, Norway. Her letters recounting that voyage appeared in the *Revue de Paris* and were later published as *Voyage d'une femme à Spitzberg*.[39] Here was a woman capable of deeply understanding Hugo's literary genius. It was unfortunate that she was married to Biard, with whom she'd had two children.

When did Victor and Léonie get together? We don't know. Victor sent Léonie an inscribed book in 1843, the year in which he lost Léopoldine. Or they might have met as early as 1841, when Hugo drafted these poetic lines, which seem to refer to Léonie: "I was thirty-nine when I met that woman. / A flame leapt out from her look full of shadow. / And I loved her."[40] Their love affair strikes us as mysterious because Hugo covered his literary tracks well, scattering his poems about Léonie in different collections and not publishing during his lifetime his most explicit verses (even though he actively published many of his poems to Juliette Drouet). It was a secret love, with clandestine assignations. Victor and Léonie did not date their letters, and his drawings related to her always took the form of a rebus.[41]

One early July night in 1845, Victor and Léonie were surprised in their rented room in the passage Saint-Roch by the bell's loud ringing. Unable to escape from the little second-floor room, they found themselves confronted by Léonie's husband and his hired detective. The Saint-Roch alleyway, near the center of Paris, was a few blocks from King Louis-Philippe's Tuileries Palace and about a mile and a half from Hugo's apartment in the Place Royale (today the Place des Vosges). Running alongside the Saint-Roch church, this path-like street was about twice as narrow and four times as shadowy then as it is now. The church bell's regular peals might have created a peaceful familiarity, but the insistent doorbell must have alarmed the lovers. Léonie, especially, had begun to fear for their safety a few days earlier, when Hugo's servants had unintentionally surprised them in his study. She had begged Victor to find a safer spot for their rendezvouses. She had good reason to worry: women caught *in flagrante delicto* were usually imprisoned in Saint-Lazare with prostitutes.[42]

Victor and Léonie may have believed their love pure, but the law didn't treat it that way. Adultery was a crime, despite the frequent extramarital affairs among nobles and artists typical of the times.[43] While still legally married, for instance, female novelist George Sand had public liaisons with such luminaries as poet Alfred de Musset and composer Frédéric Chopin. Hugo found the laws on adultery "absurd." For one thing, they favored the man over the woman. Proven cases of adultery led inevitably to the wife's imprisonment. The man caught *in flagrante delicto* would be found guilty only if the husband filed a specific complaint, which Biard did. Even so, Hugo was protected as a Peer of France and a friend of King Louis-Philippe. If charged, he would have been judged by the other 200+ Peers, an immense embarrassment, yet nothing like going to prison. In the end, Hugo escaped an official charge of adultery, apparently because the king persuaded Biard to withdraw his complaint.

Although Hugo was spared a trial, the Paris newshounds had a field day joking about this famed poet Peer caught in an adulterous liaison. But the worst for him was not being able to save Léonie, despite his connections and fame. On August 14, Biard's request to end the marriage was approved. Much worse, after a week-long trial, the woman Hugo adored was found guilty and sentenced to three months' incarceration in the Dames de Saint-Michel convent, one of the most severe establishments for prostitutes and adulteresses. Hugo did all that he could to get her released or, at least, her sentence reduced. Eventually, his and his friends' numerous interventions gained her transfer to a less inhumane convent and perhaps shortened her sentence. When she was released in early November, Léonie and Victor renewed their liaison until Hugo went into exile in late 1851.

After Léonie's trial, Hugo heeded the king's advice to stay out of the public eye for a while. He traveled a bit around France, apparently visiting some sites that would appear in *Les Misérables*. And, in his writing journal for *Les Misères* (the novel's early title), Hugo explicitly connected the dots between the summer 1845 events and *Les Misérables*. Although he scratched through this comment, aiming to obliterate it, scholars deciphered his fear that his public shame would be revived: "Abuse that I foresee after the publication of *Les Misères*: the author could have shown us the Wretchedness (*Misère* [Hugo's capitalization]) of a Peer of France and a woman caught in adulterous *flagrante delicto*."[44] Two and a half years after his calamitous exploit Hugo still felt its antagonistic fallout.

Victor Hugo's great skill at seeing others' lives was matched by his openness to understanding and feeling for others. And I believe that his observations and receptivity improved his ability to see—to recognize—the implications of his own experiences. Hugo's misery over Léopoldine's death was exacerbated by his and Léonie's public humiliation. Each event, in different ways, provoked crises for him and rocked his sense of self. Each made him delve into his conscience. Hugo's sensitivity to people's misery was very personal, as it must be for anyone who loses a child, for anyone who sees a lover suffer. Similarly, his motivations for writing *Les Misérables* were obviously humanitarian, but they may also have been very personal.

Why Forgive?

Jean Valjean (played by Hugh Jackman) accepts Bishop Myriel's candlesticks in Tom Hooper's 2012 film Les Misérables.
*Courtesy of Universal Studios Licensing LLC,
©2012 Universal City Studios Productions, LLLP*

I dream of equity, of profound truth,
Of love that wills, hope that glows, faith that builds,
And the people's enlightenment, not punishment.
I dream of kindness, goodness, pity,
And vast forgiveness. Hence my solitude.[45]

We all need compassion and new beginnings. Daily, we forgive each other for small unkindnesses or omissions, easing personal interactions and making life more pleasant. I'm impressed by a friend who regularly gives people the benefit of the doubt. When someone misses a meeting, for instance, she imagines that something urgent must have come up, instead of assuming forgetfulness or laziness. Her generous reaction feels like forgiveness in advance. But what about intentional cruelty? Why should we forgive that? How do the parents of children killed in school shootings or the families of people shot while worshipping at church forgive the murderers?[46] Some do, but being broadly beneficent is tough for most of us. The larger the hurt, of course, the harder it is to forgive.

Les Misérables tells us a lot about forgiveness, as does Hugo's life. He believed that forgiveness had the power to save both individuals and nations, and he dedicated himself to grand-scale amnesty, such as clemency for insurrectionists and condemned criminals. He sought compassion for political dissidents whether or not he agreed with their goals, as when he publicly offered refuge to the rebels involved with the failed Paris Commune. For those Communards, as we'll see later, Hugo prioritized generosity over his own well-being and once over even his family's safety. In that way, he resembled Bishop Myriel, who opened his door to a threatening ex-convict, and like Jean Valjean, who risked his security and freedom—his life, actually—when he forgave Inspector Javert.

On an individual level, the Jean-Valjean level, Hugo knew that forgiveness can free us and open new pathways in life. In fact, it frees both the forgiver and the forgiven. Today's psychology teaches us that people who pardon others release resentment and desire for vengeance.[47] Those absolved can move forward, relieved of guilt or the need for secrecy. When Bishop Myriel forgives Jean Valjean for stealing his silver—and stunningly hands him his candlesticks, too—he ultimately cures Valjean of the hatred engendered by his long, brutal prison sentence. That moment in the story *always* makes me wonder about—fear for, really—today's ex-offenders. How often do people released from American prisons have a fair chance of getting a job they're qualified for? Will landlords rent them apartments? Will they have the right to vote? Having "paid for their crimes," aren't they commonly still suspected when a new crime occurs? To what extent are we as a society capable of forgiveness? And doesn't that capacity begin with each of us as individuals? How willingly would I—or you—hire someone who's served his time?

When Bishop Myriel forgives the ex-convict, he liberates Valjean beyond physical freedom. He launches his guest on a journey that Valjean never intended: an odyssey toward his conscience, toward a better life, toward God. Just as Valjean's quest drives the entire novel, despite its many apparent digressions, his unselfish love for others and aspiration to follow his conscience draw me over and over again into *Les Misérables*. When he has at his mercy Inspector Javert, who has relentlessly tried for seventeen years to put him back into prison chains, how can Valjean so freely release him? Doesn't he hate Javert as much as the mother or father of a murdered daughter might hate her killer? How can some victims' families forgive, while others hate or desire retribution? Is forgiving really a better place to be, and, if so, how can we get there? What can we learn about ourselves from Bishop Myriel's and Jean Valjean's inordinate capacity for forgiving others and sacrificing their own desires and needs?

Hugo puts us in the shoes of the shabby, sweaty, unnamed man who arrives in the mountain village of Digne wearing tattered clothes, with bristling hair and a long beard. This man's yellow passport—his convict release statement, which he must always show officials—reveals that he has spent years in prison not only by its color but also with the words "highly dangerous." For good reason, Valjean frightens the townspeople, even though we, at our distance as readers (and with Hugo's help), can see how pitiable he is as he searches for shelter.

The news of this man's ex-convict status sweeps through the village like a brush fire. The more innkeepers and homeowners turn him away, the more angry, frustrated, and terrible he becomes. It's easy to understand his resentment. Valjean has quickly figured out that he is not really free, an irony that the *Les Mis* musical captures in the haunting soliloquy he sings after his release. The sweet line "Freedom is mine" is soon followed by his agonized realization: "And now I know how freedom feels, / The jailer always at your heels, / It is the law!" Valjean's past follows him everywhere. His chain-gang experiences and society's label have taught him to be violent. He does not seem like a man who could ever change. At this point in the story, Valjean is "weighted down by the past . . . emotionally at sea," as Hugh Jackman described him to me.

Jackman connected personally with Valjean's fear. "I have to admit, when I filmed this movie, it was very difficult. . . . No film has touched me more in terms of fear, elemental fear, because everything was required of me. Vocally, it's a very difficult role." On top of that, Jackman said, it was the first time he'd been apart from his family for so long: "It felt like the only project I could imagine justifying being away for, because this film had an opportunity to really resonate and teach people some things." Still, Jackman considered quitting: "I rang my wife, and she said, 'Hugh, if you didn't feel that way about this role, then you're the wrong person for this part. Because it should scare you. Because if you're not prepared to give *absolutely* everything to this, you're not going to be able to pull off Jean Valjean.'" Jackman agreed, telling me, "Valjean is a man at his bottom, at the worst time of his life, at his rawest. Acting-wise, I knew that to play Valjean, I needed to lay myself open, that I needed to be able to, in the right time, on the day, in the close-up, whatever it is, to be able to be completely raw."

Jackman captures how much prison has beaten down the man who had been a simple peasant tree pruner until an especially hard winter kept him unemployed. Desperate, he impulsively broke a window to steal a loaf of bread for his seven starving nieces and nephews. Sentenced to five years in the Toulon penal colony, Valjean attempted to escape each time his turn came up—"as impetuously as a wolf who finds the cage door open" (I, 2, 7)—and racked up an additional fourteen years in chains. Those years were dreadful, as Jackman learned in prepping for his role, finding that harsh nineteenth-century prisons released each man as an "animal, to serve as a living deterrent to others."[48] First prison, and then society, stole Valjean's humanity, as Hugo explains: "When he left prison, he had not shed a tear for nineteen years" (I, 2, 7).

"What had happened within this soul?" (I, 2, 6) To answer his question, Hugo flashes back to prison, where Valjean probed his conscience and analyzed both his crime and the punishment (I, 2, 7). After conscientiously examining his soul, Valjean decided that it would have been better for the children if he had tried other avenues, and that it was no good "getting out of misery by entering into infamy." But after concluding that he had done wrong, Valjean evaluated society's role—both the failure of his rigorous efforts to survive through honest labor and the severity of the punishment—and found society guilty, too. The penalty he was paying was "an outrage committed by the stronger against the weaker, a crime of society against the individual" (I, 2, 7). Valjean swore eternal hatred toward that society and condemned God, too, for having created it. Hugo makes clear his position as author: "In our civilization, there are dreadful moments: when criminal law wrecks a man. What a dismal moment, when society withdraws and irreparably abandons a sentient being!" (I, 2, 6) Jean Valjean at this point in his life is hardly inclined to forgive anyone.

Society's disgust at convicts and disdain for them leap out again at Jean Valjean—and at us—many years after his release. When Valjean and his adopted daughter, Cosette, happen on a wagonload of prisoners being transferred to Toulon, the scene takes him back thirty-five years, to when he had been one of those chained convicts (IV, 3, 8). We realize that Valjean's chain-gang experiences irretrievably traumatized him. Seeing the men exposed to the weather and to bystanders' jeers revives the galley's terrors and the anguish caused by people's repugnance. Despite Valjean's decades of freedom and respectability, he is still "24601." Hugh Jackman told me that what stuck with him in reading the novel was "how scared and repulsed Cosette was by the sight of the chain-gang prisoners" and "the huge conflict of emotions" that the prisoner transport and her reaction to it stir in Valjean.[49]

The teenaged Cosette trembles as she asks her father whether these creatures are still men. "Sometimes," answers Valjean, so distressed that he is once more *"le misérable"* in spirit, seeing himself in these men so dehumanized that Cosette had thought they were *things*:

> They had something behind them that clanked, a chain,
> and at their necks something that gleamed, an iron collar.
> Each had his own collar, but the chain was for all; so
> that these twenty-four men, if they should happen to get
> down from the dray and walk, would be subject to a sort
> of inexorable unity, and have to snake across the ground
> with the chain for a backbone, rather like centipedes. In the
> front and rear of each wagon stood two men armed with
> muskets, each with an end of the chain under his foot. The
> collars were square (IV, 3, 8).

Given people's unfailingly negative reaction to the idea of an ex-convict, it is no surprise that Valjean disdains himself, or that Hugo once called Jean Valjean "a sort of Job of the modern world."[50]

Victor Hugo was not exaggerating when depicting Valjean. He had personally investigated prison and chain gangs. Appalled by the public executions he had witnessed in childhood, Hugo in his early twenties began examining the social causes of criminality and started fighting against what he saw as state-sanctioned murder. Hugo delved into crime statistics, such as ones he provides in *Les Misérables*: "In London starvation is the immediate cause of four out of five thefts" (I, 2, 6). After studying criminals' motivations, he based his novella *Claude Gueux* (1834) on a real man whose life paralleled Jean Valjean's. Admiring the work of early prison reformers such as Cesare Beccaria (who fought the death penalty and called education the greatest weapon against crime), Hugo visited the Bicêtre prison on the southern edge of Paris when he was twenty-five, in 1827. There he witnessed men being chained together to be driven on those open wagons to Toulon, twenty-five days away, on the Mediterranean coast.

A dozen years later, on October 1, 1839, Hugo visited that Toulon penal colony while traveling with Juliette Drouet. He insisted on seeing the dungeon and didn't shrink from walking among the convicts, offering money, and entering the smithy where they forged "their own chains," as Hugo remarked. His trip journal is rich with ideas that he wove into *Les Misérables*, including his first note of his hero's original name: "Jean Tréjean."[51] Hugo's description of a convict he saw in Toulon reminds me of Valjean (although *his* hair turned white only later): "Old convict, with white hair, seated on one of the milestones, his big chain beside him. Pensive and weary." Hugo found the convicts to be "respectful, but menacing—somber," and he detailed "a staggering regimen of punishments." Prison and the criminal "justice" system labeled Jean Valjean forever a dangerous ex-convict, and most people bought into the stereotype. M. Myriel, the welcoming Monseigneur, has the rare courage and openness to look beyond the labels and to call Valjean "my brother" (I, 2, 3).

The heart and soul that the bishop is trying to cultivate are indeed embittered. In the midst of detailing prison's soul-destroying torments and Valjean's miserable state of mind, Hugo, in one of his most riveting philosophical moments, asks a key question: Are some individuals beyond forgiveness because their crimes are so heinous—or can *any* human being be forgiven? Can Valjean forgive the system for what it did to him? Can others forgive Valjean for wrongs he did to society? The question of whether forgiveness is possible lies at the core of Jean Valjean's past and future. Hugo, as narrator, sounds optimistic: "Is there not in every human soul— was there not in Jean Valjean's soul in particular—an original spark, a divine element, incorruptible in this world and immortal in the next, which goodness can nurture, stoke, kindle, and fan into a glorious blaze of brilliance, and which evil can never wholly extinguish?" (I, 2, 7)

A naïve hope, some might think, but the bishop would have answered with a resounding, "Yes!" We, however, who have seen inside Valjean's mind, are not sure *what* to think. Reading on, we decide that we were right to hesitate. Nothing good comes of Valjean's waking up to the cathedral bells chiming at 2:00 a.m. (I, 2, 10) The gratitude he had expressed while dining with the bishop and his family has evaporated, overlaid by his sense of injustice and anger. If he has a conscience, it's too weak to compete. The sense of decency that the bishop's welcome seemed to revive in Valjean is not enough to stop him from stealing silver worth double what he'd earned in nineteen years.

Yet radical mercy can have a powerful impact, as the bishop understands. When three gendarmes bring the thief back, the bishop's warm greeting to Valjean telegraphs his great love of humanity and his capacity to forgive: "Ah, there you are! I'm glad to see you. But I gave you the candlesticks, too, which are silver like the rest and would bring two hundred francs. Why didn't you take them along with your cutlery?" (I, 2, 12) Valjean has done nothing to deserve the bishop's forgiveness, and he knows it. So the bishop's forgiveness is more like grace, the "unmerited divine assistance given humans for their regeneration or sanctification."[52] The man who played Bishop Myriel in the 2012 *Les Mis* film (and who originated the role of Valjean in 1985), Colm Wilkinson, told me how much the bishop moves him: "I have *never* seen any description of a more *perfect* person in my life than this man. He was totally, unbelievably generous and so aware of the underdog, like Hugo was. . . . I've never seen a description of a more holy and honorable and saintly person. That was one of the reasons I wanted to play him."

The bishop is definitely "at work," as the chapter title tells us. But Valjean is so bitter that forgiveness flummoxes him. Trembling, distracted, bewildered, about to faint—Valjean is literally stunned by the bishop's gift and final words:

"Do not forget, ever, that you have promised me to use
this silver to become an honest man. . . . Jean Valjean, my
brother, you no longer belong to evil, but to good. It is
your soul I am ransoming for you. I withdraw it from dark
thoughts and from the spirit of perdition, and I give it to
God!" (I, 2, 12)

The bishop clearly states that he is saving Valjean's soul *for Valjean
himself*—not "from" Valjean or "for God." He is offering Valjean the
chance to save himself from spiritual ruin and become a better man.
Valjean can—he must—take responsibility for shepherding his own
soul. In forgiving Valjean, Bishop Myriel encourages this hate-filled
man to move his life toward God. And since the bishop focuses
more on love and goodness than on religious dogma (see Chapter
4), his counsel makes sense not only to the religiously faithful but
also to people who, like me, consider decency to be simply part of
our humanity.

The original musical alters Hugo's concept into a singularly Christian one by having the bishop refer to Jesus Christ's death and res-
urrection:

But remember this, my brother:
See in this some higher plan.
You must use this precious silver
To become an honest man.
By the witness of the martyrs,
By the Passion and the Blood,
God has raised you out of darkness,
I have bought your soul for God!

In his film, however, Tom Hooper deliberately made an important
lyric change: he had the bishop conclude, "I have *saved* your soul for
God." When I asked him about that decision, Hooper explained
it this way: "I got rid of the word 'bought' and changed it to 'saved'
because that felt right. The language of dealing with the devil, of buying someone's soul, the *transactional* language felt wrong." Switching
that one word brings the musical closer to Hugo's understanding,

conveying his emphasis on the soul's salvation. Some of us today don't talk much about our "soul," but isn't it closely connected to our conscience?

Victor Hugo could promote this strong message of forgiveness because he valued and practiced mercy in times that were at least as stressful as ours. The monarchies and empires that ruled nineteenth-century France each grew increasingly authoritarian until they were rocked (and sometimes changed) by frequent insurrections and revolutions, especially in Paris, where Hugo lived. He, his family, and colleagues of a similarly democratic bent followed their consciences into exile in the 1850s, after President Bonaparte's coup d'état. Even while in exile, Hugo's worked tirelessly for amnesty, which is of course forgiveness at a national level. Believing that the state does not have the right to take anyone's life, he urged foreign governments to grant clemency. For example, he exhorted the United States not to execute abolitionist John Brown and his co-conspirators for their deadly 1859 Harper's Ferry raid. Then, despite his distaste for the former dictator's politics, Hugo pressed Mexican President Juarez to commute the death sentence of vanquished Emperor Maximilian.[53] In both cases, his letters arrived too late, after the executions. (For more on Hugo's fight against the death penalty, see Chapter 7.)

Hugo invested himself more personally when he defended the insurrectionist leaders of the Paris Commune in May 1871, even though he didn't like how they had gone about promoting change. Like Hugo, the Communards wanted to eliminate human exploitation, separate church and state, increase women's rights, and secularize education. But their violent actions appalled him. Still, he offered them asylum in his home—a moral stance that provoked some people to throw rocks through his windows and try to drag him from his house, shouting, "Victor Hugo! Let's string him up!" It was not the first time that he put his life on the line for his principles. How did the situation become so grave? Why was forgiveness on a national scale so important to Hugo?

To appreciate how far Hugo climbed out on a limb, we need to know a bit about the Commune, which ruled Paris from mid-March to mid-May, 1871, a time that Karl Marx called "The Civil War in France."[54] The men and women who became the Paris Commune were of varied political stripes, including republicans, socialists, communists, anarchists. Seeking sweeping governmental change, they operated in defiance of the National Assembly, which had been elected after France's armistice with Prussia. During this brief but devastating war, Prussia had besieged Paris. Mid-September 1870 through late January 1871 was a nightmarish time when Parisians—including Hugo and his family—were reduced to eating rats, cats, dogs, and zoo animals. Blockades of wood and coal made the nights dark and cold. Commune members were angry that the Assembly had signed the armistice and were antagonistic to the body's essentially conservative make-up.

The Communards had, however, gone beyond simply holding anti-government political views. They had tried to depose the National Assembly (which had moved to Versailles), toppled the Vendôme Column, and fomented violent revolution.[55] Yet crimes were committed on both sides. For example, after the Commune executed 64 hostages, the government's troops responded by shooting 6,000 Communards. The final fighting between the Communards and National Assembly troops—the "Bloody Week"—claimed over 50,000 lives between May 21 and 28. On the last day, the army marched 147 captured Communards into Père-Lachaise cemetery and mowed them down at the eastern wall commemorated today as "le Mur des Fédérés."[56]

Hugo watched the conflict's closing days from Brussels, where he had gone to settle his son's estate after Charles died of apoplexy. With Hugo were his daughter-in-law, Alice, and his beloved grandchildren: two-and-a-half-year-old Georges and Jeanne, only twenty months old. When the official government gained the upper hand and began executing Communards, Hugo was disgusted that Belgium closed her borders to the fleeing insurrectionists. He could not help but be reminded of how President Bonaparte's forces had pursued *him* in December 1851 for his political views.

*The Communards' Wall ("Mur des Fédérés") in Père-Lachaise cemetery,
with flowers commemorating the massacre*

In a letter to the Brussels newspaper *L'Indépendance belge* published on May 26, Hugo openly opposed the insurrectionists' actions, even as he argued that they deserved clemency: "Their acts of violence filled me with indignation, just as acts of violence on the part of the opposing party would today fill me with indignation."[57] Despite his outrage, Hugo wanted the Communards to have their day in court. Moreover, in the peremptory executions of insurrectionists he saw the eternal struggle between what's moral and what's legal, the conflict he had brought to life through Jean Valjean and Inspector Javert (see Chapter 7).

"Let's wait before judging," Hugo continued in his letter. "In the first place, for civilized people, the death penalty is abominable; and in the second, execution without a trial is despicable. . . . If you kill without judging, you are a murderer." He offered the Communards asylum at his home: 4, rue de la Barricade (an aptly named street). He added, "If they come to my home to arrest a fugitive from the Commune, they'll arrest me, too. . . . And, in the defense of what's right, they'll see next to the man of the Commune, who is vanquished by the Versailles Assembly, the man of the Republic, who was exiled by Bonaparte. I will do my duty. Principles before all else. . . . In any case, I'll have my conscience."

Hugo was willing to sacrifice himself for the cause of justice, but he did not realize to what extent this public gesture risked his family's safety. Writing to *L'Indépendance belge* a few days later, his son François-Victor described what had happened at the Hugos' Brussels apartment the night after Hugo's open letter was published.[58] About a quarter after midnight that Saturday, Hugo had just put out his light and gotten into bed when the doorbell rang. Then the bell pealed again, longer and louder. Opening his second-floor window overlooking the central square, Hugo asked, "Who's there?" A voice responded, "Dombrowski," naming the Polish left-wing independence activist and military commander Jaroslav Dombrowski, who had been killed on the barricades on May 23. Remembering his letter, Hugo thought that Dombrowski might have escaped and be seeking asylum. But before he could get to the front door, a rock hit the outside wall beside his window.

Beginning to suspect what was going on, Hugo stuck his head out, saw about fifty men gathered in front of his house, and shouted, "You're a bunch of scoundrels!" (*"Vous êtes des misérables!"*) A moment after he shut the window, a chunk of paving stone flew through it about a inch above his head, showering the room with shards of glass, which by some "strange chance" (as François-Victor wrote) did not injure him. The crowd then began yelling, "Death to Victor Hugo! Down with Jean Valjean! Down with the crook!" Despite the obviously personal nature of the attack, Hugo was still not particularly worried. He was, after all, in the civilized capital of a law-abiding country. A patrol should pass by at any moment and break up the crowd. He couldn't have known that the police were tied up with a big arrest. Only later did he learn that the Belgian Interior Minister's son had orchestrated the attack.[59]

"This violent explosion" of the breaking window woke the rest of the household, but Hugo remained certain that police would disperse what had become a lynch mob. All the family, including the nanny, Mariette, went into the nursery next door, at the rear of the building. Mariette, curious, returned to look out the window, which prompted the men to hurl a third stone at her, shattering another window and tearing down the drapes. Then rocks rained on the front wall, and the family heard, "Let's break down the door!" Mariette ran down to lock the door, which, like Bishop Myriel's, had been loosely fastened with the latch. Several times the volleys stopped for as long as a quarter hour, prompting Hugo to think that the gang had given up, or that the police had finally arrived. Little Jeanne, ill, had awoken crying, and Hugo took her in his arms to reassure her. When the silence had lasted for ten minutes or so, he believed it safe to return to his room. But as soon as he entered, carrying his granddaughter, a very sharp stone crashed into the room, flying close to Jeanne's head.

François-Victor tells us that the assault lasted about two hours, starting and stopping without warning. With no way to escape (the only exit was the front door), the family was finally saved by daylight, which apparently prompted the assailants to leave. They had not been able to break through the shutters and iron bars protecting the ground floor. (Later it was reported that two policemen had

stopped men carrying toward Hugo's home a beam large enough
to ram that door open.) Hugo's courage in the face of this menacing mob is remarkable, although we might fault him for excessive
optimism. We might wonder what on earth he was thinking when
he brought Jeanne back into his room? But he would certainly have
wanted to comfort her and had reason to think that the attackers
had left. He saw them for "misérables," the type of blackguards who
would threaten to harm a man past his prime (Hugo was then 69)
and his family. In standing up to them, Hugo followed his conscience,
as he had promised in his letter to do. There's no denying that in May
1871 Hugo put his life on the line for his beliefs, as he had done
before: this time for the sake of forgiveness in the form of clemency.

As if this incident were not enough, Hugo found himself expelled
from Belgium two days later for having "insulted the country" with
his offer. Ever resolute, he continued to seek amnesty for the Communards until it was approved nearly a decade later in the French
Senate. In valuing mercy over the vengeance that so many desire,
Hugo felt himself something of a rebel, an outlier, as he wrote in the
"Fraternité" lines that open this chapter. Yet, over time, Hugo has not
been alone.

Hugo's insight into the power of absolution reflects the vision
that prompted the first Truth and Reconciliation Commission, in
South Africa under President Nelson Mandela, and underpinned its
success. He would have agreed with that Commission's chair, Nobel
Laureate Archbishop Desmond Tutu, who knew how forgiveness
opens the way to new beginnings: "Retribution leads to a cycle of
reprisal, leading to counter-reprisal in an inexorable movement, as in
Rwanda, Northern Ireland, and in the former Yugoslavia. The only
thing that can break that cycle, making possible a new beginning, is
forgiveness. Without forgiveness there is no future."

Archbishop Tutu expanded the meaning of "justice" when he
explained why South Africa had rejected the models of both the
Nuremburg Trials post-World War II and the blanket amnesty of
General Pinochet's Chile:

Our country chose a middle way of individual amnesty
for truth. Some would say, what about justice? And we say
retributive justice is not the only kind of justice. There is
also restorative justice, because we believe in Ubuntu—the
essence of being human, that idea that we are all caught up
in a delicate network of interdependence. We say, "A person
is a person through other persons." I need you in order to
be me and you need me in order to be you.[60]

Parallels between Archbishop Tutu's perspective and Hugo's are
striking. In his May 1876 Senate speech for amnesty, Hugo recognized people's interdependence, *and* he contended that clemency is a
higher level of justice—not the sort of legalistic justice that the term
sometimes implies and that Hugo found to be too often inhumane:

Clemency is none other than justice, rendered more just.
Justice sees only the offense; clemency sees the offender.
With justice, the offense appears in a sort of inexorable
isolation; with clemency, the offender appears surrounded
by innocents. He has a father, mother, wife, children,
all of whom are condemned with him and suffer his
punishment. He is imprisoned in a labor camp or in
exile; they are in poverty. Did they merit punishment?
No. Do they undergo it? Yes. So clemency finds justice
unjust. Clemency intervenes and offers mercy. Mercy is
the sublime correction that justice from above bestows on
justice from below.[61]

In Hugo's link between mercy and "justice from above," it is easy
to see an allusion to God's grace and a recommendation that forgiveness be as freely offered as grace is freely given. That freedom passes
to the person pardoned. Past wrongs can be a prison, Archbishop
Tutu believed: "Having looked the beast of the past in the eye, having asked and received forgiveness and having made amends, let us
shut the door on the past, not in order to forget it, but in order not
to allow it to imprison us."[62] Through Bishop Myriel's leniency, Jean
Valjean escapes from the prison of hate that had captured his mind.

*Justicia, Hugo's depiction of an inhumane "justice," 1857,
which he inscribed with an ironic, bloodred "JVSTICIA"
on the paving stones in front of the guillotine*

✦

Near the end of *Les Misérables*, I am astonished by Jean Valjean's forgiveness of Inspector Javert, just as Colm Wilkinson was by Bishop Myriel's goodness. Yes, these are fictional creations, and Hugo as author can make Valjean do anything. But, like all great authors, Hugo breathes recognizable humanity into his characters, vibrantly showing what Jean Valjean has to lose and how hard it is to forgive Javert. As readers, we can empathize with Valjean's challenges and be inspired by *his* choices in order to grapple with *our* hard real-life decisions. Like Desmond Tutu and Victor Hugo, Jean Valjean refuses to seek retribution when he releases Inspector Javert at the barricade, implicitly forgiving Javert for his implacable pursuit. In doing so, Valjean personifies the "ruthless forgiveness" that Hugo advocated politically and personally.[63] Even more, in doing so, Valjean risks his life as willingly as Hugo did on that May night in Brussels. He knows that Javert will never rest until he's back in prison, and that he himself would not survive a return to the penal colony.

Hugo highlights Valjean's mercy by holding us in suspense: Is this one of those moments when the hero's human flaws will win out? By this point in the novel, we've often seen Valjean struggle to make the right decision. So we, along with the inspector, might be surprised that Valjean foregoes the perfect chance to rid himself of this eternal threat. But Valjean so highly values Bishop Myriel's compassionate, redemptive forgiveness that he feels no need to explain, saying to Javert simply, "You are free." When Hugh Jackman told me how he'd come to understand and play this scene, his analysis brought me deeper insights, reminding me of how love and mercy interconnect:

> So I played that moment when I let him go by actually *loving* Javert, by seeing the humanity in him. The music is so beautiful at that point. Valjean says [Jackman sang the lyrics], "You are wrong, and always have been wrong. I'm a man, no worse than any man. You are free, and there are no conditions, no bargains or petitions. There's nothing that I

blame you for. You've done your duty, nothing more." That's all Valjean says, and I believe he really meant that. And there he frees that ghost of Javert.

In articulating the power of loving others, Jackman echoes both Archbishop Tutu's reference to Ubuntu—"that we are all caught up in a delicate network of interdependence"—and Hugo's conception of love, which we'll explore in the next chapter.

For Victor Hugo, the rewards of forgiveness are inner freedom and the chance to move forward. He reminds us that peace comes from forgiveness, as the successes of South Africa's Truth and Reconciliation Commission demonstrate. He compellingly argues that people who seem beyond forgiveness still deserve mercy, and that mercy can help them reach redemption. In *Les Misérables*, we see how difficult it can be to forgive—and to accept forgiveness. And we see how such actions release both the giver and the receiver. Yes, Hugo declares, we can draw upon our ability to love and our conscience to find good reasons to forgive, and forgiveness benefits us all.

CHAPTER 3

Love Is Action

*Victor Hugo (second from left, at rear) at one of his weekly lunches
with poor children at Hauteville House, meals that his family
began offering the spring* Les Misérables *was published*

To love is to act.[64]

"To love another person is to see the face of God." This *Les Mis* line from Jean Valjean's deathbed speech was memorably crafted *not* by Victor Hugo, as many people believe, but by lyricist Herbert Kretzmer. Still, these words do capture Hugo's sense that love and God are identical. God, Hugo tells us, is behind every sort of love: familial, romantic, altruistic. And although for some people this famous lyric seems to suggest romantic love, selfless love is what really pervades *Les Misérables*.

Les Mis creator Alain Boublil highlighted such benevolence and charity with his original words for the show's finale: "Whoever loves his fellow man is closer to God on earth."[65] Such a sentiment is true, however, only when that love translates to conscientious choices and deeds, Victor Hugo might have said. For Hugo, love demanded positive action on behalf of the beloved—from his faithfulness to the women he loved, to his generosity toward those in need, to his work for democratic movements because he broadly loved humanity. Such magnanimous love flies in the face of self-interest, for it prompts us to give to others with little regard for ourselves.

Hugo's detractors routinely taunted him for being naïve, for pressing for what they thought was an impossibly greathearted society. Yet I applaud his optimism and belief in human potential. Without a vision of a better future, how can we possibly get there? Of course, Hugo's and my hope contradicts today's sometimes frequent emphasis on self-interest over empathy or community connection. I've felt pushed to prioritize myself, and you likely have, too. Need to find a new job? "You should put yourself out there." Need to get your book published? "You must self-promote." A family member in distress? "Don't forget to take care of yourself first."

Film director Tom Hooper shared with me his belief that our Western culture has become less open to the self-sacrifice that is connected with loving others. He proposed that the appeal of *Les Misérables* is somewhat ironic because its message runs contrary to a prevailing focus on self-interest:

One of the reasons why this story still resonates is that it is strangely out of sync with the times. Of course, it *is* in sync in the sense that the theme of revolution is incredibly topical, and we had the whole Arab Spring happening as we started to make the film—and Occupy Wall Street. But where the story's out of sync is that, in the world I'm in, it feels that we're being encouraged to optimize our own self-interest. We're told consciously or unconsciously that the route to happiness is through focusing on self. In some ways, we've been sold a false dream.

There's something about *Les Misérables* which celebrates people who are devoted to the self-interest of others—an idea which, in our rather selfish age, has a powerful claim on us and a beauty that, perhaps, contemporary culture somehow isn't quite capturing. When these eternal stories come along and speak to the claim that your family makes on you, that the world makes on you, that politics makes on you, there's something incredibly noble about it, something very powerful.

Hooper didn't shy away from admiring the virtue of our acting out of love, and he alluded to the various kinds of love we can feel. I find myself drawn into Hugo's writings by his understanding of the breadth of our capacity for love. In *Les Misérables* alone, he gives us Bishop Myriel's and Jean Valjean's humanitarian love for everyone, the romantic love that propels Marius and Cosette and sparks Éponine's ultimate sacrifice, the parental love that inspires Fantine's and Valjean's selfless gifts to Cosette, the generous love that prompts Gavroche to give more than he can afford, and the patriotism that drives Enjolras and his dedicated colleagues to high levels of revolutionary idealism. Despite their wretched situations, many of Hugo's characters—in *Les Misérables* and beyond—act out of love, to the benefit of others. As Tom Hooper pointed out, Hugo's story "resonates with the beauty of what people will do in the name of love."

Love motivated Victor Hugo in many ways, too, enriching his private and public lives. At home, he showered on his four children more attention, time, and energy than most nineteenth-century parents, giving them the best possible educations and writing dozens of poems about his joy in them. In private, he gave to the women he cherished a romantic, passionate love. Both publicly and privately, Hugo poured out benevolent love on people in need. All these sorts of love interconnect, of course, and his philanthropy grew from personal feelings, as when his love for the orphaned Juliette Drouet led him to pay more attention to the plight of destitute or outcast women and to speak out on their behalf. In this, Hugo was far ahead of most men of his generation.

Hugo's first love was a strong one, an adolescent idealizing of his childhood friend, Adèle Foucher. They carried on their romance in secret because Victor's mother, believing that he could do better, had banned their courtship. Yet after she died and when Victor proved that he could support a wife, Adèle's parents approved the marriage. Victor was twenty and Adèle nineteen. They were a loving couple, but then Adèle barred Victor from her bed eight years later, in 1830, after the birth of their last child (named Adèle after her mother). With pregnancies every couple of years for nearly a decade and four lively children, Adèle must have wanted no more. It is hard to imagine that Victor was pleased with the only dependable form of birth control in those days. Still young and virile at twenty-eight, he was no longer the eighteen-year-old who had thrown his heart at Adèle's feet, proudly writing her about how he was virtuously remaining chaste for her. Nevertheless, he remained faithful to Adèle even after he realized in late 1830 that she and his best friend, famed literary critic Charles Augustin Sainte-Beuve, were having a secret love affair, with clandestine meetings. From Adèle's perspective, Charles may have been the perfect lover, as he had a physical condition that rendered him incapable of sexual intercourse.

Devastated by his sense that Adèle had withdrawn from him and grown nearer to Charles, Victor at one point offered his wife her freedom from the marriage, but she chose to stay with her husband.

Victor continued to throw himself actively into theater, attending daily play rehearsals, where he noticed the lovely actress and model Juliette Drouet in 1832. Juliette, on her own in the world, had a tiny role in Hugo's *Lucrèce Borgia* and ambitions to be a great actress, although by most accounts her beauty surpassed her talent. Before she met Victor, love affairs had helped Juliette survive financially. Her liaison with sculptor James Pradier brought her a daughter, Claire. A later lover, the physician Scipio Pinel, borrowed 20,000 francs (about $100,000 in today's money) to give Juliette expensive jewelry and "magnificent Indian cashmeres."[66] Pinel defaulted on the loan, and, despite their having split up, Juliette heroically undertook to repay 8,000 of the francs that he had borrowed. That debt became a millstone around her neck and threatened her with imprisonment until Victor managed to repay it.

Juliette was likely ready for a new lover, and Victor was a good-looking, famous man whose wife wouldn't sleep with him and loved someone else. He and Juliette spent their first night together on February 16, 1833, after she sent him this invitation:

> Monsieur Victor,
> Come pick me up this evening at Mme K's.
> I'll love you for your patience until then.
> Until this evening. Oh! this evening will be everything!
> I will give myself to you completely.[67]

Hugo pays homage to his love with Juliette by setting Marius and Cosette's wedding on the same date, "the 16th of February, 1833," as the chapter title tells us (V, 6, 1). *Les Misérables* contains dozens of such autobiographical moments and, more importantly, translates Hugo's feelings. Marius's love letter to Cosette (IV, 5, 4), for example, expresses the euphoria, anxieties, hope, and sense of the divine that we see in Hugo's letters to Adèle, then to Juliette, and later to Léonie.

Victor and Juliette cherished each other so much that they sacrificed greatly, Juliette no doubt more than Victor. Victor paid Juliette's immense debts and effectively adopted Claire, whose biological father had rejected her. Juliette not only relived her unhappy youth to help Victor with the convent scenes in *Les Misérables*, but she also

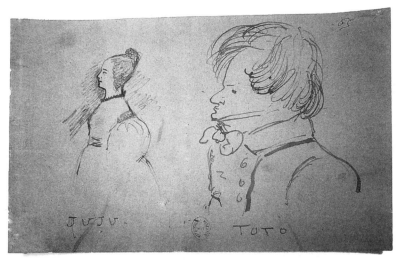

Juju et Toto: Juju and Toto, Hugo's humorous drawing of Juliette and himself, labeled with their nicknames for each other, undated but likely from the 1830s

Marine Terrace, Hugo's painting showing his and
Juliette's initials intertwined, floating over his
Jersey home, Marine Terrace, dated May 21, 1855

spent countless, happy hours making a clean copy of his novel. And then she saved him from imprisonment—or possible execution—after he resisted the 1851 presidential coup d'état. Although their love at first provoked jealousy on both sides, it convinced them in the long run to forgive each other for real and suspected lovers. Juliette gave up her theatrical career and, for some years, agreed not to go out unless Victor accompanied her. Of course unhappy about such enforced isolation, Juliette sometimes protested, but her letters to him (at least 22,000!) focus most often on her keen, steadfast love for him.[68]

Victor worked night and day to finance two families. In the long term, his trust in Juliette and their love, regardless of society's contempt, proved to be well founded: they stayed together through exile, illness, and Victor's competing romantic affairs, both of them devoted to their longstanding love and friendship. Through it all, Victor's belief in the fundamental divinity of love—a concept that permeates *Les Misérables*—underpinned his relationship with Juliette. Together with her, he found redemption through love, too, several years before he began his novel: "We've suffered much," he wrote Juliette, "we've labored much, we've made many efforts to redeem, in God's benevolent sight, the irregularity of our happiness through the sanctity of our love."[69]

As Victor loved and supported Juliette and Claire, he grew morally from his interactions with them. His empathy for the those driven into crime by poverty and ignorance widened to include downtrodden women and children, in part because Juliette cared deeply about those in distress. People in need turned to Juliette, finding her approachable and knowing that she would share their requests with the famous poet.[70] Victor became increasingly interested in all sorts of social justice issues: for instance, what causes crime; how the criminal justice system responds; how poverty affects men, women, and children; how education can help. Showing a breadth of vision beyond his time, he did research, met suffering people, and energetically cultivated his social conscience.

Angry about our capacity to ignore the destitute and to waste human potential, Hugo worked to improve society through legislation. In the Chamber of Peers (under the monarchy), he argued for workers' rights and abolition of the death penalty. Later, in the French National Assembly (during the Second Republic), Hugo spoke vociferously for free, public education for all children and worked toward improving the laws regarding child labor. He was one of the first to argue for the rights of children over those of adults. In his personal life, Hugo regularly acted out of his charitable love for others to donate money and clothes. In his will, he bequeathed 50,000 francs to the poor.[71]

Hugo undertook one of his most public, humanitarian acts of love the spring that *Les Misérables* was published. According to medical wisdom of the time, children needed a wholesome lunch, including meat and wine, in order to flourish. Many Guernsey families were too poor to provide that, as Hugo knew, and he cared about children's welfare. So he decided to help. On March 10, 1862, he and his family began offering what he called the "poor children's meal," a weekly noontime dinner at his Hauteville House home, normally on Tuesdays.[72] The children—twelve at that first meal— sat at the dining table as the Hugos and their servants waited on them. The lunches quickly expanded in size because Hugo invited more children whenever he heard about them. He even invited strangers: "A child with bare feet in the street. I called to him. That made sixteen." By the end of the year, the family fed thirty children each week, and later forty. Hugo saw these children as individuals, sometimes noting their names in his journal and keeping up with their families.

When the number of guests increased rapidly, Hugo offered engravings of some of his artwork for a special edition book to help fund the meals, even though he found it a bit ridiculous to share drawings that he had created for fun. Still, it was worth it. As he wrote to his publisher, this merging of indigent families with his own brought "the sacred democratic formula: Liberty, Equality, Fraternity" to life for both groups of people.[73] For Hugo, these meals meant loving solidarity rather than charity. He argued the point with his son Charles, who had wondered about the rightness of making such generosity public. "Alms should be secret—brotherhood should not,"[74] noted Hugo. He didn't just feed the children, he talked with them about God and prayed with them.

Not content with providing healthy meals to Guernsey's children, he gave them clothing, shoes, and toys at the annual Christmas party his family threw for them. At the 1868 gathering, Hugo proudly announced that his "propaganda" had worked: his idea of weekly dinners for poor children had spread to Switzerland, England, and, especially, America (and, the following year, to Cuba and Haiti). Such were the benefits of letting his actions be publicized, Hugo responded when a Catholic newspaper complained that he didn't know "how to do something good without being ostentatious about it." Each time Hugo visited Guernsey after his post-exile return to Paris, he revived the weekly meals and Christmas parties—and at age eighty hosted a similar children's dinner while visiting an old friend in Normandy. Consistently, however, Hugo saw these offerings as simply palliative, maintaining as he did in *Les Misérables* that "to truly help the poor we must abolish poverty."[75]

Hugo gave us the ultimate model of how to put love into action with Jean Valjean and the bishop who reawakens his conscience and educates him. We get to know Bishop Myriel in a series of slow-paced scenes that might at first seem uneventful. For instance, three days after moving into the sumptuous bishop's palace, Myriel visits the town's hospital next door. Talking with the hospital director, Myriel notes the institution's flaws: twenty-six beds closely packed together, poor ventilation, a tiny garden that could not hold all the convalescents. Acknowledging the breadth of the problem, the director sees no solution and suggests that they must resign themselves.

But the bishop has already made his decision. Standing in the palace, he asks:

> "Monsieur, how many beds do you think this hall alone would contain?"

"Your Lordship's dining hall!" exclaimed the director in amazement.

The bishop ran his eyes over the hall, measuring and calculating.

"It will hold twenty beds," he said to himself. Then, raising his voice, he said, "Listen, Monsieur le Directeur, here's what I think. Obviously this is wrong. There are twenty-six of you in five or six small rooms. Here there are three of us and space enough for sixty. That is wrong, I assure you. You have my house, and I am in yours. Give me back mine, and this will be your home" (I, 1, 2).

I delight in how the bishop decidedly redefines how each building will be used, offering a done deal, couching his offer in terms the director cannot refuse. By smilingly demanding back "his own house," Myriel points to the morality of the exchange, and his love for others shines out as he ignores or embraces his own sacrifices.

As we get to know the bishop, we learn that he easily makes such generous choices because he loves others substantially more than himself. "Outside of and, so to speak, beyond his faith, the bishop had an excess of love. . . . A serene benevolence, going beyond humans, . . . and, on occasion, extending to inanimate things" (I, 1, 13). His compassionate love inspires his sister, Jean Valjean, and many around him. But today—in our on-the-move, sped-up, digitally-connected world—feeling such love for others can seem especially hard, even if we're not driven by self-interest. Modern-day life, with its commuter culture and its demands that we relocate for professional advancement, can put physical distance between us and those we love. Many of us communicate with friends and family primarily through Facebook, Instagram, and/or the latest social media app. Co-workers leave for new positions. Keeping love alive for those we care about can be such a challenge that we might wonder whether we can possibly try to cultivate love for strangers.

Hugo, however, does not shy away from advocating such bountiful love or from acknowledging that the bishop's capacity for love is extreme. In fact, he says, the love that Bishop Charles-François-

Bienvenu Myriel bestows on everyone is so uncommonly big-hearted that "reasonable people" distrusted it. Hugo begs to differ, arguing that love can—*should*, he would say—define and develop the best in us. Myriel bestows love on the downtrodden most of all: "There are men who work to extract gold; he worked to extract pity. The misery of the universe was his mine. Grief everywhere was only a chance for good always. *Love one another*: . . . He desired nothing more and made that his whole doctrine" ("What He Thought," I, 1, 14). In doing so, Myriel differs from the power-hungry, self-serving clerics whom Hugo doesn't hesitate to condemn.

Not a fan of pomp or power, Bishop Myriel would not have chosen for himself the standard honorific title "Monseigneur." He dislikes the sense of dominance that the term "my lord" embodies, but he adores the friendly name his poor parishioners had given him: "Monseigneur Bienvenu" (I, 1, 2). By choosing from among his several given names the one that "meant the most to them," they show their affection for their bishop, who feels that "the 'welcome' meaning of 'Bienvenu' counterbalances the Monseigneur." His personal warmth is enriched by his self-deprecating humor, as when he teases his servant, Mme Magloire, about her habit of calling him "Your Highness." When he cannot to reach a book above his head, he asks her to bring him a chair because, he says, "My highness cannot reach that shelf" (I, 1, 4).

The bishop's obvious—and ongoing—*choice* to act from love inspires readers. Hugh Jackman told me this story, for instance, about the former head of World Vision Australia, an organization that for over sixty years has been fighting poverty:

> One of my mentors, Tim Costello, is sort of the moral mouthpiece of Australia. When he was the mayor of St. Kilda—an area of Melbourne that was known for drug addicts and prostitutes—he became quite a famous man, because he would go out on Friday and Saturday nights and talk with them and make sure they were okay. An *incredible* man.
>
> He's gone on now to run World Vision and keeps reminding the government here about foreign aid and

many, many good causes. He told me once, "The reason I got into what I'm doing was Victor Hugo's novel. I read it when I was seventeen, and it changed my life." And, funny enough, like me, he said it was that depiction of the bishop. That's the potential of humanity, right there.[76]

Yes, as humans we have the ability to be humane, to care about others, and to act on such feelings. Such lavish love spreads. Bishop Myriel's love and the forgiveness that grows from it can transform even a man as hate-filled as the Jean Valjean we first meet in the novel.

Valjean's transformation is very difficult (see Chapter 5), but it opens his path to an extraordinary life of conscience and love. He comes to epitomize altruism and to embody the bishop's doctrine loving one another (I, 1, 14). Valjean's about-face from evil to good comes from receiving and accepting the bishop's forgiveness. Only because he gives love, however, can he maintain his newly conscientious life.

The first beneficiaries of Valjean's renewed outward focus are the citizens of Montreuil-sur-mer, where his heroic rescue of two children reopened society's door to him. But what about after he loses the townspeople's respect and affection by confessing his past? What makes him honest and kind after Inspector Javert sends him back to prison for breaking parole? At first, his promise to the dying Fantine to save her daughter, Cosette, keeps Valjean going. Yet when he and Cosette begin afresh in Paris, we learn that Valjean still carries with him the new waves of bitterness he had felt after finding himself back in prison, this time "for doing good." Hugo enters into the novel again to express his "personal opinion" and emphasize the power of love: "Who can tell whether Jean Valjean was on the verge of discouragement and falling back into evil ways? He loved, and he grew strong again. . . . Thanks to Cosette, he could persist in virtue" (II, 4, 3).

Struck by Hugo's conception of this awakening of paternal love, director Tom Hooper neatly summarized for me Hugo's image of two "apparitions," a way of framing Valjean's experiences that again touches on the divine:

> What really excited me in the novel was discovering that Valjean has a second epiphany when he meets and takes charge of little Cosette. You have this man who's about forty-six. He's *completely* given up on the idea of living a family life where he could have children, or get married, or find love. So to discover in himself that power is extraordinary.
>
> The quote goes something like this: "This was the second white apparition that Jean Valjean had encountered; the priest had taught him *virtue*; little Cosette taught him the meaning of love." I think my *entire* take on the film, really, is expressed by that quote. I wanted the audience to understand that it's a story of a double transformation: firstly, the opening up of the heart in a compassionate relationship with the world, and then, secondly, possibly through that first opening, a second, deeper opening of love continues into his being.

Raising Cosette in Paris, Valjean renews his habit of giving alms to street beggars, a munificence that enables a disguised Javert to recognize and pursue him. Valjean risks his life to help the miserable Thénardier family and then puts himself in grave jeopardy to protect Cosette from the bandits' clutches. The benevolence that he demonstrated as M. Madeleine reappears in a new guise when he joins the students fighting at the barricade. There, his unspoken goal is *only* to protect and defend, as when he dissuades snipers by shooting their helmets, rather than aiming at them. After he offers his National Guard uniform so that one more student can escape and survive, fellow insurgent Combeferre realizes that Valjean is "a man who saves others" (V, 1, 4).

Still, Jean Valjean is far from a saint. Although superhuman in his strength, marksmanship, and capacity for escape, he is very much a man, with an array of flaws such as those we all have. Hugo implied the difference between his virtuous Bishop Myriel and his oh-so-human Jean Valjean in an 1840s' note that also indicates the archetypal nature of his characters: "Story of a saint / Story of a man / Story of a woman / Story of a doll."[77] The saint is certainly Myriel, in juxtaposition to the man Valjean, while Fantine represents the challenges facing women, and Cosette is as passive, beloved, and ultimately beautiful as a doll.

Valjean's flaws are rarely more evident than in his complicated reactions to loving Cosette. It's a powerful love, a first love, as Hooper noted. Hugo does not shy away from delving into how bewildering such new sensations can be: "Poor old Jean Valjean did not, of course, love Cosette other than as a father, but . . . into this fatherhood the very aridity of his life had introduced every type of love." The feelings of a lover, too, "the most indestructible of all, were mingled with the others, vague, ignorant, pure with the purity of blindness, unconscious, celestial, angelic, divine" (IV, 15, 1). Hugh Jackman admired how Hugo alluded to the sexuality that Valjean doesn't recognize and how the author confronted the messy confusion of "this avalanche of emotions that Valjean didn't know what to do with." And Jackman was struck by how beautifully Hugo presents Valjean's new capacity for love, which Hooper's film highlights by adding the song "Suddenly."

On the one hand, Valjean's love for Cosette almost irresistibly tempts him to be selfish. On the other, that same love propels him to the highest levels of sacrifice. Like many fathers who dote on their daughters—like Hugo, who despaired when Léopoldine married Charles Vacquerie—Valjean loves Cosette with a purity melded with self-interest and jealousy. Intensely human, Valjean agonizes when he suspects that Cosette and Marius have fallen in love. How can he lose the only person he has ever loved? Then, much worse, Valjean discovers Cosette's love letter to Marius! His conscience is put to its greatest test yet, a test that might defeat him, as Hugo warns: "Well, anyone able to see his inner core would have been compelled to admit that at this moment it was weakening. . . . He felt down to the very roots of his hair the immense awakening of egotism, and the self howled in the abyss of this man" (IV, 15, 1). All evidence points to the fact that he hates Cosette's boyfriend. Thus when Valjean grabs his rifle and heads for the barricade, we might well imagine that he is plotting Marius's death.

A master of suspense, Hugo keeps us guessing about Valjean's motives and plans throughout both the long, final barricade battle and Valjean's seemingly endless trek through the Parisian sewer muck. As he carries Marius over his shoulder, is he trying to save him as he has saved many others? Or has Valjean's hatred of this rival for Cosette's love so overcome his conscience that he plans to make sure Marius dies? Valjean did, after all, "give an interior cry of horrible joy" when he read in Marius's letter that he expected to die on the barricade. Valjean "had before his eyes that splendor, the death of the hated being" (IV, 15, 3). We cannot be sure of Valjean's motives until he comes to a locked gate that he cannot force open. Feeling close to death, "Of whom did he think in this overwhelming dejection? Neither of himself nor of Marius. He thought of Cosette" (V, 3, 7). It's clear now: Valjean has been acting from his all-encompassing love for Cosette. Everything he's done was aimed to save Marius, and his intentions are so strong that he convinces Inspector Javert to help him.

Valjean's conscience and love face one more monstrously tough test after Marius and Cosette marry and warmly invite him to live in their home. With his perceptions tainted by society's disgust for former convicts, Valjean expects his past arise again and shame his daughter. His conscience pushes him to leave, but he struggles, waffling between his desire to be near Cosette—although he now sees that as a self-centered love—and his altruistic love for her, a feeling strengthened by his conscience. Yet his conscience is working under society's baleful inability to believe in positive change or to see Valjean's overwhelming good actions. When Valjean does reveal his ex-convict past, Marius's shock and disgust reflect society's narrowmindedness. For us as readers, it's agonizing and ironic to watch Marius in his blinders reject his savior even as he energetically seeks to reward the mysterious man who saved his life. Marius's reaction confirms Valjean's suspicions. Choosing to protect Cosette by sacrificing his happiness, Valjean tears himself away, to live alone and lonely.

Without Cosette to receive his love, Valjean has no reason to live. As he nears death, his mind wanders, skipping to and from various life events, as often happens with the ill or elderly. Bishop Myriel is present in spirit. Even though it's still daytime, Valjean lights candles in the silver candlesticks the bishop had given him, practically the only possession Valjean had kept aside from young Cosette's mourning clothes. When the doorkeeper asks whether he would like a priest, Valjean responds that he already has one, pointing somewhere above his head. "It is probable that the bishop was indeed present at this hour of death" (V, 9, 5), Hugo tells us, hinting at a scene director Tom Hooper brought into his film, where the bishop welcomes Valjean's soul. With his last words to Cosette and Marius—which is in effect his last will and testament—Valjean makes clear that Cosette's inheritance was honestly earned, tells Cosette of her mother's boundless love for her, and implicitly forgives Marius for his antagonism. Valjean's key message? He bequeaths to them the love and sustenance that Bishop Myriel had given him: "Always love each other deeply. There is scarcely anything else in the world but that: to love one another" (V, 9, 5).

"The end of the film *Les Misérables* is about love," director Tom Hooper told me. "It's saying that through love we achieve our highest possible communion in this world." Victor Hugo lived that sort of communion, seeing love as a manifestation of God within everyone, believing that love motivates our best selves if we recognize and follow it. Alain Boublil remarked, too, on how Hugo expressed the divine nature of love in all its aspects: "Victor Hugo saw religion as a way to pacify, as a way to link people through a message of love. Sometimes, I think, there is even a very healthy and *healing* confusion in the way he speaks of physical love, love between human beings, and a broader love of everyone. That's what attracted us, Claude-Michel and me, to the novel." By the time Hugo had written most of *Les Misérables* and spent several years in exile, he was explicitly connecting God and love, much as he connects God and conscience in his novel. "God has only one face: Light! And only one name: Love!," he wrote in the last stanza of his unfinished poem *Dieu* (more on *Dieu* and the world's religions in the following chapter).[78] His daughter Adèle expanded

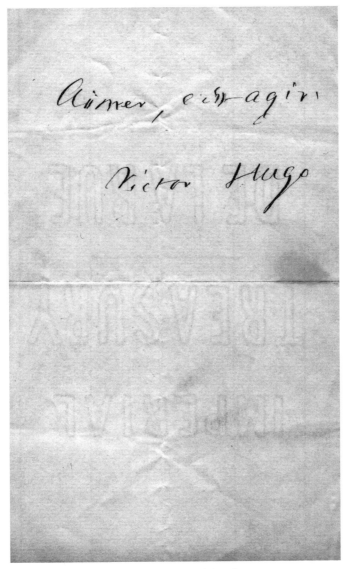

"Aimer, c'est agir" in Hugo's handwriting,
May 19, 1885

on this quotation in the journal comments she wrote after Hugo had read *Dieu* aloud to family and friends: "My father arrives finally at his own religion, which is summarized in this great word: *Love* [Adèle's emphasis]."[79] Thirty years later, three days before his death at age 83, Hugo still focused on love. "To love is to act" were practically the last words he wrote.

In Bishop Myriel, Hugo discloses a spiritual life in which individuals bond with God through love and conscience, a spiritual life that parallels Hugo's own, in which the writer's desire to act from his feelings of love played out in both his humanitarian quest for justice and his personal life. The bishop—with his "excess of love"—inspires Valjean's strong love for Cosette and his charitable love of humanity. The idea of such bountiful, giving love, Hugo tells us when he introduces Bishop Myriel, amused "reasonable people," those who wanted to dismiss the bishop and everything he stood for.

Similarly, when the *Les Misérables* film appeared in cinemas, many critics found it "sappy" and "manipulative." *New Yorker* writers were dismissive. David Denby called it "sentimental," and Anthony Lane labeled it "bombast." Such reactions "confused" Hooper, and they saddened me. First, Hooper:

> I put my faith and trust in the audience. I definitely make
> films for them, just like *The King's Speech*. The greatest
> reward is sitting in the audience and hearing the reaction
> at the end. . . . The time we live in is a postmodern age
> where a certain amount of irony is expected. This film is
> made without irony. A friend of mine who lost his father in
> October said the film's ending made him feel better about
> his dad, that he felt closer to him. It's as if the musical
> holds up a mirror to the suffering in our lives.[80]

For me, Hugo's openness to love's power and his frank simplicity in having love and conscience drive his novel refreshingly contradicts contemporary disillusionment and cynicism. In *Les Misérables*, Hugo preaches compassionate humanity as the best way to engage not only with our personal tragedies but also with tragedies that affect hundreds or thousands. In the past decade, the world has experienced such devastating war and revolution that migration is at an all-time high. Terrorism can strike anywhere with no warning. Over one-fifth of America's children live in poverty.[81] What would happen if more of us connected with our potential to love and acted on it? Do we make time to feel benevolent or empathetic toward others—and to act on our feelings in meaningful ways? Bishop Myriel's and Jean Valjean's accomplishments make a strong case for why living through love can make a difference and is worth the effort.

Seeking—and Finding—God

*Victor Hugo in his Hauteville House study in the look-out's
antechamber. Taken by an anonymous photographer
between 1859 and 1861, the period during which
Hugo revised and finished* Les Misérables.

Solitude! Ocean! Its somber nature draws me
imperiously and pulls me toward the dazzling
shadows of infinity. I spend whole nights
sometimes dreaming on my rooftop in the
presence of the abyss, I feel as though God is
overwhelming me, and at last I can do nothing
but cry out, "Stars! Stars! Stars!"[82]

Watching what's going on in our country, I see that I'm not the only one with questions about spirituality. As I read the news and talk with others, I feel what a 2019 Pew Research Center study showed: that the U.S. religious landscape "continues to change at a rapid clip." The percentage of American adults who call themselves Christians dropped by nearly twelve points from 2009 to 2019. At the same time, the percent of "people who describe their religious identity as atheist, agnostic or 'nothing in particular/none,' grew to 26% (from 17% in 2009). Most striking, perhaps, is the finding that "only half of Millennials (49%) describe themselves as Christians; four-in-ten are religious 'nones,' and one-in-ten Millennials identify with non-Christian faiths."[83]

At the same time, the internet teams with stories from people who so want to find out who they are or why they exist that they have traveled to India, Israel, Indonesia, and beyond. CNN's Jessica Ravitz, for instance, found many Westerners seeking higher meaning in life among gurus and their followers in Rishikesh, India. On the web, too, is a rich trove of questions, ideas, and wonderment about what it means to be spiritual or how to do it. Krista Tippett's National Public Radio interview program, "On Being," explores in broad ways "the animating questions at the center of human life: What does it mean to be human, and how do we want to live?"[84]

TED talks have exploded with different perspectives on religion and spirituality. There Alain de Botton, for example, encourages atheists to experience transcendence in religious ritual, what he calls "Atheism 2.0."[85] Even as some Americans continue their established religious practice, others meld spiritual practices from diverse sources and look beyond defined religions. And, for some of us, traditional boundaries between religions more and more blur, in a way that illuminates the connections between religious and spiritual beliefs.

Victor Hugo distinguished between spirituality and organized religion, and I am inspired by his notion to make a similar distinction. When I refer to ideas about the divine, the term "religious" indicates those connected to organized religion, and "spiritual" connotes those which do not come from institutionalized religion. Hugo confirmed his deep faith in God even as he separated the Divine Spirit from churches in his draft notes for his last will and testament:

> I believe in God.
>
> I feel myself, immortal soul, in the presence of God.
>
> I implore him to admit me, together with those I love and those who love me, into the better life.
>
> All religions are true and false: true by God, false by dogma. Each one wants to be the only one, hence untruths. I hope that God will not exclude these religions from the vast pardon that he will grant.
>
> I do not accept any funeral prayers from churches; I ask every soul for their prayer.
>
> I implore the eternal God.[86]

God, like love, is nearly everywhere in *Les Misérables*. So pervasive that I can imagine how the novel might seem fantastical, ridiculous, or offensive to atheists. But for me—someone who spent several years as an agnostic, who speculated that atheism might be the right way to go, who studied world religions, and who tried attending various Christian churches—Victor Hugo's novel has been a clear path to a belief in and personal sense of a divine spirit beyond us. Hugo creates in his story a connection to God that resonates with people who belong to no organized religion as strongly as it resonates with those who see the Christian allusions, which Hugo brings into a novel written for a majority French Catholic audience. How did he open his novel to so many, I wondered, and what does his vision bring to us today? What does a sense of a Higher Power give those of us who want to live so conscientiously that we help improve ourselves and society? I wanted to know whether Hugo includes ideas from religious traditions other than Catholic, Protestant, or Evangelical, ideas that might not pop out to readers from Christian cultures. Most importantly, how did Hugo himself seek and understand God?

Like many of us, Victor Hugo searched for the spiritual meaning of life, not only in private meditation, but also publicly in his poetry and in *Les Misérables*. The spiritual complexities that Hugo weaves through his epic novel are echoed in contradictions in his life, particularly during his early adult years. Raised in an overwhelmingly Catholic country, Hugo loved the Bible and knew it inside out. In his poem "Aux Feuillantines," he tells how, as a young boy, he adventured into the attic, climbed to the top of a cupboard, and found himself intrigued by what turned out to be an old Bible smelling of incense. "Pictures everywhere! what happiness! what ecstasy!" he wrote.[87] Forgetting to play, he says, he and his brothers plunged into the book, charmed by everything they read. As an adult, Hugo had a lifelong habit of prayer and built poems around biblical stories—and also around stories from other religious traditions, especially in *La Légende des siècles*. He knew Catholic ritual well and wove it into many of his books, such as *Notre-Dame de Paris* and *Les Châtiments*.

But Hugo was never baptized. He and his father had to rely on personal relationships to obtain the documents that permitted Victor to marry Adèle Foucher in the Catholic Church of Saint-Sulpice. In practical terms, it can be argued, Hugo was never Catholic.[88] Aside from weddings and other formal occasions, he hardly ever attended mass. Yes, in his early twenties he inherently supported the Church-monarchy affiliation when he was invited to King Charles V's coronation. But his railings against similar Catholic associations with the Second Empire twenty-five years later brought him fire from the Vatican. For most of his life, Hugo questioned established religion. The older he grew—and the more time he spent surrounded by the sea in exile—the more Hugo sought

From his fourth-floor look-out in Hauteville House on Guernsey,
Hugo watched the ever-changing sea.

direct connection with and understanding of God. As he did so, he broadened his sense of the Universal Spirit, or Supreme Being, even though he often continued to use the traditional word God (*Dieu* in French). This familiar term is, of course, convenient and understandable, even though it may not completely capture Hugo's sense of a deity who is, at once, pervasive in and around us, yet intangible. So I use *God* where Hugo wrote *Dieu*, but I choose other words, where possible, in an attempt to better express Hugo's sense of the divine reality and its unity.[89]

As he searched, Hugo rejected religion and dogma ever more decidedly. "We must destroy all religions in order to rebuild God. I mean: to build him up again in mankind," he wrote to a friend.[90] Such sentiments parallel the ideas in his "philosophical preface" to *Les Misérables*. Hugo drafted that long essay, which is a sort of brainstorming about his novel's purpose, as he deliberated about how to revise his manuscript. "The book that you are going to read is a religious book," he tells us right off the bat. And he soon makes clear that he means "religious" in its broadest spiritual sense: "The author—and he is speaking here by right of free conscience—does not belong to any of today's prevailing religions."[91] Instead, Hugo dazzles us with sweeping examples of the immensity of the universe and the incredible number of creatures that exist in a seashell, for instance. From his appreciation of nature's prodigies and the intelligent power of the "infinite" that created them comes his belief in a universal divine power, a belief at once spiritual and metaphysical.

"There's no religion that doesn't blaspheme a little," Hugo wrote in *Religions et religion*, his book-length poem drafted during his hiatus from *Les Misérables* in the mid-1850s.[92] He rejected Catholicism along with all others. With such an anti-religion rhetoric, Hugo went beyond standard republican anti-clericalism. He riled the Vatican, for instance, by consistently lobbying each pope to care about the poor and work toward social justice more than he suspected they did. (Today's Pope Francis, on the other hand, regularly acts in many ways that remind me of Bishop Myriel.[93]) As Hugo continued to clarify his view of the disconnection between God and religion, he contradicted the positions of both atheists and devout Catholics.

But *Les Misérables*—especially as seen through the *Les Mis* musical—looks to many people like a completely Christian story. Hugo's novel begins, of course, with the Catholic Bishop Myriel, whose actions in many ways drive the novel, even though we rarely hear of him throughout the remaining 1,300 pages. To create Bishop Myriel, Hugo drew upon the life of a historical—although atypical—Catholic bishop. Monseigneur Charles-François-Melchior-Bienvenu de Miollis was the real-life Bishop of Digne in 1815.[94] He served there 33 years, until his retirement at age 80, just as Bishop Charles-François-Bienvenu Myriel does in the novel. De Miollis was so large-hearted that he helped an ex-convict named Pierre Maurin find a new start in life, inviting him into his home despite his frightening appearance, just as Bishop Myriel does for Jean Valjean. Both the real and the fictional bishop chose to help the poor by foregoing their personal comfort and rejecting the ostentatious wealth that some bishops displayed.

Hugo's adult son Charles was surprised to see his father portray a bishop in such a positive light, as were author George Sand and other friends. Like most republicans—who found the Catholic Church's support of the French kings' divine right to rule contradictory to democratic ideals—Hugo and his family were staunchly anti-clerical. In 1849, for example, a few years after beginning *Les Misérables*, Hugo argued vociferously that clerics should not control the French educational system, foreseeing laws for secular education that were passed in the 1880s. Thus Charles had reason to be surprised at Bishop Myriel's central role in the novel. In fact, he complained that making such a pivotal character a bishop gave too much credit to the Catholic Church. His father disagreed, contending that "this pure, noble representation of the true priest is the sharpest satire of today's priests."[95] Hugo's distinction between what he thought a Christian spiritual leader should be and what he often saw in real life underlies his gently humorous depiction of the humble Myriel. Hugo extols Myriel's virtue and wisdom while pointedly condemning clerics who profited from their religious positions.

In modeling Bishop Myriel on Bishop de Miollis, Hugo immortalized the real bishop's kindness and integrity. So we might assume that those who had known such a saintly man would be pleased to find his contributions celebrated. That's not how members of de Miollis family saw it in 1862 when they recognized their relative in Bishop Myriel. They were mightily offended. They and other Catholics objected to what they saw as non-Catholic aspects of Bishop Myriel's beliefs and actions. But wait! The bishop doesn't seem Catholic? My students think he is. Today's bloggers think he is. John Caird, who co-directed the original British 1985 musical with Trevor Nunn, said that "Valjean's story is fundamentally a New Testament Christian tale."[96] It's true that the *Les Mis* bishop *never* seems *not* Catholic during the three minutes he's on stage. How can the novel at once be deeply Catholic or Christian, as many believe, *and* have offended believing Catholics and Christians?

One scene in particular touched a nerve: the bishop's encounter with a man everyone calls an atheist (I, 1, 10), what Bishop Miollis's nephew called a "free-thinker."[97] This outcast, known only as "G.," had been a member of the Convention, the Revolutionary body that had condemned King Louis XVI to the guillotine in January 1793. Although G. had not voted for the King's death, the people of Digne reviled him as a murderer, indeed, a monster: a despicable *Conventionnel*. The townspeople refuse to meet him, and the bishop has every religious and social reason to avoid G. Monseigneur Bienvenu, too, sees the former *Conventionnel* as "an outlaw almost, even outside the law of charity." In spite of Myriel's great benevolence and love for others, he feels for G. a contempt that he does not try to hide when they meet.

To understand the significance of the bishop's encounter with G., we need a bit of historical context. We are, after all, reading this novel over two centuries after the 1789 French Revolution. In 1815, a generation after the Revolution, the bishop's parishioners—most of France, in fact—would still have been reeling from its social and political upheavals. King Louis XVIII's coming to the throne after

Emperor Napoleon had abdicated was a moment of intense feeling. Many monarchists remembered the excesses of the Revolution that had overthrown King Louis XVI and eventually led to Napoleon's decade-long empire. They were horrified by anyone connected to the Revolution. And, of course, the Catholic Church was offended by any affront to the monarchy, since the Church claimed that French kings' right to rule came from God through his agent, the pope, under the theory of divine right.

Even worse, by 1793, the Revolution—originally spurred by the Enlightenment—had become controlled by extremists. The ruling Convention decreed "terror" to be the order of the day, and at least 16,000 French citizens, nobles and commoners alike, died by the guillotine. Thus "93" became shorthand for the horrors that followed the French Revolution, including the execution of King Louis XVI and Queen Marie-Antoinette, as well as the Reign of Terror and the death of ten-year-old Louis XVII in the Temple Prison in 1795.

With the overthrow of the monarchy, Myriel's family had lost their fortune, and anti-clerical revolutionaries had desecrated churches. G. had been one of those revolutionaries. So, as saintly as the bishop is, he has never visited G. Hugo doesn't hesitate to show the bishop's human weaknesses. Even after the bishop learns that G. is dying, he continues to procrastinate. In the end, after vacillating and struggling with his conscience—and despite his distaste for G.— the bishop decides to do his duty, to offer final rites to a dying man. He makes the hour-long walk to G.'s impoverished hut and greets the former *Conventionnel* with none of his usual warmth and humor.

The bishop begins with biting comments about G.'s past but soon finds himself in dialogue about the meaning of the Revolution, grudgingly listening to G.'s perspective on progress and humanity. G. argues that progress is by nature brutal and that the French monarchy had committed many atrocities equal to those of 1793. When the bishop confronts G. with the death of the imprisoned ten-year-old prince, G. asks why the death of a royal child should matter more than another young boy's torture and execution simply because his brother was a famous highwayman. Seeing G.'s point, the bishop "almost regretted that he had come, and yet he felt strangely and inexplicably moved."

Bishop Myriel's openness to discomfort brings him to a great self-realization as he really listens to this "atheist's" ideas about a subject close to the hearts and minds of both men: God. The bishop launches the topic aggressively, implying that G. *must* be an atheist since he supported the Revolution, saying, "Progress ought to believe in God. The good cannot have an impious servant. An atheist is an evil leader of the human race." But G.'s reaction and response powerfully affect Bishop Myriel:

> The old representative of the people . . . trembled once, briefly. He looked up at the sky, and a tear slowly gathered in that upturned gaze. The tear, filling his eye, trickled down his pallid cheek, and talking to himself in an undertone, his gaze lost in the remote depths, he said almost stammering, "Oh you the ideal! You alone exist!"
>
> The bishop experienced a sort of inexpressible turmoil.
>
> After a pause, the old man raised a finger skyward and said, "The infinite exists. It is there. If the infinite had no selfhood, selfhood would set a limit upon it; it would not be infinite. In other words, there would be no such thing. Yet exist it does. So it has a self. That selfhood of the infinite is God."

The intensity with which G. declares his belief in an infinite God seems to have used up much of his failing energy. The bishop knows that death is near and takes the old man's hand in his. Monseigneur Bienvenu feels inside himself that "from extreme coldness of heart he had gone gradually to extreme emotion." He says, "This moment belongs to God. Don't you think it would be a pity if we had met in vain?" As readers, we assume that the bishop is about to offer to bless G. or perform the last rites, or both. Not so. In a role reversal that shocked readers of the period, the bishop sinks to his knees, asking G. for *his* blessing. Too late. When the bishop looks up, he realizes that G. has died, with a noble expression on his face.

When the bishop bows before G.'s vision of a God disconnected from any religion, he utterly fails to uphold Catholic doctrine. No wonder the book was banned! The nephew of the historical Bishop Miollis was horrified at the idea of "episcopal dignity" kneeling before a *Conventionnel*. But today this scene deepens our respect for the bishop. Acknowledging and ultimately accepting G.'s unconventional spirituality takes great effort. The bishop is shaken by the feeling that he is being initiated into a new understanding—and he's not sure he likes it. Despite his discomfiture, however, he tenaciously engages with G. The chapter title, "The Bishop in the Presence of an Unknown Light," hints at Myriel's unease while emphasizing Hugo's admiration of the *Conventionnel*'s faith, since Hugo often links radiance to the Divine Spirit, whose unknowability or distance is a gloomy abyss. Talking with G. has enlightened Monseigneur Bienvenu and aided his personal development: "No one could say that the passing of that soul in his presence, and the reflection of that great conscience on his own, had not had its effect upon his approach to perfection."

In the *Conventionnel*, as in the bishop, Hugo gives us something of his own sense of the universal, divine spirit. He is even more direct in "Prayer" (II, 7, 5), a chapter in which he steps back from his fictional story to share his thoughts. Hugo begins by raising the question, "To pray to God, what do those words mean?" He then expands upon his character G.'s rather mystical declaration about the infinite or, as he says, "two infinites":

> While there is an infinite beyond ourselves, is there not
> at the same time an infinite within ourselves? Are these
> two infinites (what an alarming plural!) not superimposed
> one on top of the other? . . . If these two infinites are
> intelligent, they each have an element of will, and there
> is an I in the infinite above as there is an I in the infinite
> below. The I below is the soul, the I above is God.
> To place the infinite below in contact with the infinite
> above by the medium of thought, that is called praying.

By defining such a meditational connection with God—especially alongside G.'s nebulous, semi-philosophical expression of God's infinity and selfhood—Hugo reveals his desire to explore the puzzling mystery of the Divine beyond and within us. And he shows us something of his growing personal sense of an all-pervasive force, an indescribable entity that differs somewhat from the idea of an almighty power watching over humanity.

Wanting to comprehend the intangible and inaccessible, Hugo sought and experienced God directly through nature, not unlike other Romantics in that way. Spending much time alone outside, he loved contemplating the sea and sky surrounding his Channel Island exile homes. He and his family lived from 1852 to 1855 in the reputedly haunted Marine Terrace, a sprawling white house on Jersey's south coast. After he settled on the wilder, less cultured Guernsey, Hugo found that the ocean and seclusion for writing made his long exile tolerable: "I'm a storm bird," he wrote to a friend. "I begin to feel the need of clouds, foam, and hurricanes. It would now be difficult for me to live completely in town. I would miss the ocean."[98] He would also have missed the mystery of Guernsey's and Jersey's megalithic dolmens, especially the one at Rozel Bay, where he set a famous poem that we'll look at later in this chapter. Apparently ritual burial sites, these standing stones remain enigmatic today. Hugo connected them to the divine and found them inspirational.

He saw divinity, too, in the ocean's apparently infinite nature and eternal movement. And Hugo explicitly associated his fascination with the ocean with his writing, as he detailed in this personal journal entry after he'd lived on Guernsey for several months:

> I live in a splendid solitude, as though I were perched
> on a rock peak, with all the waves' vast foam and all
> the sky's great clouds under my window; I live in this
> immense dream of the ocean, I'm becoming little by little
> a sleepwalker of the sea. From time to time, I awaken from
> this eternal contemplation to write. There's always on my
> stanza or my page a little of the cloud's shadow and the

sea's saliva; my thoughts float and come and go, as though loosed by this giant swaying of the infinite.

What doesn't float, what doesn't vacillate is the soul face to face with eternity, it is conscience face to face with truth.[99]

A fan of the productive power of dreaming, or musing, Hugo—who had been used to walking miles in Paris while contemplating writing ideas—in exile found his creative juices flowing even more strongly. As he poetically describes his new situation, though, he doesn't let go of his essential focus on his conscience and on what is right, the truth.

Enthralled by nature and appreciating how the Supreme Being permeates our world, Hugo could be talking about himself when he tells how the bishop experiences divinity in his garden: Bishop Myriel "seemed to be thoughtfully seeking—beyond life as we know it—its cause, its explanation, or its excuse. . . . He examined without passion . . . the quantity of chaos which there is yet in nature" (I, 1, 13). Hugo delves into that natural chaos through his visionary poetry in Les Contemplations and beyond. In his beautiful "Clearing Sky," for example, all nature—from the ocean waves to the smallest blade of grass, from a sparrow to the distant horizon—embodies the peace and love for humanity that flows from what G. called the infinite's self.[100]

Not modest about his spiritual insights, Hugo writes about channeling the divine through nature, as in "Yes, I'm the Dreamer . . .":

> Often, in May, when branches swell with perfumes,
> I converse with the gillyflowers.
> I take counsel from the ivy and the cornflower.
> The mysterious being—whom you believe silent—
> Leans over me and writes with my pen."[101]

During that same poetic communion, he blithely remarks, "Don't be surprised by all that nature tells me with ineffable sighs. I converse with all the voices that metempsychosis offers." Hugo embraced metempsychosis, or the transmigration of souls, the idea that souls

The End of the Temporary Breakwater on Guernsey, as Seen from my Look-out (L'extrémité du brise-lames provisoire à Guernesey, vue de mon look-out), Hugo's pen-and-brown-ink wash dated January 13, 1865

are reborn in plants or objects as well as in animals or people. Belief in such reincarnation appears in other French Romantics' poetry and in Edgar Allan Poe's work, which found favor first in France. The idea dates back to Greek philosophy and the theologies of such Eastern religions as Hinduism, Buddhism, and Jainism.[102] Hugo's acceptance of metempsychosis is but one sign of his broader sense of what is commonly called "God," as well as evidence of his interest in spiritual traditions other than Christianity. His Guernsey Hauteville House library contained a French translation of the *Qur'an* and a large book treating Eastern religious thought, including Hinduism's "Laws of Manu," Confucianism, and Islam, along with multiple copies of the Bible and the Psalms.[103]

Hugo's efforts to comprehend a power that he believed to be both above and within us went beyond studying assorted religions, however. Perhaps because of his crisis of faith after Léopoldine's death and/or because of the upheaval of exile, he intensively sought understanding during the 1850s, the period between drafting *Les Misérables* in the mid 1840s and finishing it in 1860-62. When fascination with séances swept through the United States and Europe, his close friend Delphine de Girardin brought the craze to Jersey. Hugo was interested but skeptical. His family was tempted to try reaching the spirits, though, as they still grieved over Léopoldine and hoped to communicate with her. They accepted de Girardin's offer to hold séances, despite Hugo's reluctance.

The first attempt failed. Then, on September 11, 1853, the Hugos and five friends were deeply moved to receive a message from Léopoldine. They were certain that it must be her because the information communicated was known only to Madame Hugo and her daughter. From then on, through October 8, 1855, séances took place most evenings. In their version of table-tilting (called in French "les tables tournantes"), a small, three-legged pedestal table responded to questions by tapping once for "yes" and twice for "no," or by spelling out messages with one tap for "A," two for "B," and so on. Charles Hugo proved to be an excellent medium for transmitting messages purportedly from the spirits of the dead. Different family members or friends took turns scrupulously transcribing what the spirits said.[104]

These séance transcripts pose the classic chicken-or-egg problem: Hugo's poetry from the mid-1850s parallels in both style and content what the spirits tapped out. Which caused which? Charles never exhibited the sort of literary skill that would have enabled him to make it all up. But had Charles so imbibed his father's poetic rhetoric that he channeled it in occult words? Or did 110 different spirits—including such unexpected beings as Shakespeare, the Lion of Androcles, and Galileo—really talk via the table? Remarkably, the spirits all spoke in French, although Victor Hugo was fluent in Latin, Greek, and Spanish, and he understood English. How much was Hugo influenced by the spirits? On the other hand, to what extent did his strong personality and ideas influence the séances? We will likely never know.

Still, the séance experiences matter for our reading of Les Misérables. Bishop Myriel's appreciation of the Conventionnel's unconventional sense of what many people call "God" reverberates with the awareness of the infinite that flows through Hugo's mystical poetry. The poet's spirituality echoes in the bishop's devotion to finding the divine in the starry skies he contemplates each evening from his garden. Hugo's quest to understand the infinite, to touch the divine as closely as possible, was enhanced by séance conversations with what purported to be the spirit world. Neither Hugo nor his Bishop Myriel shut any doors but, instead, remained open to listening to whatever the universe would tell them.

The poetry Hugo wrote during the séance years sheds light on questions and ideas that drove Hugo as he revised Les Misérables a few years later. He made great strides in defining his cosmology not only in Les Contemplations but also in Dieu (titled God in English), an even more complex visionary poem in which Hugo seeks to define God. There, he probes numerous religious and philosophical traditions, beginning each investigation with the same line: "And I saw above my head a black speck."[105] This speck infinitely far off represents the mystery of the divine. One by one the poet listens to and then rejects eight different perceptions of God, including those embodied in atheism, skepticism, paganism, *and* Christianity.

Never finding a definitive answer, Hugo contends that God is ultimately unknowable. In fact, he describes anyone claiming to have solved the mysteries of the universe in this way: "Blind man who thinks he reads, fool who thinks he knows!"[106] The final section of *Dieu* consists of nothing more than the "black-speck" line followed by many dots, which led his daughter Adèle to write that the poem ends only at "the brink of the infinite." When Hugo read "The Ocean of the Heights" section aloud to friends and family, his listeners demanded that he continue well beyond midnight. Adèle noted that it was half past two when Hugo finished "this account of the religions which tried to find God without ever succeeding."[107] As we saw in the previous chapter, that night Hugo explicitly defined "his own religion" as love—Bishop Myriel's driving force. Hugo may have consciously decided not to finish *Dieu*, since he spent his life seeking to comprehend, yet reveling in wonder. Nine years later, he was still musing: "Beyond the visible the invisible, beyond the invisible the unknown. Everywhere, always, at the zenith, at the nadir, in front, behind, above, below, up on high, down below, the formidable dark infinite."[108]

The French artists who originally adapted Hugo's novel into a musical recognized the magnitude of Hugo's message and the story's broad spirituality. Working from a deep knowledge and cultural experience of *Les Misérables*, composer Claude-Michel Schönberg and librettist/book author Alain Boublil found Hugo's spirituality to be distinct from established religion. Boublil, for instance, declines song-rights permission for anything religiously linked in an overt manner "because that is not why we wrote that musical. We never felt that the Christianity in *Les Misérables* was somehow church-related. I certainly appreciate that people sometimes tell us, 'I have to return to see the show because for me it's as healing as going to a service in a church.' That's wonderful. It means we have captured the essence of the novel." Schönberg, too, commented on that core

element of the novel. As "a Jewish boy educated by Jesuits," Schönberg calls himself an agnostic who believes in "personal spirituality,
the radiance of individual people." Thinking of that radiance, he
wondered, "Maybe such people have God in them, I don't know. I am
sure that Victor Hugo believed there was something out there other
than what we see. There is a *huge* spiritual side to the story—a belief
in something other than what we see."

Hugo's relationship with Christianity both in his life and in his
portrait of Bishop Myriel is at once complicated and simple. In
Myriel, Hugo gives us a man "illuminated by his heart" more than
by any religious tradition (I, 1, 14). He tells us that Bishop Myriel
follows the Gospel—Jesus Christ's life and teachings—as a shortcut
to perfection, and in myriad ways Hugo shows how Myriel's actions
parallel Christ's. At the same time, Hugo condemns the actions of
most priests and devotes practically no time to detailing the bishop's
dedication to performing Catholic ritual. This apparent contradic-
tion becomes clear, however, in a straightforward, staggering statement that Hugo wrote to historian Jules Michelet in 1856: "I remove
Christ from Christianity."[109] Much as Thomas Jefferson created *The
Life and Morals of Jesus of Nazareth* (more commonly known as *The
Jefferson Bible*), Hugo admired Jesus's life and actions and, in *Les
Misérables*, alluded to them throughout the novel.[110]

To underscore the breadth of the bishop's spirituality and
approach to life, Hugo explicitly draws upon multiple major world
religions and philosophies (I, 1, 13-14). As he describes the bishop's
compassion for non-human creatures, he compares Myriel not only
to the Catholic St. Francis of Assisi but also to the Hindu Brahmin
and the pagan, Roman Stoic philosopher Marcus Aurelius, thus suggesting religions' interrelationships. Of course, acting out of love for
others is a key tenet for a variety of religions. The *Qur'an*, for example, repeatedly encourages Muslims to do good. In Hinduism, "compassion is one of the highest virtues." Today's Dalai Lama, believing
that our purpose in life is to be happy, has "found that the greatest
degree of inner tranquility comes from the development of love and
compassion."[111] Certainly, as Hugo points out, Bishop Myriel goes
"outside of and beyond his faith."

Like Hugo (who wrote a poem honoring spiders and stinging net-
tles), Myriel pities creatures that most people find horrible. He loves
all living things, choosing to sprain his ankle rather than crush an
ant: "The Bishop of Digne had none of this unconsidered severity
toward animals peculiar to most priests. He did not go as far as the
Brahmin, but he appeared to have pondered these words of Ecclesiastes: 'Do we know where animals' souls go?'" (I, 1, 13) Hugo recast
that biblical verse in everyday words, choosing to have the bishop
think of "souls" rather than "spirits" (the usual translation of *spiritus*).[112] By seeing souls in animals, the bishop flies in the face of the
formal, centuries-old religious dogma that people alone have souls.
We feel a breath of Hugo's belief in metempsychosis.

The bishop's attention to and love for nature, animals, and even
inanimate objects is consonant, moreover, with the Hindu belief that
all things in the universe *are* the Supreme Being. To put it another
way, given the unity of being, distinctions are illusory.[113] Nature is at
once the creation and the embodiment of the Divine Reality, a sense
enhanced by how Bishop Myriel loves spending time in his garden,
"meditating in the presence of the great spectacle of the starry firma-
ment. . . . He was out there alone with himself, composed, tranquil,
adoring, comparing the serenity of his heart with the serenity of the
skies, moved in the darkness by the visible splendors of the constel-
lations and the invisible splendors of God, opening his soul to the
thoughts that fall from the unknown" (I, 1, 13). Hugo focuses as
much on the bishop's communing with nature as on his celebrating
Communion, and he makes clear his sense of how divinity pervades
and envelopes everything, even as he uses the traditional term *God*.

Hugo brilliantly wove into *Les Misérables* the Christian ethos of
his culture while simultaneously incorporating his personal sense of
an unknowable Being who permeates the universe constitutes our
conscience and our capacity to love. Director Tom Hooper, recognizing the breadth of Hugo's vision, wanted to make the film "in an
inclusive way, not an exclusive way":

The first time I saw the musical thinking that I might make
a film of it, I noticed that last line, "To love another person
is to see the face of God." When I experienced it sitting in
the audience, I was thinking, "My job as director is to make
that line resonate, to make that line belong to *everyone*,
and not make people who are not specifically Christian, or
specifically Catholic, feel excluded by that line."

Hooper tapped on the table as he emphasized that he wanted to
reach all people. "And I think I kind of achieved it, with Hugh's help."
Hugh Jackman confirmed that he does indeed see *Les Misérables* as
"a human story":

It speaks to the heart of what it is to be human, the trials
and tribulations of being human, and the ideals that we
should be striving for. I believe that at the heart of all
the world's religions right now—any kind of Christian,
Buddhist, Muslim, whatever—there's this sense of
devotion to something greater than our separate self—
something that connects all of us—and to the basic tenets
of "Do unto others as you would have them do unto you,"
these simple kind of laws. It's the same in every religion,
and that's what *Les Misérables* is speaking to.

Claude-Michel Schönberg put it this way in conversation with University of Virginia graduate students in drama: "When you play *Les
Misérables* in Japan, where the culture and the understanding of God
is *completely* different, the audience reaction is the same as in the U.S.
or England."

Victor Hugo spent decades on a quest to better comprehend why
we live, what death is, and where and how we might fathom God. In
the end, he developed an expansive spirituality and a mystical sense
of the Divine, Universal Spirit, which is in everything, including in
ourselves, in our consciences (see Chapter 6), and in the love we
feel. Hugo shares in *Les Misérables* his keen belief in love as a direct
route to God. In my journey to better grasp the impact of his epic

around the world, I now understand why a story that many consider a Christian allegory moves people of other faiths, as well as those of less faith. Spirituality—an awareness of something beyond ourselves—can touch us, whether or not we follow an organized religion.

Is Change Possible?

*Jean Valjean with Petit-Gervais, from the
1957 Pathé film starring Jean Gabin*

To believe in virtue, freedom, progress, and
enlightenment is to believe in God.[114]

I've been a teacher for over forty years, first as a graduate student teaching elementary French and then as a professor of literature. Of thousands of students, one especially stands out. My story with him reveals one reason why I regard *Les Misérables* so highly.

About twenty years ago, at the University of Virginia, one of the brightest students I've ever known was often a problem—a pain even—in my French composition course. Let's call him Joe. He would roll into class late, sometimes looking bored or hungover, and would answer questions with ease. Having him in class was *wonderful*: he was perceptive, creative, and able to express profound ideas in ways that his classmates comprehended (and in French!). Having him in class was *awful*: he visibly didn't do half the work, and his attitude set a bad example. Joe seemed uninterested in applying his obvious intelligence to learning the skills in the course he'd *chosen* to take. Here was an A-quality brain doing C-level work—what was up?

I won't bore you with my efforts to rouse his interest and focus his mind, except to say that they didn't seem to work. About three-quarters of the way through the semester, Joe stopped coming to class altogether. When that happens, I make every effort to discover what's going on. I called the phone number from his information sheet, and his housemate breathed an audible sigh of relief. "Oh, Professor Barnett," she said, "thank goodness! Joe won't get out of bed, and yours is the only class he was going to."

So I tracked Joe down and cajoled him into finishing the course. At the end of the semester, his imaginative video project brought his classmates great pleasure, as their enthusiastic applause showed. But that course was the only one he completed that semester. I think that he must have worked hard at failing the others, a failure which resulted in his automatic, immediate withdrawal from the university.

I soon lost touch with Joe. When he called me once from California, apparently just to say "hi," I got the impression that he was moving around the country quite a bit, without a steady job. In his early twenties, he had left home. I guessed that he was staying with friends. Hard to forget, this guy who had demonstrated such potential, who seemed not to care, who avoided help. Once or twice a year, a memory of Joe would suddenly come to me, for no apparent reason, and I'd muse on why he had made such choices and what had happened to him.

Flash forward to a few years ago. I'm in my office on a balmy spring day, when a thirty-something-year-old man knocks on the door. I don't recognize him for a few seconds. But as soon as he says, "Hello, Professor Barnett, you probably don't remember me," I immediately know. "Hi, Joe." He summarizes his past decade-plus in a few words: drifting, working unskilled jobs, coming to recognize what he had given up in leaving school. With the help of his academic dean, he'd returned to finish his undergraduate degree and was smoothly on his way to graduating. A couple of years later, he had completed a master's degree.

It matters to me that he came by to share his appreciation for my support all those years ago. What matters more is that Joe changed for the better, completely turning his life around. He did it through his own inner strength and intelligence. But he was able to do it, too, because others helped him: his housemates, his academic dean, me a little—his friends, too, no doubt. No one is irretrievably lost. I saw that in Joe's story—but Bishop Myriel and Jean Valjean taught me that first.

"A story of redemption," my friend Kate said when I told her about how Joe had successfully resumed his studies. "A story of change," I responded. Not such different interpretations, really. Victor Hugo's conception of redemption includes and then goes beyond the notion of atonement so often associated with redeeming oneself. In Jean Valjean's redemption, in particular, Hugo offers a compelling case for people's capacity to remake themselves and lift themselves morally. For Valjean, that moral progress means not only doing good, but also growing closer to God—in a personal way that resonates with people who believe in a higher power. Certainly, as we saw in the previous chapter, Hugo seeks and welcomes the divine in *Les*

Misérables. At the same time, he illustrates in down-to-earth ways how tough personal change can be, both because we all have human flaws and because society sometimes tends to label people as good or bad and to consider some irredeemable. Recognizing that social status defined people and that past mistakes dogged their lives, Hugo worked both as a writer and legislator to improve that world.

Hugo's and Valjean's society was not so different from our own. Yes, some people are able to build a life that's better than the one they inherited from family or place of birth, but others find themselves shackled by the culture into which they were born. Contemporary memoirs and news articles regularly recount both types of stories. Shaka Senghor in *Writing My Wrongs* graphically tells how young black inner-city boys descend into drug dealing and crime. J. D. Vance in *Hillbilly Elegy* analyzes the history and culture of the Scots-Irish in Appalachia and beyond. *The New York Times* blogger Nicholas Kristof brings readers into the lives of people struggling to work their way out of poverty around the world, despite the huge structural obstacles they face. In the United States, notwithstanding the promises of the American Dream, over 38 million people (one-eighth of the population) lived in poverty in 2018, according to the U.S. Census Bureau.[115]

Whether hillbilly white, inner-city black, or born into poverty, some people rise up despite negative expectations. Yet society unfortunately has endless power to block people's progress, from certain laws to some individuals' simple (and devastating) assumption that people cannot change. In some ways, we have not progressed since Jean Valjean's time, when the prevailing assumption was that ex-convicts were lost causes. Examples are everywhere. Laws that block ex-felons from voting keep them from participating fully in society. Lack of mental health clinics can impede sufferers' recovery. Regulations that require job applicants to list prior convictions often knock such applicants out of the pool. The past—even if overcome—adversely affects the present and future. Too many people seem to be like the "absolute" Inspector Javert, who admits no exceptions and has "nothing but disdain, aversion, and disgust for all who had once overstepped the bounds of the law" (I, 5, 5). How many times have

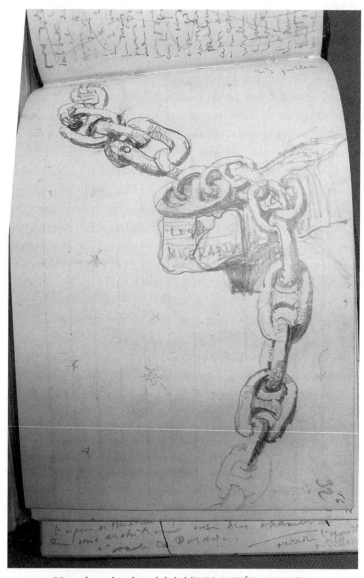

Hugo drew this chain labeled "LES MISÉRABLES" as a possible frontispiece for his novel (undated).

we heard similar reactions to people simply because they were immigrants and refugees?

Like those who feel trapped by their life situations, Jean Valjean is trapped by people's perceptions of him, sensing that he can never shed the shame of that "ex-convict" label. Those making *Les Mis* understood well his plight. Actor Hugh Jackman recognized the power of such stigma, describing it to me this way:

> In everything he did, Valjean was haunted by Javert and
> by his past. And the power that Javert has over him, really,
> right up until the end, is that Javert represents Valjean's
> deepest fears of himself: "That actually you're right: I am
> still an animal, I am still that bad guy. No matter how
> hard I try, I really am worthless. I really am an animal, you
> know." And Valjean tries in everything he does to get out of
> that place.

Director Tom Hooper emphasized that sense of conflict in the "What Have I Done?" scene (when Valjean soliloquizes over his theft and the bishop's unexpected forgiveness), a scene that Hooper set in the bishop's chapel. When I asked him about the symbolism of Valjean's moving back and forth through the light and darkness so significant to Hugo, Hooper explained, "Partly, it was luck in the sense that there was the arch he walked through. That happened naturally, but I wanted to set up a physical dynamic with the altar, where Valjean would make an approach and feel like he'd got closer than he deserved and so back away and then be pulled back in." Hugh Jackman similarly recognized what a trial it was for Valjean to work his way toward God, and he admired Valjean's tenacity in striving to be a better man:

> After that first lightning bolt of virtue [the bishop's
> forgiveness and gift of the candlesticks] comes this
> constant mountain to climb, this constant ideal, a constant
> sort of Holy Grail that he's trying to reach, and/or measure

up to, which is, you know, God. . . . I always feel that
Valjean's humility comes from the feeling that, no matter
what he does, it's never quite enough.

Tenacity is essential for those who want to change. Other people
doubt that someone like Jean Valjean could choose to follow a new
path in life. Such suspicion can make him think that he must repeatedly atone for his crime, as minor as it was. But, at the same time,
Valjean recognizes (both in prison and after his release) that he has
already expiated that theft and his attempted escapes. He has *more*
than atoned since the punishment was much greater than his crimes
warranted. In fact, Valjean's desire for improvement goes beyond the
idea of redemption as atonement. In Valjean's case, redemption is
lifelong personal growth. Such moral progress was one definition
of *rédemption* in nineteenth-century France, just as "regeneration or
renewal" is an aspect of the contemporary French definition.[116] For
Valjean, redemption means continuing to remake himself in real,
positive ways. Director Tom Hooper appreciated the inspirational
nature of both Valjean's impetus to recreate himself and his ability
to do so:

> What I find very inspiring about the story is this idea that
> it's possible in a defined and intense instant of time to
> remake yourself. We live in an age where so many types of
> courses that people might go on as adults—whether it's
> therapy, counseling, yoga, meditation—promise some level
> of giving you back the power to transform yourself. And
> this story seems to me like the ultimate example of contact
> with a great person allowing this extraordinary change to
> happen. I found that very powerful.

What Hooper calls "a defined and intense instant of time" is key
to appreciating Hugo's understanding of the complexity of the challenge facing Valjean. Yes, the bishop's loving, self-sacrificing forgiveness launches the arc of Valjean's inspirational story: such great mercy

must spawn change. In the *Les Mis* musical, the bishop's forgiveness prompts Valjean's "What Have I Done?" soliloquy. Given the necessary compression of the stage and screen, that heart-wrenching self-questioning transforms Valjean in just over three minutes. But, as Hugo makes clear, in the real world, more would be necessary before Valjean does change—not only because he has fallen to great depths, but also because personal development is very difficult. In the novel, Bishop Myriel's forgiveness starts the process, but the "intense instant" is Valjean's coming face to face with what he has become—after he steals again.

When Bishop Myriel forgives Valjean's theft and hands him his candlesticks, he disrupts Valjean's decided hatred and reawakens his conscience. Such generosity stuns Valjean, leaving him dumbfounded and faint. The bishop has so rocked his expectations that he hardly knows where he is or what he's doing, and he leaves the city "as if he were escaping." Walking in a daze, he's "prey to a mass of new emotions" (I, 2, 13). Valjean is, among other things, angry, without knowing at whom. "He could not have said whether he was touched or humiliated. At times, there comes over him a strange relenting, which he tries to resist with the hardening of his past twenty years." Far from transformed at this point, Valjean is working hard to hang onto his hostility. Tired, full of inexpressible feelings, he does not notice the itinerant young chimney sweep who's passing by, singing and tossing his coins in the air. One forty-sou piece escapes and lands near Valjean, who puts his foot on it.

When Petit-Gervais innocently asks this savage-looking man for his coin, Valjean demands his name but otherwise "does not seem to understand." Petit-Gervais tries to move Valjean's foot, but the ex-convict looks at the boy "with an air of bewilderment," wondering who is there. Then, for no apparent reason, he frightens the sobbing boy into running off. Valjean just sits and stares unseeingly until the evening cold makes him shiver and move his foot, which reveals the coin. "What is that?" he asks, hit by an electric shock when he realizes what it is. For a few seconds he stares at the coin, "as if the thing that glistened there in the shadows were an open eye staring at him." Valjean's next actions show that his conscience has finally—

and suddenly—revived. He convulsively seizes the money and peers in all directions, "trembling like a frightened animal seeking refuge." Repenting of his unintended action, he runs after Petit-Gervais, shouting his name, desperately trying to return these few cents that he had automatically, unknowingly taken.

Valjean could not have explained why he took the coin, but he realizes that he has nonetheless stolen it. When he cannot find Petit-Gervais, he sinks to the ground "with the weight of his bad conscience," and cries out, "I'm such a miserable man!" ("*Je suis un misérable!*") In a flash, he sees himself "face to face," as "the hideous convict Jean Valjean." That theft in response to the bishop's pardon, as it were, makes Valjean realize how immoral and wretched he has become. Such consciousness of oneself, Hugo clearly implies, is closely associated with having a moral conscience—a connection made palpable in French, where the word *conscience* first means "awareness" and "consciousness" and only then refers to "the moral faculty of conscience."[117] Valjean sees a "light dawning on his conscience" because he is outside himself, in "a kind of ecstasy." The light is the bishop, he realizes, and Valjean feels his hatred and misdeeds fade away in the bishop's presence. He weeps for the first time in nineteen years, feeling defenseless and frightened. The last we see of Valjean for a long time, he is "kneeling in prayer, on the pavement in the dark, before Monseigneur Bienvenu's door" (I, 2, 13).

To make big changes we may need multiple, soul-shaking experiences such as those Valjean undergoes. Sometimes our conscience gets so buried—or is so overwhelmed by anger, hate, or despair—that only a jolt can reawaken it and help us become willing to listen to it. Most of us don't talk publicly about such personal ordeals, but former felon Shaka Senghor does on the TED stage and in his memoir, *Writing My Wrongs: Life, Death, and Redemption in an American Prison.* The ways in which his life and metamorphosis parallel Jean Valjean's underline the truth of Hugo's insights and testify to people's power to remake themselves. As Senghor puts it, "Anybody can have a transformation if we create the space for that to happen."[118]

In 2010, Shaka Senghor was paroled after serving nineteen years for second-degree murder. During those prison years, he had attempted to escape, lived "in hell," assaulted an officer, spent over five years in solitary confinement, witnessed unspeakable brutality, and missed seeing his son be born and develop into a man. In his memoir, he details how he had grown from the twelve-year-old who dreamed of becoming a physician, to the fourteen-year-old drug hustler, to the angry seventeen-year-old who got himself shot in an argument over a girlfriend, to the fearful nineteen-year-old who killed another drug dealer. Most interestingly for me, he describes with insight and honesty his many efforts to change and the shock that finally provoked his transformation.

Senghor recounts his redemption as a series of small turning points, such as when he decided that if he didn't forgive everyone he was angry with and rid himself of "destructive force," he would become as crazy as some he had met in solitary confinement. But one-time forgiveness wasn't powerful enough. The real shifts came when he started keeping a journal, writing about his anger: "It's hard to express how much this process of examination began to change me. Within the lined pages of my notepads, I got in touch with a part of me that didn't feel fear whenever something didn't go my way—a part of me that was capable of feeling compassion for the men around me."[119]

But his "true awakening" came when his ten-year-old son pleaded with him in a letter: "MY MOM TOLD ME WHY YOU'RE IN JAIL, BECAUSE OF MURDER! DON'T KILL DAD PLEASE THAT IS A SIN." Senghor found himself trembling violently, worrying that everything inside himself might break apart:

> For the first time in my incarceration, I was hit with the
> truth that my son would grow up to see me as a murderer. . . .
> When I finished reading, I was scared for Li'l Jay and all of
> the other young men who had fathers like me—fathers who
> were languishing away in prison cells while their sons grew
> up lost and angry. I had acknowledged my guilt years before,
> but there was a difference between that and accepting

responsibility for my actions. My son's words made me take
that final step on my road to redemption.

Senghor wrote his son that he would not murder again. "When I
finished writing the letter, I was emotionally drained and spiritually
exhausted—but I felt better than I had at any other point in my life.
Something in me had changed."[120]

Only when Senghor, like Jean Valjean, was forced to face what
he really had become and experience the emotions provoked
by that realization did he truly evolve. Senghor puts it this way:
"Real change comes only when you are completely and thoroughly
disgusted with your actions and the consequences that they pro-
duce."[121] Valjean's transformation is immediate, Hugo tells us: "It
was a strange phenomenon, possible only in his current condition,
but the fact is that in stealing this money from that child, he had
done something of which he was no longer capable" (I, 2, 13). Both
of these real and the fictional redemptions thrive, too, on the power
of love and a conscious desire to work toward becoming a better
person. Valjean found courage in his love for Cosette and in the
memory of the bishop's love symbolized by his candlesticks. Senghor credits his love for his children and for Ebony Roberts, who
gave him unfailing support.

Much as Victor Hugo wrote his novel to inspire people to make
society better, Shaka Senghor sees his life work as mentoring young
people, sharing his story to dissuade others from going down the
dangerous, wrong path he took. He relives and retells horrific life
events to help others and prove that personal progress is possible.
"That's the thing about hope," he writes. "In the moment it can feel
foolish or sentimental or disconnected from reality. But hope knows
that people change on a timeline we can't predict."[122] Senghor's is one
of many voices today pushing back against what Hugo showed as
people's tendency to label others. Both writers argue against societies whose cultures reject the idea that people can redeem themselves
and whose rules inhibit such renewal. Senghor might easily be referring to Jean Valjean when he says, "Our worst deeds don't define who
we are or what we can contribute to the world."[123] Or as a policeman

friend of mine who's known hundreds of offenders puts it, "It's about who you are now, not who you were."

Redemption for a Shaka Senghor or a Jean Valjean means working to build the most productive, helpful, generous life possible—to be the best person one can be. For Valjean, redemption also means growing ever closer to God. In remaking himself, Valjean aims beyond the already lofty goal of goodness. As he realizes during his first major crisis of conscience (see Chapter 6), Valjean's ultimate life goal is to "return to God," to "enter into holiness in God's eyes" (I, 7, 3). In fact, during the ex-convict's all-night war with his conscience, Hugo again steps into the story, telling us that Valjean's altered attitude after encountering Bishop Myriel and Petit-Gervais, Hugo writes, was "more than a transformation—it was a transfiguration." As such, his shift is spiritual, since "transfiguration" is "an exalting, glorifying, or spiritual change" or "a change in form or appearance, especially one that elevates or idealizes."[124] Several religious traditions contain stories of transfiguration, including those of the Buddha and the Hindu Krishna. Christian doctrine finds divinity in Jesus Christ's mountaintop transfiguration into someone shining with bright rays of light (as told in Matthew 17:1-9, Mark 9:2-8, and Luke 9:28-36). By calling Valjean's metamorphosis a *transfiguration*, then, Hugo simultaneously emphasizes the elevating nature of Valjean's development and his progress toward the Supreme Being.

In the character of Jean Valjean, Hugo merges the ideas of transformation and redemption and hints at his own complex notion of the latter. On the one hand, Hugo connected redemption to atonement, as when he wrote Juliette Drouet of his hope that the sincere goodness of their love, together with their suffering, made up for that love's illegitimacy in society's eyes (see Chapter 3). But a decade later, after being forced into exile, Hugo had the time and inclination to muse ever more deeply on the meaning of life and death. His ideas evolved during his long, meditative walks in nature, as he explains here, writing about himself in the third person: "Since he is at the seaside, let him gain from it. Let this constant motion beneath the infinite give him wisdom. Let him meditate on the eternal uprising of the waves against the shore, and of imposture against the truth."[125] Inspired by both the ocean's eternal presence during his Channel Island life and by the séances related to his grief over Léopoldine's death, Hugo developed his visionary disposition. As he expanded his spiritual thinking beyond the Bible reading he'd done in his youth, he delved into his multiple books about world religions.

Beginning primarily in the 1850s, Hugo mused about his broad understanding of redemption in a number of poems, where he offers his cosmology, or theory of the universe. Hugo's conception echoes with aspects of cosmologies associated with several world religions but follows none. Several of his visionary poems appear in *Les Contemplations*, including his famous, apocalyptic "Ce que dit la bouche d'ombre" ("What the Shadow Mouth Said"), a work inspired by séance experiences. Hugo recognized the importance of "Ce que dit la bouche d'ombre" within his work, calling it a "poem about universal fate and universal hope."[126] In it, Hugo explains that God created the universe, but not evil, which comes from the universe itself. When souls commit evil acts, they come closer to the shadow and the matter that constitute the universe and thus move farther from God. Hugo suspected along with Jean Reynaud (just one of the philosophers whose works those he read) that eternal hell does not exist. Instead, in a sort of reincarnation, souls redeem their bad actions through expiation, moving from planet to planet as they progress toward infinity—an infinity that is God. Souls who do good also move closer to light and spirit, that is, closer to God. For Hugo, the opportunity to advance toward God is a source of hope.

Hugo confessed his own distance from God and his ultimate reconciliation when he finally wrote about Léopoldine's untimely death. He revealed his enormous crisis of faith after the tragedy and his hard-won return to God, a redemptive change of heart, in a series of poems in *Les Contemplations*. There, Hugo's love for his daughter and his grief, anger, and fears are as vibrant as any we might read in our tell-all culture today. He explicitly aimed for such candor, telling us in the preface that he would have called the book *Memoirs of a Soul*, "if doing so had not been too pretentious."

The Dolmen Where the Mouth of The Shadow Spoke to Me
(Le Dolmen où m'a parlé la bouche d'ombre),
which Hugo drew in 1855 probably

Hugo's personal growth came only at the cost of heart-wrenching grief and anguish. In "Demain, dès l'aube . . ." ("Tomorrow, at dawn . . ."), we walk alongside the poet on his lengthy, somber trip to what we eventually learn is the grave of someone he loved. He is bereft, his eyes are so fixed on his thoughts that he sees and hears nothing, his heart so distressed that day seems to him like night. The misery of this now-classic poem is both reinforced and rocked by Hugo's anger in "Trois Ans Après" ("Three Years After"), which is set three years after Léopoldine's death. Here the poet rails at God for having taken so many of his beloved family members. Hugo, who had long believed even more strongly than most other Romantic poets that his was a divine calling, wonders why he should continue writing in order to serve such a God. He rejects the conception of a loving God and hints that our lives might be driven by some sort of malicious fate or destiny rather than by a benevolent higher power.

But then, in "À Villequier" ("In Villequier"), Hugo worked through his emotions, expressing his willingness and ability to develop, even when in despair—or perhaps because of it. Hugo wrote this moving poem a month after visiting Léopoldine's grave in Villequier for the first time.[127] We read of his daughter's fine qualities, his loss and sadness, and his resentment of God. He speaks directly to God, saying, for instance, "I know that . . . a child who dies, bringing her mother despair, doesn't matter to you—not to *you!*"[128] But Hugo eventually comes to accept Léopoldine's death and shows how his sorrow brought him a richer understanding of life and death and a renewed closeness with God. In this intensely intimate poem, Hugo engages us with the recognizable, complex emotions of grief. At the same time, he testifies to our potential to move forward from doubt and disbelief. No matter how far we might have fallen, Hugo tells us with his own story and with Valjean's, we *can* change for the better.

Still, moral transformation is tough. "Progress is not made overnight" (III, 3, 6). Personal progress takes ongoing courage, effort, and inspiration—which together make for tenacity. It might require a life-changing moment and/or the angst that comes from seeing clearly our faults or bad actions. We might have to sink lower before we rise. And once set out in a new direction, we can rarely rest on our laurels. Sticking to our resolution to grow requires ongoing attention, work, and, often, others' support—not to mention the resolve and resilience we'll explore in Chapter 8. Hugo is up front about how hard self-improvement can be.

When my students and I follow Jean Valjean's journey, they are sometimes dismayed to see, for instance, how much Valjean hates Marius as the suitor for his daughter's hand. Or how Valjean vacillates about what to do when he learns that Marius is fighting on the barricade. Some of these young people are idealists; others have expectations driven by the musical and its need to tell an immense story in under three hours. Whatever the reason, many of them expect Jean Valjean to be perfectly good after he has met the bishop. Hugh Jackman told me how much he appreciated director Tom Hooper's grasp of Valjean's complexity:

> Tom kept saying, "With Valjean, we have to play the long
> game. In the musical, really, the game is over from the
> time he's the mayor. From that point on, Valjean sings
> beautifully, but he's the hero, and he's the saint. We must
> play the long game. There can be no resolution to him and
> to who he is until the very end."

Les Misérables inspires, in great measure, because Valjean (despite his uncanny physical strength) is deeply human, in both positive and negative senses of the word. In him we see, on the one hand, the mix of good and bad intentions that sometimes makes us struggle to do what is right. Yet, on the other hand, alongside such natural flaws, in Valjean we find the profound compassion and love that prompt him to sacrifice for others, qualities that in part define our humanity.

Valjean's tenacity in following his conscience and striving for goodness in the face of great challenges generates hope from the hopelessness that he had felt before his transformation. Such capacity for change or redemption gives all of us a potent reason to be optimistic. Jean Valjean epitomizes what an individual can do, but, Hugo argues, that same hope exists for societies. Valjean's moral growth reflects the capability for society to move forward. Some of the novel's philosophical sections (which are not the digressions they might seem to be) make clear that civilization's potential parallels Valjean's. Hugo's robust confidence in a better future appears, for example, in "The Two Duties: To Watch and To Hope." In that chapter, Hugo makes the case that, given the "imperishability of humanity," the world's wretched have reason for hope:

> Ideas no more flow backward than do rivers.
> Just let those who don't want the future reflect on this.
> By saying no to progress, they are condemning not the
> future, but themselves. They give themselves a dark illness;
> they infect themselves with the past. There's only one way
> to refuse Tomorrow, and that's to die (IV, 7, 4).

Growth is like a stream, which may eddy and even briefly flow backward, yet always goes on to its outlet—the sea, which symbolizes the generous, altruistic, peaceful future that Hugo envisions. Hugo's trust in our divinely-created capacity to love and to change for the better underpins his belief in humanity and his optimism. Convinced that people—and hence cultures—are moving toward God, Hugo brings us the hope that comes from knowing that progress is as inevitable as it is beneficial.

CHAPTER 6

Listening to Our Best Selves

Conscience before a Bad Action (LA CONSCIENCE
DEVANT UNE MAUVAISE ACTION),
which Hugo drew and captioned in 1866

Conscience is the internal moral solar spectrum.
Sun lights the body. God lights the mind.
It's as though a sort of God's moon exists deep in
every human brain.[129]

Victor Hugo must have felt at the top of his game as he headed home after a scintillating dinner party with his good friends, the publisher Émile de Girardin and his wife, Delphine. After all, only two days earlier (on January 7, 1841), he'd been elected to the prestigious French Academy, a goal he'd sought for five years. Now he was one of the forty members of the national body overseeing the French language, one of the "immortals." That election added to the fame he already had as the acknowledged leader of French Romanticism—a successful playwright and much-published poet who would soon be called "*le Maître*" ("the Master"). Academy members could also run for public office, and Hugo had political aspirations. Proud of his hard-won reputation, he had reasons to protect it. So it's no surprise that he found himself wrangling with his conscience when he encountered an ethical dilemma that evening.

Because heavy snow made walking home in his fancy shoes a bad idea, Hugo was looking to hire a carriage when a violent scene erupted. He saw an expensively dressed man plunge a huge fistful of snow down the back of a woman standing on the corner in a low-cut gown. She was most certainly a prostitute. Just as Hugo's Fantine does when similarly attacked in *Les Misérables*, the woman let out a piercing scream and struck the man, who hit her back. The ensuing fight brought the police running. As Hugo reported, "They seized the woman and didn't touch the man."[130]

At first Hugo did not intervene. Even though he sometimes associated with prostitutes (as his writing notes indicate), it would not do to be publicly seen with one. Hugo joined the crowd following the officers and their suspect to the station. Then, like the onlookers he disparages in his novel, Hugo watched the proceedings through the window. The two sergeants—unknowingly serving as models for Inspector Javert—ignored the woman's protestations of innocence, her grief, and her accusations against the man who had attacked her. Hugo later reported to his wife that he had hesitated to enter the police station, recounting to himself the reasons he shouldn't. He was well known, and the newspapers were full of stories about his recent Academy election. Let reporters know that he was mixed up in this sordid affair, and he would be getting the *wrong* sort of publicity. No need to give fodder to other writers who already resented his success, either.

When the police promised the woman six months in prison, she sobbed, threw herself on the floor, and tore at her hair. Hugo, overtaken by compassion, reflected on the situation—and decided to listen to his conscience. Walking into the station, he told the police that he had witnessed the scene and wanted to testify on the prostitute's behalf. But oral testimony wasn't enough. Because the police had begun their report, the commissioner said, he could release the woman only if Hugo signed a statement. To win an innocent person's freedom, Hugo agreed to sign. Committing himself to getting truly involved was the right thing to do, he knew.

In just such ways, conscience pushes us to act out of love and to prioritize others' well-being over our own. Hugo felt his conscience pricked that snowy evening, and he had to battle with himself before he chose justice at the risk of his reputation and public embarrassment. In *Les Misérables*, Hugo depicts with heartrending reality how conscience connects with caring and how harrowing it can be to follow our conscience. His characters struggle with conscience in some of the novel's most thought-provoking scenes—internal confrontations that intrigue my students. These young people argue vociferously about whether and why Marius should save the father of the woman he loves *or* help the man his dying father asked him to protect. They agonize with Jean Valjean over whether he should ruin his life in order to save an innocent man. And they appreciate Inspector Javert's anguish when he senses that what he believed to be his conscience was false. Year after year, students enthusiastically debate these fictional characters' ethical dilemmas and address real-life contemporary ethical questions along the way.[131]

Outside of classrooms, plenty of issues call on our conscience, on us personally as well as on us as a society. How should we deal with refugees from war-torn countries? What is my role in a country ever more polarized between conservative and liberal, black and white, urban and rural? What should I think when I learn that a well-connected friend who admitted defrauding a widow of millions goes free? I know that less well-off people who commit relatively minor crimes spend years in prison. What does my conscience say about such situations, and how do I act? How much does my personal conscience affect my social conscience?

Some people have famously followed their conscience, at great personal sacrifice, as they often seem villains to some even as they are heroes to others. Think of Mahatma Gandhi, Dr. Martin Luther King, Jr., Nelson Mandela, or Malala Yousafzai, to name just a few. In the long run—or from an international perspective—their work for social justice and the public good is applauded as admirable. In the short term and locally, however, they have been arrested, shot at, imprisoned, exiled. Many were as explicit as Hugo about the power of conscience:

- Mahatma Gandhi: "There is a higher court than courts of justice and that is the court of conscience. It supersedes all other courts."

- Martin Luther King, Jr.: "There comes a time when one must take the position that is neither safe nor politic nor popular, but he must do it because conscience tells him it is right."

- Edward Snowden: "I'm willing to sacrifice [my former life] because I can't in good conscience allow the U.S. government to destroy privacy, internet freedom and basic liberties for people around the world with this massive surveillance machine they're secretly building."[132]

As these modern examples remind us, people who visibly follow their conscience can be polemical, polarizing influences even when they prompt positive changes. Victor Hugo, too, unleashed controversy when he publicly expressed his conscientious political decisions, as we'll see in his long fight against Napoleon III. In *Les Misérables*, though, Hugo steps back from such public displays of conscience to delve into how difficult it can be simply to hear what our conscience is saying and make the morally right decision, putting care for others above our self-interest.

Watching Jean Valjean struggle with his conscience is an intriguing, agonizing, and provocative experience—especially when he faces an impossible dilemma, as he does more than once. In the chapter aptly called "A Storm Inside a Mind" (I, 7, 3), Hugo brings us for the first time into Valjean's thoughts as he vacillates between listening to his conscience and fighting with it. Eight years have passed since Valjean's transformative experience with Bishop Myriel and Petit-Gervais, when he became conscious of his conscience (see Chapter 5). Valjean now lives in Montreuil-sur-mer, where his inventive, inexpensive manufacturing of imitation jet beads and trinkets brings his workers high wages. He enriches his fellow citizens' lives and develops a well-deserved reputation for philanthropy: "His pockets full of money when he went out, and empty when he returned" (I, 5, 3). About fifty years old, loved and admired by many, he is known as M. Madeleine.[133] The townspeople convince him to become mayor. Valjean has been able to succeed, however, only by hiding his galley-slave past.

Madeleine believed he had buried forever the name "Jean Valjean"—until a new police inspector arrives and changes Valjean's life forever. Inspector Javert thinks he recognizes in the mayor a former convict he'd guarded at Toulon. (The police seek Valjean because he broke parole by stealing from Petit-Gervais and by not showing his yellow passport in Montreuil.) M. Madeleine responds to Javert's frequent, annoying stare with his usual easy kindness. He even knowingly risks betraying his identity by using his superhuman strength to lift a heavy wagon off a man. Javert *does* recognize Valjean but thinks he must be wrong, as he tells Madeleine, because a man recently arrested for stealing apples has been identified as the "real Valjean." The accused, known as Champmathieu, will likely be condemned to life at hard labor after his trial in Arras the following day.

What is Madeleine/Valjean to do? He realizes that he would maintain his safe, comfortable life if he simply left everything to fate—or to God's will, as he sometimes calls it (especially when it favors his self-interest). Once Champmathieu is imprisoned as Jean Valjean, Madeleine could never be identified as the ex-convict. Yet Valjean's sense of honor and duty push him to tell the truth, which would send him back to the horrors of perpetual hard labor. But doesn't he also have a duty to the hundreds of employees who depend on him for their income? And what would become of Fantine and Cosette if he left? What about himself? Is saving his life and freedom worth destroying his soul by letting someone be condemned in his place? He even momentarily toys with the vain hope that his "crimes" might be forgiven because of his good works. Almost as soon as Valjean thinks he's settled the question, he looks at the situation from another side—and there are many sides.

Throughout one terrible night and the following, angst-filled day, Valjean searches his soul. At times, Hugo draws more or less subtle parallels between Valjean's torment and Jesus Christ's Gethsemane agony over his looming sacrifice on the cross.[134] For some readers, such allusions prove that Hugo wrote a Christian book. To readers like me, they emphasize Hugo's sense of the divine source of conscience *and* Valjean's desire to grow closer to God with no religion as intermediary. Each time Valjean resolves on either confessing or remaining quiet, he sees how that choice would harm either people depending on him or Champmathieu. For Valjean personally, one decision would be "the death agony of his happiness" and the other "the death agony of his virtue" (I, 7, 3). Over and over again, he finds himself thrown back into his crisis of conscience. Hugo brilliantly describes Valjean's apparently conscientious arguments that tempt him to do what his more egocentric self *wants* to do. Such recognizable rationalizations let us see ourselves in Valjean. With a wonderfully human inconsistency, too, Valjean fights both to listen to his conscience and to skirt around it at the same time.

As Valjean grapples with the ramifications of Javert's news, he tries to hide in the dark, but to no avail: "Alas! What he wanted to keep outside had come in, what he wanted to blind was looking at him. His conscience. His conscience, or God" (I, 7, 3).[135] Valjean instantly understands that his self-preservation instinct conflicts with the right, honest thing to do. And he senses that he cannot hide from his conscience and God—because his conscience is God manifested inside himself.

Director Tom Hooper makes visible such inner struggles between our self-serving and other-focused selves through his Les Mis "Who Am I?" scene. There, Hugh Jackman sings sometimes as his mirrored reflection and sometimes directly into the camera. Commenting on that performance, Jackman found Hooper's idea "a genius decision to film that in the reflection of the mirror."[136] We literally see Valjean's generous morality debating with his self-interest as he is internally torn between doing what's right and doing what's comfortable.

Les Mis producer Cameron Mackintosh added another dimension to the meaning of this scene—whether in the film or the stage musical—when he talked with me about what are known as "the magic notes."[137] These are the four descending notes that repeat and crescendo between the Prologue and "The End of the Day" scene and then reappear throughout the show. "The magic notes are always used to open a new chapter, pivotal moments when Jean Valjean moves to another place in his life," Mackintosh pointed out. They are especially unmistakable in "Who Am I?", where their repetition slowly grows in intensity as Valjean moves closer to choosing to follow his conscience. Mackintosh observed that "Who Am I?" has more musical resonance because of the "magic notes," which connect this scene to the rest of the show. "There something heavenly about those magic notes," he continued. "It's like they are notes from God, so God plays a part."

God's role is still more evident in the novel. Valjean knows that he is wrestling with a decision made impossible by the ironic disjuncture between God's wishes and human understanding. As singer/

actor Colm Wilkinson remarked: "To play Valjean, you had to feel that anguished, conscious dilemma he was going through." Doing the right thing would save Valjean's soul, which he has made his life goal. Incongruously, turning himself in would make him repugnant and criminal in the eyes of society. He would be "condemned" to both prison and public disgrace, as he sings in "Who Am I?" Yet protecting his reputation and successful life would, from God's perspective, "damn" him. "Painful fate! He could enter holiness in God's eyes only by returning to infamy in other people's!" (I, 7, 3) Despite his natural horror at rejoining the chain gang, Valjean recognizes that confessing is his best chance to continue his progress from immorality toward divinity.

Since his encounters with the bishop and Petit-Gervais, Valjean realizes, two thoughts have directed his actions: "to conceal his name, and to sanctify his life; to escape from men and to return to God" (I, 7, 3). For eight years, those goals have mostly worked in tandem. When they conflicted, Valjean never hesitated to sacrifice his safety to his virtue. He "thought—following the example of all those wise, holy, and just men of the past—that his highest duty was not toward himself" (1, 7, 3). But now, when the stakes are great, he knows that the same society that had condemned him to a miserable prison existence will neither comprehend nor value his sacrifice.

Hugo vividly portrays what conscience does *to* and *for* us—and also engages us with the human agony of his hero's dilemma. Nothing is more terrifying than contemplating the depths of someone's conscience, "the soul's interior," Hugo writes. "Nowhere can the mind's eye find anything more dazzling or more obscure than in man; it can focus on nothing more awe-inspiring, more complex, more mysterious, or more infinite." Hugo dives into these depths with some emotion and trepidation, he tells us, finding in the dark infinity inside us "giants doing battle as in Homer, mêlées of dragons and hydras, and clouds of phantoms as in Milton, ghostly spirals as in Dante." Still, entering into such depths is essential: "To write the poem of the human conscience, though only of one man, even the most insignificant man, would be to swallow up all epics in a superior and definitive epic" (1, 7, 3).

By delving so deeply into the darkness and light of human conscience and by plunging us into the anguish and strength of choosing love over self-interest, Hugo reveals the potential grandeur of the human spirit. Jean Valjean's willingness to heed his conscience—to sacrifice himself repeatedly for the good of others—is key to why many find *Les Misérables* uplifting and inspiring. Claude-Michel Schönberg pondered Valjean's generosity when he answered a University of Virginia student's question about Valjean's death:

> Our lynchpin is Valjean. So take our show as a biography of Jean Valjean. And we all know that by the end of biographies, it's never a happy ending. So we have the death of Valjean, but we see that he didn't die for nothing. All the good that he did in his life—he opened up hope and the future, virtually their humanity, for a number of characters. Cosette and Marius have the future, and they will live on the legacy of Jean Valjean.

And it is natural, then, to ask ourselves: "Who would not want to leave such a legacy?"

For Hugo, personally, listening to his conscience was fundamental to living well. As he once flatly stated, "Obeying my conscience is my rule, a rule with no exceptions."[138] He was adamant in his belief that conscience is personal, that one is answerable to God but not to other people. Hugo's commitment to his principles manifested itself in sometimes highly visible or startling choices, some of which we might disagree with—for example, rejecting amnesty from exile despite his family's desire to return to France, or hiding from Juliette Drouet the fact that he and Léonie d'Aunet were lovers. Hugo did not flinch from doing what he thought best, however, and he attributed to his conscience many of his legislative stances and actions. His most consequential, public acts of conscience were arguably those related to his nineteen-year exile from his beloved France. After choosing exile when President Louis-Napoleon Bonaparte usurped

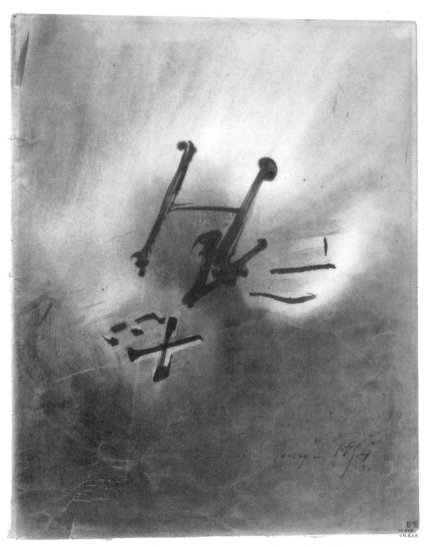

*In this drawing done on Jersey in 1854, Hugo embraced
his initials with the letters of the word for "exile."*

the French government, Hugo rejected the general amnesty eight years later, preferring exile over capitulation. Here's how it happened.

As a member of the French National Assembly after the 1848 revolution, Victor Hugo had supported for president Louis-Napoleon Bonaparte, the nephew of the first Emperor Napoleon. Bonaparte had authored *Extinction of Poverty*, espousing progressive ideas resembling Hugo's.[139] All in all, Bonaparte seemed a better option than his opponent, General Cavaignac, who had earned the nickname "June Butcher" after he had brutally suppressed a workers' insurgency. Yet two years later Hugo was disgusted by Bonaparte's efforts to revise the constitution in order to prolong his presidency. Hugo famously denounced the president's ambitions: "What! Because we had Napoleon the Great, we must have Napoleon the Small (*Napoléon le Petit*)!"[140]

Hugo had reason to worry. When Bonaparte proclaimed himself president without term on December 2, 1851, he dissolved the National Assembly and had more than eighty legislators arrested. Hugo and a small group of other Assembly members organized to resist this coup d'état. That very day, Hugo wrote, signed, and had displayed around Paris a proclamation calling on the army to oppose the coup. Bonaparte had smashed the Constitution, he declared, and you soldiers should stop aiding and abetting his crime! Everyone would condemn the coup as immoral, he believed: "One more step on this path of aggression, one more day with Louis Bonaparte, and you will be ruined in the eyes of universal conscience."[141] Standing by his principles, Hugo instigated barricade building despite the government's threat: "Any individual found constructing or defending a barricade, or with arms, WILL BE SHOT."

Hugo's exhortations sounded much like those of the student insurrectionists in *Les Misérables*, all of them sure that people would rebel against governmental usurpation. But that December, as in the novel, the people did not rise, and the barricades fell. Hugo learned from a frightened Adèle that men had come to arrest him the night after the coup. For three days, he and his colleagues met surreptitiously, moving their meeting place every few hours. Unable to return home safely, Hugo took refuge with Juliette Drouet's friends and continued working with other Assembly members to reclaim the government.[142]

His friend Alexandre Dumas let him know that the price on his head was 25,000 francs (at least $125,000 in today's dollars).[143] On Parisian streets, encouraging workers and other fighters, Hugo saw massacres by government troops, who blew up barricades and carried out summary executions. One of the most nightmarish scenes of the dead and dying appeared at the intersection of rue Montmartre and rue Montorgueil, where Hugo later set the students' last stand in *Les Misérables*. Juliette, desperately searching for Victor on December 4, saw carnage, too, and narrowly escaped through an open door after a soldier took aim at her. By that evening, it was clear that the efforts to restore the Republic had failed. Former legislators were dead, arrested, or missing. For six days, Victor and Juliette eluded the police while her friends obtained a passport in the name of Jacques-Firmin Lanvin, a typographer who had legitimate reason to travel to Brussels. On December 11, in disguise, Victor Hugo boarded the night train.

Welcomed by Juliette's friends in Brussels, he immediately wrote Adèle that he was safe. His letter to Juliette brought her the next day to Brussels, with his trunk full of manuscripts. A week later, Adèle joined Hugo for a couple of days before returning to Paris to pack for exile and sell what the family could not take. His December 14 letter to his wife reveals that Hugo proudly found comfort in following his conscience: "For twelve days, I existed between life and death, but I had never a moment of distress. I was pleased with myself. And besides, I know that I did my duty and that I did it completely. That brings happiness."[144] Hugo was neither surprised nor fazed when, on January 9, 1852, Bonaparte's government officially expelled him and 65 other deputies from France.

So when on August 16, 1859, Emperor Napoleon III granted general amnesty to all exiles even while accusing them of having committed "crimes and political offenses," Hugo immediately published his disdain:

My Destiny (Ma destinée), Hugo's pen-and-ink wash
vision of his challenging life, especially his exile, dated 1857

No one will expect that I would give a moment of my
  attention to the thing called amnesty.
In the situation in which France finds herself, absolute,
  inflexible, and eternal protest is my duty.
Faithful in my commitment to my conscience, I will share
  liberty's exile right to the end. When liberty returns to
  France, I will return."
VICTOR HUGO.
Hauteville-House, 18 August 1859.[145]

Given his previous publication of *Napoléon le petit*, Hugo had no
need to detail here his defiant opposition to the Second Empire. He
had, in fact, foreseen this moment nearly seven years earlier, when he
wrote his penultimate *Les Châtiments* poem, "Ultima Verba" (Latin
for "Final Words"). Beginning with the line "Human conscience is
dead," Hugo draws a horrifying image of the emperor reveling over
conscience's corpse, as in an orgy. Throughout the poem, Hugo
repeats that he will resist such tyranny, whether he is one of thousands, or hundreds, or, as he famously concludes, "And if only one
remains, I will be that one!"[146]

Along with Hugo, other well-known exiles rejected this amnesty.
Yet Hugo did not question the personal decisions of those who
accepted it. To Dr. Terrier, for instance, who had successfully treated
Adèle and François-Victor, Hugo wrote, "Return with the happiness
of a serene conscience, and with our blessings, our memories, our
affectionate and deep esteem, and your eight years of exile proudly
borne."[147] Practically speaking, Hugo knew that many exiles had
struggled financially. Morally—as he implied in his letter—he recognized that each of us needs to listen to our own conscience. And
he seems to have understood his own family's frustration with this
apparently endless exile. Finding his actions to be self-centered
and even tyrannical, his wife and his sons began taking ever longer
sojourns away from Guernsey.[148] How much of their resentment was
caused by Hugo's strong personality and how much by his unwaver-
ing commitment to his conscience is hard to say.

.✦.

Victor Hugo's ideas about conscience as *essential* to human existence find echoes in those of many modern freedom fighters. I am
especially struck by Nelson Mandela's lifetime of conscientious
resistance to South African apartheid and by his ability to forgive.
While working as a lawyer in Johannesburg in the early 1940s,
Mandela became involved in anti-colonial and African nationalist
politics. Although initially committed to non-violent protest, he
eventually resisted more actively. He could not ignore the inequities
around him: "The racial policies of the government have pricked the
conscience of all men of goodwill and have aroused their deepest
indignation."[149]

Repeatedly arrested for seditious activities, Mandela led a sabo-
tage campaign against the government in 1961. The following year,
he was arrested for conspiring to overthrow the state. At the subsequent Rivonia Trial, he defended himself, using the courtroom to
argue for equality among all South Africans. Mandela made clear the
depth of his commitment to his conscience and ensuing duty:

> During my lifetime I have dedicated my life to this
> struggle of the African people. I have fought against white
> domination, and I have fought against black domination.
> I have cherished the ideal of a democratic and free society
> in which all persons will live together in harmony and with
> equal opportunities. It is an ideal which I hope to live for
> and to see realised. But, My Lord, if it needs be, it is an
> ideal for which I am prepared to die.[150]

The trial resulted in Mandela's being sentenced to life imprisonment. He ultimately spent twenty-seven years in three prisons for
resisting the South African governmental policy of apartheid and for
promoting black Africans' self-determination. Just as Hugo's voice
found more power in exile, Mandela's detention did not stop dis-
semination of his ideas. Domestic and international pressure on the
South African government increased until President F. W. de Klerk

released Mandela in 1990. Then he and de Klerk negotiated an end to apartheid and organized a multiracial general election in 1994, through which Mandela was elected president. Working to help create that "democratic and free society," he appointed Archbishop Desmond Tutu to lead South Africa's Truth and Reconciliation Commission, still a world-wide model for the power of forgiveness (see Chapter 2).

Both Mandela and Hugo found moral satisfaction worth the personal and physical hardships associated with their conscientious choices. Mandela, who loved family life, acknowledged sacrifice:

> It has not been easy for me during the past period to separate myself from my wife and children, to say good-bye to the good old days when, at the end of a strenuous day at the office I could look forward to joining my family at the dinner table, and instead to take up the life of a man hunted continuously by the police, living separated from those who are closest to me, in my own country, facing continually the hazards of detection and of arrest.[151]

For Hugo, one of the toughest consequences of following his conscience was exile, as he made clear: "A man so ruined that he has only his honor, so stripped that he has only his conscience, so isolated that he has only fairness by his side, so rejected that he has only truth to accompany him, so thrown into the shadows that only the sun remains for him—that's what an exile is."[152]

And because they are fighting against inequities or dishonesty that some people accept, conscientious people can find themselves labeled outlaws—a label some embrace. Nelson Mandela had his outlaw status in mind when he told the Rivonia Trial court that the African National Congress (ANC) policy of democracy and what they called "nonracialism" reflected his deepest convictions: "I explained how as a lawyer I was often forced to choose between compliance with the law and accommodating my conscience." Citing the conviction of Bertrand Russell for protesting against Britain's nuclear weapons policy, Mandela continued:

> I would say that the whole life of any thinking African in this country drives him continuously to a conflict between his conscience on the one hand and the law on the other. This is not a conflict peculiar to this country. The conflict arises for conscience, for men who think and who feel deeply in every country. . . . Men, I think, are not capable of doing nothing, saying nothing, of not reacting to injustice, of not protesting against oppression, of not striving for the good society and the good life in the ways they see it.[153]

Victor Hugo not only wrote often about the clashes he saw between law and morality but also wove his understanding deeply into *Les Misérables*, as we'll see in the following chapter. Exiles are righteous outlaws, Hugo argued, as in this quote from his essay "What an Exile Is": "The exile's power consists of two elements: one is the injustice of his destiny, the other is the justice of his cause. These two contradictory forces lean on each other, a formidable situation that can be summarized in a word or two: Outside the law, within what's right."[154] In the end, Hugo and Mandela did what they did because their consciences permitted no other action.

In our world of selfies, self-awareness, and exhortations to self-reliance, where does conscience fit? *Les Misérables* shows us. As director Tom Hooper noted, Hugo "celebrates people who are devoted to the self-interest of *others*." As Hugo applauds those who show such generous love—Bishop Myriel, Jean Valjean, Fantine, Éponine, the barricade fighters, and many others—he does so without cringing from the tortuous realities of conscience. Yet, as Hooper's comment implies, issues of conscience do not need to be such big ones as questions of social inequities, apartheid, or the life-and-death decisions that Valjean faced. Conscience is equally crucial in our everyday decisions, as it is central to our developing character. Even if we don't pay attention to it, "We are never done with conscience," as Hugo remarks near the end of his story, since "conscience is bottomless, being God" (V, 6, 4). Personally, I'd never thought of conscience as divine. But it appears that most people have a conscience, whether it comes from God, from their parents or community, or from some sort of internal source that we don't quite understand. Wherever conscience originates, Hugo makes a thought-provoking case for realizing what our conscience is telling us and—knowing how very hard it might be to follow its dictates—do our best to listen.

CHAPTER 7

Either Valjean or Javert!

Javert (Terence Mann) and Valjean (Colm Wilkinson) confront each other in the 1987 original Broadway production of Les Misérables. *Photograph by Michael Le Poer Trench,* © *Cameron Mackintosh Ltd.*

His conscience forced him permanently,
perpetually to confront the laws that men make
with the law that makes men.[155]

Will Inspector Javert capture Jean Valjean during his nighttime chase across Paris? Will he permanently imprison Valjean, or will the ex-convict remain free? Will Valjean manage to convince the inspector that he is a changed man? Failing that, will Valjean execute Javert as the spy he was at the barricade? In the end, will Inspector Javert or Jean Valjean triumph? The ongoing confrontation between these two men intrigues most *Les Misérables* readers and fascinates Boublil and Schönberg's *Les Mis* audiences. The characters themselves know that one must win and one must lose. Indeed, as the inspector sings in *Les Mis*, "it is either Valjean or Javert!"

Yet their contest goes far deeper than the struggle between hunter and hunted. In Valjean's and Javert's opposing worldviews we recognize the ways in which what is legal and what is right can clash. And we discover how rigidity conflicts with humanity. Humane people are compassionate, generous, and merciful because, Hugo argues, their sense of what's right comes directly from God into their conscience. Following their conscience, those who are fair-minded look beyond the letter of the law and care about the people involved. In acting out of love for others and forgiving when possible, they seek true justice rather than a legalistic, avenging justice.

Unfortunately, actions prompted by the law do not always meet this standard of moral integrity, a reality that the bishop encounters when he ministers to a man condemned to the guillotine. Laws can be unfair and misapplied, as when Javert arrests Fantine, assuming that she must be in the wrong because she is a prostitute. A bit ironically—since, logically, humans should be humane—laws created by people do not always align with our God-given sense of morality, or what Hugo might term in English "rightness." Not a word commonly used in American English, "rightness" means, according to the Oxford English Dictionary, "the quality or condition of being morally right or good; justice, rectitude; righteousness, integrity." In

Valjean's and Javert's polar-opposite senses of duty, we see the stark distinction between humaneness and mercy on the one hand, and unthinking rule-following on the other.

The relationship between what's legal and what's right remains as complicated today as when Jean Valjean and Inspector Javert vied over whether Fantine should go to prison, whether Javert should arrest Valjean, or whether it was right for Valjean to spare Javert. The news is rife with stories of injustice. Innocent people go to jail because their attorneys recommend that they accept a plea bargain. People wrongly convicted spend years working to prove that they deserve a new hearing. Reformed criminals cannot get parole. The story of "Colorado's own Jean Valjean," Rene Lima-Marin, for example, exposes major flaws and inequities in the criminal justice system, including extreme sentences and a complete disregard for a former criminal's reformation.[156]

That the United States faces a criminal justice crisis is more and more evident.[157] In the twenty-first century, America has the world's highest incarceration rate. Why do American prisons hold nearly one-quarter of the world's prisoners when the U.S. has only about five percent of the world's population? Examples of unfair laws and prison terms abound in almost any context we might consider. Do we really want judgments that send people to prison for life for writing a bad check? How could people selling marijuana in Virginia have received years-long mandatory prison sentences when marijuana was legal in eight other states? Are people really "violent felons" if they have not committed violence? Should a fourteen-year-old be condemned to die in prison for starting a deadly fire by accident?[158]

Bryan Stevenson, one of today's best-known advocates for justice, reminds me at times of Victor Hugo. In his best-selling book, *Just Mercy*, Stevenson writes about his powerful experiences working as a young lawyer for the Southern Prisoners Defense Committee (SPDC) in Alabama. He introduces us to women erroneously condemned to death after their babies were stillborn, to teenagers on death row, and to poor people who were convicted without access to qualified defense attorneys. When he realized through his SPDC work the desperate need of the poor, the wrongly condemned, the mentally ill, and women and children trapped in the criminal justice system, Stevenson founded the Equal Justice Initiative (EJI).[159] Under his leadership, EJI gives legal representation to people who have been illegally convicted, unfairly sentenced, or abused in state jails and prisons. The organization provides re-entry assistance to formerly incarcerated people, and, like Hugo, EJI staff challenge the death penalty and excessive punishment.

Not only do Stevenson's astute insights about what's legal and what's right resemble Hugo's but Stevenson, too, works to bring justice into an unjust system, aiming to make laws conform more closely to rightness. The main story running through *Just Mercy* is the case of Walter McMillian, who was sentenced to the death penalty for committing a murder he knew nothing about. The case against McMillian—as Stevenson and his colleagues discovered after months of research and interviews—was a tangle of false testimony, antagonism toward a black man who'd had a relationship with a white woman, and determined rejection of relevant facts. After spending three years researching, interviewing, writing briefs, and laying out the evidence at hearings, Stevenson succeeded in gaining McMillian's release, with his innocence acknowledged. Still, McMillian had spent six long years watching fellow prisoners walk to their executions and expecting the same for himself, an experience clearly detrimental to his health.

Stevenson felt the need to explain what he had learned from Walter McMillian: "Walter made me understand why we have to reform a system of criminal justice that continues to treat people better if they are rich and guilty than if they are poor and innocent." Beyond the specifics of criminal justice, however, *Just Mercy* explicitly links true justice with mercy through its title and in its stories. "Mercy" is a rich word, including as it does the ideas of both compassion and a disposition to forgive. "Mercy is just when it is rooted in hopefulness and freely given. Mercy is most empowering, liberating, and transformative when it is directed at the undeserving," Stevenson tells us, pinpointing the inherent connection between mercy and grace. To be truly just, then, we must be humane and behave fairly toward *every-one*. Working with so many people who have been unfairly treated, Stevenson concludes:

> I've come to believe that the true measure of our
> commitment to justice, the character of our society, our
> commitment to the rule of law, fairness, and equality
> cannot be measured by how we treat the rich, powerful,
> privileged, and the respected among us. The true measure
> of our character is how we treat the poor, the disfavored,
> the accused, the incarcerated, and the condemned.[160]

Victor Hugo went a bit farther than Stevenson does here, proclaiming, "The rights of all the weak make up the duties of all the strong."[161]

Jean Valjean, strong in his position as the mayor of Montreuil, finds it his duty to intervene on behalf of the downtrodden Fantine when she is condemned by the law in the person of Inspector Javert (I, 5, 13). This police inspector is not a bad person, as Alain Boublil noted in summarizing Javert's motivations for my students:

> With the songs "Stars" and "The Confrontation," we can
> see first of all that Javert was acting out of a sense of
> mission, and, second, he had come from a very, very bad
> background, which makes him want to be the opposite of
> that background. That's a very common feeling today. How
> many people come from a very poor or a very difficult part
> of the world and want to escape, to be people completely
> different from what their parents had been? But when
> Javert dies, he acknowledges that he's been mistaken—
> mistaken for his whole life. So he's a kind of white knight
> in his own way.

Javert's sense of duty, however, runs diametrically opposite to Valjean's.

The inspector is so narrowly focused on keeping order that he is blind to the human side of situations. So of course he unhesitatingly arrests Fantine after coming upon a brawl in the streets. As Javert sees it, "A prostitute just assaulted a respectable citizen." Because M. Bamatabois is a property owner, he could not be in the wrong—even though we readers know that he first attacked Fantine. The inspector applies the legal statute: six months in prison. He can act as judge and jury because, as Hugo explains, "under our laws, women of this class are placed entirely in the hands of the police." Javert ignores the fight's larger context, too, remaining unmoved either by Fantine's testimony or by her begging for "Mercy!" She insists that Bamatabois had repeatedly insulted her before pushing snow down her dress, and she explains her situation, pleading that she must work to save her daughter. "She would have softened a heart of granite, but the heart of a man without feeling cannot be softened," Hugo tells us. On the one hand, Javert not only applies the law unthinkingly; on the other, his assumptions about social class color his perceptions in ways that would mean disaster for Fantine *and* Cosette.

Into this scene arrives Valjean (as the mayor, M. Madeleine), who takes a role similar to Hugo's when he saw a prostitute arrested (see Chapter 6). Because he interviewed witnesses, Madeleine knows that Bamatabois had so severely provoked the young woman that she had fought back. Seeing Fantine as a human being with a soul, looking beyond her profession and condition, he demands her release in the name of fairness.[162] He even declines to prosecute her after she spits in his face. (She blames Madeleine for the job loss that had ultimately pushed her into prostitution.) Madeleine counters point by point Javert's insistence on applying the rule of law. Javert takes this confrontation personally since he views himself as "the personification of law, order, morality, government, the whole of society." When Madeleine says, "Inspector Javert, the highest law is conscience," the distinction between what's legal and what's right leaps out. We begin to comprehend—but Javert does not—that, with his habit of applying the law intransigently, he has come to embody the rigidity and inhumanity of bad laws. Terribly confused, Javert confesses, "I don't understand what I'm seeing." Madeleine quells him only by appealing to the law that makes the mayor the judge in municipal police matters. Unlike Javert, Fantine recognizes the mayor's humanity and feels "joy, trust, love" when she realizes that the mayor has set her free.

We must keep our hearts open, Hugo argues, in order to be truly just. But human beings are flawed not only with prejudices about class, race, ethnic origin, and so on, but also in our limited capacity to craft appropriate laws and apply them fairly and reasonably. Bad laws and poorly applied laws can and do ruin innocent people's lives. Bryan Stevenson, of course, knows this, and his insights at the end of *Just Mercy* echo Valjean's indignation about Fantine's false arrest and her worry about how jail would devastate her daughter's life:

> I often had this feeling when I worked on Walter's case, that if the anguish of all the stressed lives, the pain of all the oppressed people in all of the menaced spaces of Monroe County [Alabama] could be gathered in some carefully constructed receptacle, it could power something extraordinary, operate as some astonishing alternative fuel capable of igniting previously impossible action. And who knew what might come of it—righteous disruption or transformational redemption? Maybe both.[163]

Unfortunately, we see too often today what prompts Javert's choice to believe Bamatabois: assumptions about people's social status. For Javert, Bamatabois is the "voter who owns that handsome three-story freestone house with a balcony that stands on the corner of the parade." As Bryan Stevenson shows us in his analysis of Walter McMillian's case, privilege still has a big impact on the "justice" system.

In *his* ongoing fight for justice, Hugo was sure that we are each capable of sensing what is right. Yet prioritizing true justice can provoke negative repercussions. When, for instance, he protested the president's government takeover in 1851 and, at other times, opposed legal statutes on the grounds of justice, Hugo found himself branded an outlaw and pushed into exile. Like Jean Valjean, however, Hugo followed his moral compass, even when that meant trampling on the law.

Laws (*les lois*), he knew, run the risk of being as flawed as the human beings who write them. Hugo's definitive essay on the sub-ject—"Le Droit et la loi" ("Right and Law")—serves as the intro-duction to his four-volume *Actes et paroles*, the compilation of his speeches and other public statements. As my translation of the essay title shows, it's difficult to render easily in English the precise French sense of "le droit" as Hugo intends it. *Le droit*, after all, is often trans-lated as "law" in a broad sense, as in "she studies law" (*elle étudie le droit*). Yet Hugo's meaning of the word in contrast to *la loi* is evident in the first definition offered by the *Trésor de la langue française*, the comprehensive etymological and historical French dictionary: *le droit* is "the foundation of the rules that govern people's social relation-ships, implying a fair division of possessions, prerogatives, and free-doms."[164] Hugo indeed believed that what's right, or just, is fair and should underpin laws.

He needed to distinguish explicitly between what's right and what's legal because people tend to conflate "justice" with "law," as other dictionary definitions indicate. Hugo even turned to the Latin he knew so well in an effort to clarify his distinction. Because, as he declared, one of the formulas of his public life was *"Pro jure contra legem"* ("For what's right against the law"), his conscience pushed him to build rightness into proposed laws.[165] By contrasting the Latin terms "iūs, iūris" and "lex, legis," Hugo unequivocally connected what's right with what's just. Not only does the Latin word *jure* over-whelmingly refer to "what's right, just, and dutiful," but the root of the French or English word "justice" is also visible in the traditional spelling, with initial "j," that Hugo chose here. Hugo made the same point more subtly in *Les Misérables* by entitling the book about the bishop "Un Juste," thus focusing on his qualities as a just, or fair man.

Hugo was certain that what's right is divine. Therefore, laws should correspond to morality. What he saw happening around him, however, was an eternal battle between what's right and what's legal. That's a dangerous situation, he noted in "Le Droit et la loi," since such antagonism between rightness and law breeds catastrophes. Only their harmony brings order. To buttress his point, Hugo listed numerous ways in which what's right and what's legal in society are often polar opposites, for example:

The sacredness of human life, freedom, peace, nothing
that cannot be undone, nothing irrevocable, nothing
irreparable: that is how right is.

The scaffold, the sword and the scepter, war, every
type of yoke, from marriage without possibility of divorce
for families to the state of siege for cities: that is how
law is. . . .

The act of judgment is the law. Justice is the right.

Take the measure of what separates them.

The law has the liquidity, the floods, the invasiveness
and the anarchy of water, often roiled; but rightness is
unsinkable.[166]

That "unsinkable" nature of what's right comes from its source in
God and its life in human conscience, as Hugo points out: "In order
for everything to be saved, all that is needed is for the right to rise to
the surface of a conscience. God cannot be drowned."[167]

For Hugo, doing what's right is doing what God would wish:
loving one another, caring for the unfortunate especially if we are
fortunate, forgiving others, and giving others the same freedoms we
wish for ourselves. Five years before he died, arguing yet again in the
French Senate for amnesty for the Communards, Hugo envisioned
the sort of future he had promoted in *Les Misérables*: "When we
understand—using the words in their absolute senses—that every
human action is a divine action, then everything will have been said,
and the world will have only to progress tranquilly toward the superb
future."[168] (For the story of Hugo's defense of the Communards, see
Chapter 2.) That future will include liberty, Hugo said, because for
him liberty was "the highest expression of what is right."[169] Personal
freedom exists deep in our souls, he was sure, because God is there.

Hugo's most tenacious, vehement argument that what's right
should determine what's legal is embodied in his lifelong struggle to
abolish the death penalty. He had never forgotten the horrors he witnessed at age ten, when his family visited Spain: a gallows in Burgos,

a condemned man on his way to execution, and, in Segovia, a crucified, dismembered corpse, still bloody.[170] The right to life, Hugo
believed, is the most inviolable of human rights. Not only should
governments not commit murder, but executions destroyed the convicted person's chance for redemption. Bryan Stevenson came to
similar conclusions after working on Walter McMillian's case: "The
real question of capital punishment in this country is, *Do we deserve
to kill?*" Ultimately, he argues, executing people is wrong because, as
McMillian put it, "People are supposed to die on God's schedule."[171]

Hugo used the same reasoning in 1848 during a famous legislative speech in which he demanded the "pure, simple, and definitive abolition of the death penalty": "You open the constitution's
preamble with 'In God's presence,' and you would begin by stealing
from God this right that belongs only to Him, the right of life and
death. Gentlemen, three things belong to God and not to man: the
irrevocable, the irreparable, the indissoluble."[172] France abolished the
death penalty in 1981, 133 years after Hugo spoke, a decision due
in great measure to Minister of Justice Robert Badinter's compelling
National Assembly speech. Often invited to speak about Hugo and
abolition, Badinter has said that he had always had in mind Hugo's
"*Pure, simple et définitive!*" because he found the poet's unambiguous
stance decisive.[173]

Hugo spoke against the death penalty from his early twenties
until he was eighty. When only twenty-six, he made his case against
the inhumanity of executions with a stunningly modern depiction
of a condemned man's thoughts and feelings in *Le Dernier Jour d'un
condamné* (*The Last Day of a Condemned Man*). In this stream-of-
consciousness novella, so ingenious that Hugo was accused of pla-
giarism, we cannot escape the agony of the young unnamed murderer as he thinks of what his unnatural death will mean to his small
daughter and as he recognizes the futility of hope.

Hugo also wrote governments public letters arguing against executions of high-profile offenders, including the U.S. abolitionist
John Brown and the vanquished Mexican Emperor Maximilian (see
Chapter 2). As a young man in Paris, Hugo had sometimes come
upon guillotine preparations and even executions in the Place de

Ecce Lex (*Latin for* Behold the Law), *by Victor Hugo,*
who drew four different versions of this hanged man
as protests against the death penalty [1854]

Grève, spectacles he never wanted to witness again—neither the horror of such deaths nor the crowd's fascination with them. He disclosed his distress over "legal murder" through Myriel's thoughts after the bishop volunteered to comfort a condemned man in his last hours: "I didn't realize it was so monstrous. It's wrong to be so deeply absorbed in divine law that you become unaware of human law. Death depends on God alone" (I, 1, 4).

So Hugo was eager to defend his son Charles, who had been arrested and would be tried for opposing the death penalty. In an effort to control the press, Louis-Napoleon Bonaparte's government had imposed increasingly repressive regulations, including requiring authors to sign their articles about politics, religion, or philosophy. In that way, government lawyers could prosecute dissidents. After Charles Hugo published "The Execution of Montcharmont" in the Hugo family's newspaper *L'Événement*, he and the newspaper's manager were charged with contempt of the law for questioning the decency of state-sponsored killing. Having grown up with his father's certainty that the death penalty was immoral—no matter how serious the crime or certain the guilt—Charles hadn't hesitated to make his position public. Besides, such a brutal execution had horrified him. His article described in striking detail how twenty-nine-year-old Claude Montcharmont had begged for his life and had fought with such great force that the guards had been unable to drag him to the guillotine. Not until they had found reinforcements, after dark, were they able to force Montcharmont's head under the blade.[174]

Victor Hugo received permission to defend his son and went before the court on June 11, 1851. He began by analyzing the basis for the government's case. Since Charles Hugo was accused of "a lack of respect for the law," Hugo asked rhetorically, "What does 'respect for the law' mean?" It must mean, he explained, obeying the law. It cannot mean, as the accusation implies, that laws are above criticism. If we don't critique or question or reproach bad, unjust, or even barbarous laws, how can we improve them? If we eliminate criticism, we might as well abolish the legislature—and the court wasn't arguing for that, he wondered, was it? Laughter rang out in the courtroom.

Having made that point, Hugo moved on to discuss the law that his son had questioned: a law, he noted, that Beccaria had declared "impious" and that Franklin had called "abominable."[175] Hugo's catalog of arguments against the morality of the death penalty included a reminder of countries that had abolished it, former King Louis-Philippe's enduring opposition to it, and the fact that two abolition bills had recently been filed in the National Assembly. Of course, everyone knew which law he was talking about, but he named it only after listing those many criticisms: "this law before which human conscience recoils with an anxiety that grows deeper every day—the death penalty."[176]

Hugo grounded this speech in his belief that we all belong to a moral, "universal" conscience that knows what is right. "Conscience," "right," and "God" are constant themes. After retelling how horribly Montcharmont had died, Hugo claimed that such a scene had caused "a shiver to emanate from all consciences. Never had legal murder appeared with more cynicism and abomination."[177] He connected people's right to fight the death penalty with our rights of freedom of speech and freedom of the press. Over and over again, Hugo called on his listeners' sense of morality, putting his dramatic, rhetorical, and poetic skills into action, as you see in these excerpts:

> What! Is this what we've come to? What! Are we to be so
> driven by society's encroachments on common sense, on
> reason, on freedom of thought, and on natural rights that
> we would be forced to give moral respect to penalties that
> open abysses in our consciences, penalties that make any
> thinking person blanch, penalties that religion abhors? . . .
> No! No! No! We have not come to such a point! No!

Such impious punishments, he insisted, "make us doubt humanity when they strike a guilty person—and make us doubt God when they strike the innocent."[178]

Hugo lost the case, and it wasn't clear whether his long peroration helped or hurt. Charles was condemned to six months in prison in the Conciergerie and a 500-franc fine. Still, his sentence was not as stiff as those of his colleagues. A few weeks later, his brother and their friend Paul Meurice—defended not by the abolitionist poet but by lawyers—received nine months in prison and fines of 2,000 and 3,000 francs respectively. Together with the third editor, Auguste Vacquerie, who was arrested in September and found guilty, they were still imprisoned in the Conciergerie when Bonaparte seized the government on December 2. Until the coup, Victor Hugo regularly dined with them inside the prison's thick walls, a high quality of visitation rights not available to today's inmates—or to Fantine, if she had been unjustly imprisoned by Inspector Javert.

Inspector Javert does not consider himself unjust, however. He is, in fact, honest and honorable, as Hugo tells us and then shows us. In what director Tom Hooper calls "one of the great scenes in the book," Javert demands that the mayor fire him because he believes he has erroneously accused Madeleine of being the former convict Jean Valjean. Hooper finds the scene remarkable because "Javert is honorable enough to fall on his sword because he thinks he's made a mistake—he believes that he's not above his own law." Javert treats himself as harshly as anyone else who's done something wrong. As Claude-Michel Schönberg explained to my students, "Javert is not a villain. He does what he has to. Javert is a very pure character, who thinks that he has a duty—he has to follow the law, he has a mission to accomplish." What Javert doesn't realize is that there is something beyond the law.

Jean Valjean does understand. He had, after all, experienced the law from the other side, and he had the benefit of Bishop Myriel's mercy and grace, gifts which restored Valjean's humanity. Because he now follows his conscience, Valjean shows Javert mercy by freeing him at the barricade. Because he is honorable, Javert notices and acknowledges Valjean's action, although he does not comprehend why Valjean doesn't execute him as the spy he is. Javert's limited worldview is obvious, too, in his expectation that this convict who's unlawfully at large would of course kill his pursuer. Yet when

The Conciergerie prison along the Seine in Paris

Valjean releases the man who has unremittingly hunted him, he freely bestows what Javert neither deserves nor earns. So Javert cannot help but get a sense of Valjean's unambiguous moral framework, even though it seems that the inspector never totally fathoms Valjean's motivations.

Although Javert continues to act almost as usual, he shows subtle signs that Valjean's humanity has shaken him. For instance, the inspector unconsciously uses the polite "vous" form when he says, "You irritate me. Kill me instead" (V, I, 6). In doing so, he indicates his budding respect for the man he has always denigrated by calling him "tu." Then, after Javert captures Valjean again, he seems "preoccupied," at times in "a savage reverie" (V, 3, 9). With barely a word, Javert permits Valjean to save the nearly dead Marius and say goodbye to Cosette. And then he mysteriously disappears, leaving Valjean free.

Why did Javert act so mercifully? He doesn't quite know why himself, as we discover when Hugo plunges deeply into Javert's mind in the book called "Javert Derailed" (V, 4). There we learn how completely Valjean's love, forgiveness, and mercy have knocked the single-minded, law-enforcing Javert off track, rocking his sense of himself and the world. Javert has always defined himself as a law enforcer. "His conscience was bound up in his usefulness; his religion in his duties . . ." (I, 5, 5). "He had placed almost all his religion in the police," and "He had a superior, M. Gisquet; he had scarcely thought, until today, of that other superior, God" (V, 4). But Valjean's actions—and now Javert's own surprising choice to release Valjean—make Javert suspect for the first time that something exists above and beyond the law.

The inspector finds himself musing about both what Valjean's and his own actions might mean and how doing what's right can conflict with the law:

> A whole new world was revealing itself to his soul;
> kindnesses accepted and repaid, self-sacrifice, mercy,
> leniency, . . . no more outright condemnation, no more
> damnation, the possibility of a tear in the law's eye, some

sort of justice laid down by God running counter to justice laid down by men.

Javert feels the love Valjean has offered him, but, as Alain Boublil told me, "Love comes too late to Javert, and he cannot stand to see it in others and cannot accept it." Unlike Valjean, whose experience with Petit-Gervais shocks him into accepting the bishop's mercy, Javert recoils from his unfamiliar awareness:

> Everything he had believed was disintegrating. . . . He
> must from now on be a different man. He suffered the
> strange pangs of a conscience that has suddenly undergone
> a cataract operation. He saw what he shrank from seeing.
> He felt drained, useless, out of joint with his past life,
> dismissed, dissolved. Authority was dead within him. He
> no longer had any reason for being. (V, 4)

Hugh Jackman, who spent months being Valjean and thinking about Javert, put it this way:

> Javert has gone against everything he believes in by walking
> away and leaving a criminal. He was touched by Valjean's
> humanity, that thing that he doesn't understand. The
> simple fact that he walked away from Valjean in a moment
> of insanity or whatever it was, his life is over. He cannot
> reconcile with his belief system what he's done by releasing
> Valjean, he cannot.

Javert cannot endure his new realization that a criminal might actually be in the right. He is mightily distressed that he collaborated with Valjean in doing what's right in opposition to the law. Finding that he cannot make his new recognition of God's justice align with his lifelong, rigid stance, Javert reacts in his usual way: he seeks his dismissal, as he did with M. Madeleine (I, 6, 2). "But how to manage to send in his resignation to God," this new superior revealed by Valjean's humanity? By killing himself, of course. But before throwing himself into the Seine, Javert calmly composes for his fellow policemen what Hugh Jackman calls "one of the most brilliant suicide notes ever written." The inspector's "Observations for the Benefit of the Service" proposes new rules that indicate his conflicted mind, rules that oscillate between the severe (such as ways to better maintain officers' authority) and the humane (such as his recommendation that prisoners be allowed chairs).

When faced with the realization that their beliefs about life have been wrong, these two men make diametrically opposite decisions. Inspector Javert commits suicide, and Jean Valjean reverses the course of his life. Both are like owls dazzled by an unexpected light, Hugo says. Javert, horrified and afraid, flinches and pulls back (V, 4). Valjean, stunned by virtue and aware that his experience with the bishop has changed him, knows that he must move forward (I, 2, 13).[179] "They are exactly in the same situation. It's a turning point in their lives," Claude-Michel Schönberg explains. He and Alain Boublil built this parallel into *Les Mis* by originally titling both men's self-reflective songs "Soliloquy" and by beginning both with the same melody. These two men, whose surnames suggest each other in reverse (JaVe and VaJe), illustrate two distinctively different ways of living.[180] Inspector Javert's inflexible loyalty to the law and inability to change form a powerful counterpoint to Jean Valjean's moral progress and commitment to what is right. But Javert's legalistic mantra fails in the face of Valjean's humanity. We might find that a fitting end for a man whose lack of a first name seems to signal his dearth of human feeling.

The dominance of Valjean's worldview over Javert's—the recognition that God tells us through our consciences what's right—is fundamental to Hugo's vision of *Les Misérables*, as one of his early drafts of the epigraph (what he called "préface") confirms: "As long as man believes he has the right to introduce the indestructible into mores and the irreparable into law, books such as this one may not be useless. This book is a protest against the inexorable and nothing else."[181] Inspector Javert and the law that drives his actions are indeed relentless in their narrowness and lack of humanity. As Hugo shows so poignantly, laws that ruin the life of a hungry bread thief or imprison a woman reduced to prostitution by society's disdain are inhumane. And as Bryan Stevenson concludes about life in twenty-first century America, "The closer we get to mass incarceration and extreme levels of punishment, the more I believe it's necessary to recognize that we all need mercy, we all need justice, and—perhaps—we all need some measure of unmerited grace."[182]

The interconnectedness of mercy, grace, justice, and love defines Jean Valjean's actions and Hugo's message about humanity. As Cameron Mackintosh expressed it, "With the survival of the human spirit at its core, *Les Misérables* shows the majesty that the human spirit is capable of." But Valjean could not quite succeed in helping Inspector Javert, whose singlemindedness runs straight into—and breaks against—God: "God, always within man and refractory, being the true conscience, defying the false, forbidding the spark to die out, . . . inalienable humanity, inamissible human feeling, that splendid phenomenon, perhaps the finest of all our inner marvels—did Javert understand this?" (V, 4) No, Javert never did really understand. He didn't realize that God is ungovernable and always with us, never to be lost, as the rather obscure word "inamissible" makes clear in both French and English. In the end, Javert rejected the humanity that God deeply and divinely embedded in us. The rest of us can, however, like Jean Valjean, appreciate Hugo's idea: with God and love alive in our consciences, we need only to pay attention to know *and* to do what is right.

CHAPTER 8

Finding Strength to Carry On

"Gavroche Dreamer" ("Gavroche rêveur"),
Hugo's undated pen-and-brown-ink wash

Almost the entire secret of great hearts
is in this word: Persevering.[183]

Victor Hugo rebounded after many frankly tragic experiences. Put yourself in his place for a moment and imagine watching your first-born son die when he was three months old, and then your first grandson die of meningitis before the age of one. Seeing your older brother have a nervous breakdown on your wedding day. Losing your nineteen-year-old daughter, Léopoldine, in a nonsensical boating accident. Figuring out that your wife and best friend have fallen in love and suspecting, correctly, that they have been secretly meeting. Hearing that there's a price on your head and being forced to flee into exile—over and over again—with government spies watching your movements, even after you'd left Europe for the Channel Islands. Realizing that your thirty-three-year-old daughter, Adèle, has run away to Nova Scotia, following the British lieutenant she obsessively, unrequitedly loves. Learning, after you announce her marriage, that her report of it was untrue. Discovering when she returns nine years later that she's lost touch with reality, and that the doctors recommend you not visit her.[184] Having both your sons die decades before you do. Alongside these personal tragedies, too, you face and surmount numerous professional setbacks and failures in the theater and in national politics.

After every blow, Hugo recovered and moved forward remarkably quickly, although Léopoldine's drowning depressed him for several years. But his resilience wasn't automatic. He had a philosophical perspective on resilience and resolve, one that he reveals in *Les Misérables*. Hugo believed that love and conscience—together or separately—are not only keys to our humanity but also give us strength that helps us through tough times. Whether it's cherishing another, feeling someone else's love for us, or having a mission or purpose in life, such commitments prompt us to find the grit to keep going. Investing in something or someone outside ourselves empowers us.

Hugo's inspirational *Les Misérables* characters show what it takes to carry on. For instance, Jean Valjean both resolutely fights for the freedom to raise his beloved Cosette *and* finds ever new ways to fulfill his goal of being good. As Hugh Jackman put it, Valjean has the "tenacity to fight through his regrets and his pain and continue to commit himself to a higher ideal, something other than himself." Gavroche and Éponine overcome their parents' vicious legacy through their surprising capacity for compassion, love, and human decency. More characters than we can explore here rise above adverse circumstances: Enjolras defends his ideals against impossible odds; Fantine sacrifices all for her daughter; undeterred by losing everything he values, the elderly M. Mabeuf unfailingly assists others.

Life tosses us difficult and unexpected challenges. Whether it be a job loss, a serious illness, a criminal attack, or the sudden death of someone we love, we all face times when it would be easier to throw in the towel. How do we pick ourselves back up and get on with our lives? It's not easy. That's why many books and websites exhort us to build resilience and offer how-to advice. And people's lives around us can show how it's done. In pondering how Hugo's characters have stirred me and my students, I remembered my mother's resilient spirit and the compassionate parenting skills that she had, despite her stepmother's abuse.

As a child I learned that when my Mom was five years old, her beloved "Mama" had died, a victim of the 1918 Spanish influenza epidemic. She explained that if my grandfather hadn't remarried quickly, his brothers and sisters were going to "adopt" his four children—and get the oldest (who were five and six) working on their farms. A hundred years ago, people assumed that a widower could not raise such young children alone. What I didn't learn until later was that under such pressure my Grandpa Tut married someone more cut out to be a businesswoman than a mother. In the "life history" that my Mom wrote in her eighties, she told of the verbal and physical abuse that she and her older brother had suffered. This new "Mother" firmly believed that children "should work and obey" and that "no crime, whether fact or fiction, should ever go unpunished." The razor-strap beatings and endless household tasks were perhaps less devastating, though, than "Mother's" ongoing derogatory comments, which remind me of the insults Madame Thénardier hurled at Cosette.

How did my Mom not only endure but overcome such a childhood to be the first in her family to graduate from college and then to become a loving parent and my best friend? How could she have grown to express empathy for her stepmother, concluding that someone who prized a neat, clean, organized house might indeed be stressed by a family with four children aged seven and under? When I asked Mom how she had come through it all incredibly grounded and caring, she credited her siblings' shared love and support and the quiet help from teachers, neighbors, aunts, and uncles. Knowing her analytical, philosophical nature, I would also credit her attention to words of wisdom from such literary giants as Shakespeare. His "There is nothing either good or bad, but thinking makes it so" echoed through my childhood, so often did Mom quote Hamlet's words to Rosencrantz and Guildenstern (II, 2). Mom may have chosen to decide that such harsh experiences had made her stronger, giving her and her older brother the courage to set out on their own in their mid-teens.

Absorbing Shakespeare's idea might have made *me* more receptive to *Man's Search for Meaning* by Austrian neurologist and psychiatrist Viktor Frankl. Frankl found the will to go on while imprisoned in multiple Nazi concentration camps, including Auschwitz. When, in college, I read his description of the horrors he had experienced and witnessed, I was immediately struck by his breakthrough realization, which broadens Shakespeare's memorable aphorism: "Everything can be taken from a man but one thing: the last of the human freedoms—to choose one's attitude in any given set of circumstances, to choose one's own way." (It doesn't bother me that Frankl, like Hugo, wrote at a time when writers used the term man/men to refer to either men or people of whatever gender.) After more observation, Frankl decided that, along with the freedom to choose how we see things, our ability to survive such hellish circumstances comes from having a mission, "a task waiting for [us] to fulfill." Having a purpose—or someone to love—makes us responsible in a way that makes us resilient: "A man who becomes conscious of the responsibility he bears toward a human being who affectionately waits for him, or to an unfinished work, will never be able to throw away his life. He knows the 'why' for his existence, and will be able to bear almost any 'how.'" Quoting Nietzsche here, Frankl notes that he finds "much wisdom" in the philosopher's acknowledgment that knowing that one has a meaning in one's life can enable one to survive even the worst conditions. Suffering is endurable when we have a reason to endure it.[185]

Viktor Frankl is one of hundreds who have investigated resilience through personal experience, case studies, and research. As I explored other perspectives, I was particularly taken with two more recent stories. Sheryl Sandberg, working with organizational psychologist Adam Grant, found ways to build resilience and find joy after her husband died suddenly from heart failure. And Malala Yousafzai continues her activism on behalf of free, universal education after surviving a Taliban member's gunshot to her head when she was fifteen. Through their experiences, each writes, they discovered effective ways, first, to recover and, then, to move forward with energy. Yousafzai tells how she saw herself in Dorothy when she read *The Wizard of Oz*. Dorothy "had to overcome a lot of obstacles to get where she was going, and I thought if you want to achieve a goal, there will be hurdles in your way, but you must continue." Sandberg found that using multiple positive ways to respond to tragedy leads to "post-traumatic growth," what she and co-author Adam Grant call "bounce forward."[186]

Psychologists propose numerous other strategies. Focusing on neuroscience, health psychologist Kelly McGonigal finds that "when we help others, or focus on our bigger-than-self goals, it changes our neurochemistry and physical stress response from one of fear and overwhelm to the biology of hope and courage." Martin Seligman echoes Frankl when he says, "We plant the seeds of resilience in the ways we process negative events." And Rick Hanson explains how resilience perpetuates itself—how the sense of well-being that it fosters builds inner strengths that promote more resilience.[187]

Still, Frankl's perspective endures and resonates especially strongly with me. I find hope and the will to persist—even in writing this book!—when I choose how to think about an event and when I remember the people and goals that matter to me. What is more, Frankl's view parallels Hugo's major message in *Les Misérables* about our humanity. For Frankl, committing ourselves to someone or something beyond ourselves is key to being human: "Being human always points, and is directed, to something, or someone, other than oneself . . . The more one forgets himself—by giving himself to a cause to serve or another person to love—the more human he is and the more he actualizes himself."[188] Frankl calls this outward-facing commitment "self-transcendence of human existence," and Hugo's characters show how we can build more of it into our lives.

We have already seen how, after Javert re-imprisons him, Jean Valjean bounces back by devoting himself to Cosette and his goal of caring for her in Fantine's place. Valjean is a model of resolve and tenacity. But the character who most shouts "resilient" to me is young Gavroche. He leaves his personal miseries behind by caring about others, even when they don't care about him—and by being very funny, too! Gavroche has the capacity for a much greater self-transcendent love than we would expect, given his past experiences and present circumstances as the Thénardiers' son. Gavroche and, later, his little brothers, were ignored and then abandoned by their cold, manipulative father and by their horrific mother, who preferred her girls. Gavroche began living on the street when he was about six years old. Although he was kicked out by his parents, his situation is reminiscent of those children who escape abuse today by running away from home. Gavroche survives it all, however. His sense of humor and compassion combine to make him tough and buoyant.

Hugo introduces Gavroche as an example of the Paris street urchins, whom he calls *gamins*, the ingenious, independent creatures who manage somehow to get along—until they don't. Eleven or twelve years old now, Gavroche is "a boisterous, pallid, resourceful, smart, cheeky boy, animated yet sickly-looking," and like all gamins full of "inexhaustible initiative." He is cheerful because he is free (III, 1, 13). *Les Mis* creator Alain Boublil was struck by the spirit of such young *misérables* and their revolutionary potential, as Hugo describes it. In fact, Gavroche was the launching point for the musical, as Boublil disclosed in answering a student's question about how the musical came to be:

> One night in London watching *Oliver!*, I was struck like lightning. Suddenly in my head the scene was divided in two. I was seeing Oliver on stage, and I was imagining Gavroche doing the same moves on another stage, so, really, in the stage of my mind I was watching two shows. The idea of *Les Misérables* the musical all began with Gavroche—so we started from a character who was emblematic in France of an idea, of what revolution, poverty, and being abandoned meant in those times.

A hero of the insurrection, beloved by the "barricade boys" and by generations of *Les Misérables* readers, Gavroche embodies the idea of revolution not only in his enthusiasm for the barricade fight but also in his insolent yet deeply caring approach to life.

When we first see him in action, Gavroche is cheerfully shivering in his rags in a freezing northerly wind and rain. As he studies a barbershop window, considering whether he can "lift" a bar of soap to sell for something to eat—he figures that he hasn't eaten for three days—he sees two younger boys chased from the shop. They are crying, their teeth chattering with cold. So Gavroche runs after them, asking what's wrong, stopping their tears with his facetiousness and gentle protectiveness: Nowhere to sleep? Not a problem. "Is that anything to cry about? What ninnies!" (IV, 6, 2) As we'll see, Gavroche's lighthearted air and kindly authority calm these two unnamed boys, who have gotten lost by accident. In one of his coincidental twists, Hugo reveals to us that they are Gavroche's brothers, although neither he nor they know it.

As though virtually adopting these two is not enough, Gavroche stops on the way home when he sees a shivering teenage beggar girl in a too-short skirt. She is blue with cold. "Poor girl!" he says,

"Without even a pair of breeches. Here, take this at least." And he wraps around her the wool muffler he'd had at his neck, his one warm piece of clothing. Now, of course, colder and wetter than ever, he talks to the rain, joking, "If it goes on like this, I'm cancelling my subscription." After buying a bit of bread with his last *sou* (worth just a few cents) and generously giving the larger pieces to the small boys, Gavroche takes his charges back to his place. There we see his humor and positive outlook at work, even in the face of starvation.

Gavroche lives inside a structure that actually existed—a life-size wood-and-plaster elephant that was meant to be a fountain, like so many still working in Paris. The Emperor Napoleon had ordered this mock-up of his planned fountain to be put in the Place de la Bastille in honor of his successful Egyptian campaign. By the time Gavroche takes up residence in 1832, the elephant has been left to fall into disrepair for over twenty years (and it wasn't removed until 1846).[189] Blackened by the elements, as Hugo explains, this "grandiose carcass of Napoleon's ideas" is forty feet high, cracked, surrounded by weeds, and "foul, despised, repellent and superb" (IV, 6, 2).

Gavroche easily scrambles up the elephant's leg through a hole into its belly and then helps the boys climb a rope. Inside, Gavroche continually draws on his sense of humor and, as Frankl recommends, chooses how to think about the situation. Mocking his strange abode, Gavroche jokes with his guests—"Let's begin by telling the porter we're not at home"—as he pulls a plank over the hole. He goes on to show us a great deal about how to remain resilient, using techniques that reflect what experts today recommend.

Gavroche makes the best of what he has, in effect employing Sandberg and Grant's "Option B" technique. For instance, Gavroche has fabricated a tent to protect himself from drips (the elephant leaks) and from the thousands of rats who have taken up residence in the rotting structure. He reduces or eliminates his own discomfort by empathizing with the five-year-old, who is frightened by hearing the rats gnawing at the tent. Calming the little boy down by telling him they're mice, Gavroche encourages him to hold his hand, passing on his "courage and strength" (IV, 6, 2). Gavroche also uses what my husband and I call the "Brightside-Barnett" technique, a version

*Gavroche helps his little brothers inside the Bastille elephant
in this 1862 illustration by Gustave Brion.*

of Sandberg and Grant's focusing on worst-case scenarios: when something goes wrong, it can help to recognize how things could be worse.[190] Hearing the boys worry that it's dark inside the elephant, Gavroche makes the point that, because they have a candle, being inside the elephant is better than being outside where it's seriously dark—and where they would be much more uncomfortable in the rain and cold.

Gavroche has a devil-may-care attitude that stands him in good stead later that night. A boy on the streets is an outlaw in the making, Hugo argues, and Gavroche knows several underworld characters. As a result, when the thief and murderer Montparnasse requests his assistance, Gavroche is not surprised (IV, 6, 3). Always up for an adventure, Gavroche readily agrees to climb three stories up through a narrow flue carrying a rope to an unnamed man breaking out of prison. Even when he sees that he will be risking his life for his uncaring father, Gavroche doesn't hesitate: "Fancy that! It's my father! Oh, not that it makes any difference." And Gavroche is right: it doesn't make a bit of difference to Thénardier that his son has rescued him. Thénardier is focused on pulling off his next robbery and doesn't recognize his son. In the boy's response, I see the wisdom of the first words of Reinhold Niebuhr's well-known prayer: "God, grant me the serenity to accept the things I cannot change."[191] Gavroche waits "a few moments—maybe his father might turn to him—and then puts his shoes back on" and leaves, saying only, "I've got to go and get my kids up." Gavroche's strength comes in part from his ability to accept things as he finds them and move on.

Gavroche obviously loves people, and his empathy and compassion contribute to his resilience. In the end, though, his desire to help others and his irreverent attitude take him to his death, as all novel readers and Les Mis fans remember. When the student insurrectionists at the barricade realize that they are running out of ammunition, Gavroche decides to retrieve cartridges from slain soldiers' pouches. He leaps over the barricade before anyone can stop him. The soldiers' firing at him and the bullets' striking right beside him seem to spur Gavroche to keep up his collecting and to "tease the rifles" by singing a satirical popular song. Undaunted, he quips, "I'll be blowed!

Someone's trying to kill my corpses" (V, I, 15). A few soldiers laugh—until a marksman's two bullets cut short Gavroche's song. Hugo's final sentence emphasizes Gavroche's nobleness of character and seems to remove him from the story: "That great little soul has just flown."

But the next chapter carries on Gavroche's spirit when we find ourselves with his two little brothers, lost and hungry, wandering through the Luxembourg Garden, a thirty-minute walk from the barricade. After a bourgeois gentleman tosses a partly-eaten brioche towards the swans on the pond, the seven-year-old successfully retrieves it before the birds do. Breaking it in half, he takes the smaller piece, just as Gavroche had done at the bakery. Giving the larger chunk to his little brother, he says, again just as Gavroche had said to him and adopting his mentor's street slang, "Ram that down your muzzle" (V, 1, 16). Gavroche's resilient spirit lives on in his brother, much as it continues to inspire many who meet this young man in *Les Misérables*.

Throughout his life, Victor Hugo rebounded from his personal tragedies, driven or inspired by his sense of mission for causes and by the people he cared for. His motto, "*Perseverando*," announced his conscious dedication to keeping his commitment and resolve alive. Fluent in Latin, Hugo would have known that *perseverando* can be interpreted in two related yet different ways, and he might have applied both meanings to himself. On the one hand, Hugo often said that it's "by persevering" that we get things done, that perseverance is a useful tool one might choose to use. On the other hand, his motto implied that he naturally responded to life's events "by persevering," that is, that his default response was to persist. Hugo first used "*Perseverando*" in 1827 as the epigraph for "To my friend S.-B.," a poem which he composed the year he became best friends with the talented literary critic, Charles Augustin Sainte-Beuve. In this ode to genius, Hugo encourages Sainte-Beuve to pursue his lyrical ambitions, although he must already have seen that Sainte-Beuve was unlikely to reach the poetic peaks envisioned in this exhortation to persistence.[192] (See Chapter 3 for more about Sainte-Beuve.)

Hugo urged other writers to persevere in order to stimulate them to more or better literary production. As his fame grew, Hugo received numerous requests for advice from aspiring poets, letters that he answered with kindness and generosity. For instance, in 1833, remarking that he was still pretty young himself, Hugo wrote to an even younger Strasbourg poet who had sought stylistic recommendations. His suggestions came along with this encouragement: "Work. You have what it takes to succeed; work. Don't get discouraged and don't get tired. Do you know the secret of every success in the world when you're strong?—it's this: *perseverando*."[192] Hearing from the French Romantic leader must have motivated the struggling writer.

We might wonder whether Hugo's sons equally appreciated similar counsel. It seems that both Charles and his younger brother, François-Victor, sometimes took their time about getting down to work, which prompted their father to remind them about the power of perseverance. When François-Victor was still imprisoned in the Conciergerie (see Chapter 7), Hugo wrote him from exile, applauding his outline of a proposed book on minority European political parties: "Now seize your idea with both hands, and don't let go. You know my motto: *perseverando*."[193]

All of which might lead us to suspect that Hugo was buoying *himself* with his motto. After all, he had many obstacles to overcome in order to succeed—beyond his personal tragedies, he faced fierce literary enemies and ongoing governmental upheaval. Not to mention nineteen years in exile! All the French republicans must have endured a great deal, Hugo perhaps less than others during the times he had his family with him. He was, for example, able to publish his apolitical works in France and earn a living. After Hugo rejected the general amnesty, however, his wife, daughter, and sons more or less deserted him to spend more and more time in Paris and Brussels (see Chapter 6). During the 1860s, at the height of the Second Empire, Hugo had every reason to imagine that he might die in exile, never again to see his beloved France—and that must have been very hard.

It is not surprising, then, that Hugo inscribed exhortations to survive and thrive right into his exile home, Hauteville House, where he designed the interior except for his family's bedrooms. He carried out his plans with help from Guernsey craftsmen (most often his cabinetmaker, Tom Mauger) and from Juliette Drouet, who frequented junk-and-antique shops with him. As Charles Hugo described it, "Victor Hugo scattered throughout his house maxims that summarize his life's experiences and ordeals."[194] Several of these messages encourage perseverance. Visiting Hauteville House today we can see carved in tall capital letters on the lower half of the oak gallery double doors the Latin imperatives "PERGE" ("Proceed" or "Persist") and "SURGE" ("Get up" or "Rise up"). Hugo recorded this work in his Guernsey Agenda notebook eleven days after rejecting the general amnesty (on August 18, 1859): "I traced, and Mauger highlighted in gilt the inscription PERGE — SURGE on my apartment door."[195] Hugo biographer Jean-Marc Hovasse confirms that these words were provoked by Hugo's new status as a voluntary exile. That same year, in his ground-floor studio, or smoking-room, Hugo had Mauger inscribe high up on the sideboard, where it is half hidden under the molding, the Latin phrase "AD AUGUSTA PER ANGUSTA."[196] Meaning "Toward elevated goals via narrow paths," this phrase prompts resolve and dedication.

Hugo articulates his conception of resilience in probably the greatest detail—and definitely most poetically—in his novel *Les Travailleurs de la mer*. Because the hero, Gilliatt, hopes to win the woman he loves, Déruchette, he tenaciously pursues a seemingly impossible task: recovering the steam engine from her uncle's wrecked ship. Déruchette's uncle has, in typical nineteenth-century fashion, offered her hand in marriage to the man who can save his shipping company by salvaging the engine. For weeks, running out of food and water, Gilliatt works in the English Channel around the dangerous Douvres rocks, which Hugo calls "a granite dragon" (II, 2, 4). Everything is against Gilliatt. He is isolated, abandoned, weakened, forgotten, endlessly battered by ocean waves. "Thirsty and hungry by day, cold by night, covered with wounds and rags," Gilliatt has torn hands, bloody feet, thin limbs, a pale face, a flame in his eyes. It's that flame that matters:

Hugo's interior design: PERGE & SURGE *at Hauteville House,*
photo © Jean Baptiste Hugo

Hugo's interior design: "AD AUGUSTA PER ANGUSTA,"
photo © Jean Baptiste Hugo

A superb flame, the will made visible. Man's eye is made
in such a way that we can perceive his virtue there. Our
gaze tells how much of a man there is in us. . . . Small
consciences blink their eyes, but great ones flash lightning.
If nothing shines out from under the eyelashes, it's because
the brain doesn't think, it's because the heart doesn't love.
The person who loves desires, and the person who desires
lights up and bursts. Resolve puts fire in one's look, an
admirable fire that burns away all timid thoughts.

Obstinate people are sublime. . . . Almost the entire
secret of great hearts is in this word: *Perseverando*.
Perseverance is for courage what a wheel is for a lever: a
fulcrum that is always moving. Whether the goal is on
earth or in heaven, going straight to that goal is everything;
. . . Not letting our conscience be debated or our will be
subdued, that's how we achieve suffering—and triumph."[197]

Strikingly, in this tribute to perseverance, courage, conscience, and
love, Hugo welcomes anguish alongside triumph. More than that, he
implies that suffering is glorious, something that we *achieve*, a path
to victory. Viktor Frankl found suffering essential in a somewhat different way: "If there is a meaning in life at all, then there must be a
meaning in suffering. Suffering is an ineradicable part of life, even as
fate and death. Without suffering and death human life cannot be
complete."[198] Certainly, as we have seen, Hugo's dedication to following his conscience brought him much pain, and his *Les Misérables*
characters accept the pain that sometimes accompanies their caring,
conscientious actions. Gavroche doesn't mind being colder than he
was if he can help the freezing young woman. Likewise, although
Jean Valjean's choices agonize him, he goes ahead and saves Champmathieu from prison, Marius from death, and Cosette from any infa-
mous connection to an ex-convict. The satisfaction of doing the right
thing, or of accomplishing one's mission, provides the will to move
forward and makes hardship and anguish worthwhile.

In the end, Hugo surprises me a bit by what I understand would
be *his* answer to my initial question: What does *Les Misérables* say

about having the strength to go on despite setbacks, despite pain, despite loss? For Hugo, my question might barely make sense. Because he saw pain as natural, acceptable, and productive in the cause of conscientious action, there would be no "despite suffering" for him. Suffering is evidently a logical corollary to conscience, he might say, and the strength that we gain from both is admirable.

Love, fortified by conscience, prompts the resolve and perseverance that bring us through suffering to success. Whether we love another person or care for those less well off than ourselves, feeling such outward-facing commitment gives us meaningful goals and increases our resilience. Beyond supplying us with a mission and courage, however, love is key to our humanity. And our humanity, Hugo argues, is indomitable and imperishable. We all have within us "inalienable humanity, inamissible human feeling, that splendid phenomenon, perhaps the finest of all our inner marvels" (V, 4). Love connects us together, and love invites us to accept our own and others' failings. Reinforced by conscience, love pushes us to do the best we can, despite our shortcomings.

Why does such a tragic story as *Les Misérables* uplift and inspire so many who read it or see the musical? Because we can see our potential in the characters who overcome impossible odds and who sacrifice greatly to help others. By surmounting their human flaws to reach unexpected heights of generosity, characters such as Bishop Myriel, Jean Valjean, Gavroche, Fantine, and Éponine help us realize that we, too, can be better than we have been.

Critics sometimes complain that Hugo's characters, especially in *Les Misérables*, are not realistic, are "nothing but archetypes"—the good-hearted criminal, the fallen woman, the idealistic revolutionary. Yet when you want to richly portray human beings and their humanity and when you want your readers to recognize themselves, why not turn to archetypes, the "pervasive ideas, images, or symbols that form part of the collective unconscious"?[199] As producer Cameron Mackintosh said to me, "The story and the genius of Hugo's characters is that he wrote archetypal characters that live in every generation and every country in the world. The triumph of the human spirit embodied by Jean Valjean's story is the ultimate emotional high that you can have for any story." Along with bringing us that emotional high, Hugo gives us a vision of how powerfully positive our human spirit truly can be.

Himself driven by his humanity, Victor Hugo never gave up in his efforts to make the world a better place. As he tells us in his epigraph, he explicitly wrote *Les Misérables* to spur people to improve society. Yet the social change that he imagined horrified some contemporaries, including long-time friend, fellow poet Alphonse de Lamartine, who had been a government minister. Appalled to find the novel almost seditious, Lamartine believed it preached what he called "egalitarian socialism." "Socialism" is an equally provocative idea for some today. But the term had a different meaning for Hugo and for many of his contemporaries. For Hugo socialism meant "encouraging the rich and protecting the poor" by creating wealth and paying equitable wages (IV, 1, 4)—not by taking money from the rich to give to the poor. M. Madeleine's factory, whose work and profits benefited his workers and the town as well as himself, was a model of what Hugo had in mind.

Still, Lamartine worried. "*Les Misérables* shows a sublime talent," he wrote, "an honest intention; and it is a very dangerous book in two ways: not only because it makes the fortunate fear too much, but also because it makes the unfortunate hope too much."[200] Lamartine believed that Hugo's novel would tempt people to hope for the "ideal," what he called an "impossible" chance to live a better life. They would inevitably fail to achieve what they hope, he believed, and they would revolt—by virtue of reading *Les Misérables*. Before publishing his condemnation, Lamartine requested Hugo's understanding.

In his response, Hugo emphasized his determination to fight for the best in humanity. To get his point across, he even associated himself with radicalism, a political movement to which he did not belong, but which was in line with several of his key positions, including separation of church and state and everyone's right to be educated and vote:[201]

My illustrious friend,

If the radical is the ideal, then, yes, I am a radical. . . .
Yes, a society that accepts poverty; yes, a religion that
accepts hell; yes, a humanity that accepts war—all seem
to me inferior as society, as religion, and as humanity; and
I'm striving toward a society on high, toward a humanity
on high, and toward a religion on high: society without
a king, humanity without boundaries, religion without a
book. . . . The goal is distant. But is that any reason not to
march toward it? . . . Yes, as much as a man is permitted
to want, I want to destroy human fate; I condemn slavery,
I drive out poverty, I enlighten ignorance, I treat illness, I
illuminate the night, I hate hatred.

That's what I am, and that's why I made *Les Misérables*.

To my way of thinking, *Les Misérables* is nothing less
than a book with brotherhood as its core and progress as
its summit.[202]

With unceasing visionary idealism and optimism (together with a
surprisingly vigorous *naïveté*), Hugo insisted on believing in people's
ultimate goodness and capacity for progress. He imagined a world
where people watch out for each other, where their ability to love
generously leads to mercy, where God and conscience matter, and
where everyone has a voice in society and a true chance to grow and
thrive. His unflinching faith in humanity is life-affirming and spiritually regenerating. Convinced that people can be better than they
are, Hugo refused to accept the status quo as right or desirable. A
caring man of conscience who searched and questioned his life—and
the universe—to help his readers find meaning as individuals and as
societies, Victor Hugo shares in *Les Misérables* his hard-won understanding, inspiring us to connect with our own consciences and act
out of love.

APPENDIX A
Time Line of Victor Hugo's Life, Works, French History, and *Les Misérables* Actions[204]

"Hugo's Work" includes primarily his publications, but also some of his plays' premiere performances or revivals. I have not included his graphic art. Abbreviations: P = poetry; N = novel; T = theater; S = speeches and political statements; E = essays.

DATES & SOME KEY EVENTS IN HUGO'S LIFE	HUGO'S WORKS, FOLLOWED BY SOME FRENCH HISTORICAL EVENTS	LES MISÉRABLES ACTIONS, WITH REFERENCES TO CHAPTERS
1795	France abolishes slavery in her territories and establishes freedom of worship. General Napoleon Bonaparte leads the rout of Parisian counter-revolutionaries, beginning his rise to power.	Jean Valjean steals a loaf of bread and is arrested in his village, Faverolles. He is sentenced to five years at hard labor. (I, 2, 6)
1796		Jean Valjean is one of the many convicts who make the many day trip to the Toulon prison galleys in chains. (I, 2, 6)
1802: Victor-Marie Hugo is born in Besançon on February 26. Brothers Abel and Eugène were born in 1798 and 1800, respectively.	Napoleon Bonaparte's position as First Consul is made a lifetime appointment.	Jean Valjean tries to escape when his turn comes up, in both 1800 and 1802. Each time he is recaptured, his prison sentence is lengthened. (I, 2, 6)
1803: Adèle Foucher, Victor's future wife, is born in Paris on November 28.		
1804: Charles Augustin Sainte-Beuve, future poet and literary critic and friend of the Hugos, is born on December 23.	Crowned Emperor, Napoleon introduces the Civil Code, commonly known as the Code Napoléon.	Father Myriel is the parish priest at Brignolles in Provence. He meets the new emperor around the time of his coronation. (I, 1, 1)
1806: Juliette Drouet (baptized Julienne Joséphine Gauvain), Victor's future lover, companion, muse, and lifelong friend, is born on April 10.		Myriel is named Bishop of Digne. (I, 1, 1) Jean Valjean makes a third attempt to escape from the Toulon prison. (I, 2, 6)
1804-12: Victor's parents (Joseph Léopold Sigisbert Hugo and Sophie Françoise Trébuchet Hugo) live mostly apart. He, his mother, and his brothers spend time with his father in Italy (1808) and Spain (1811).	Napoleon conquers Italy, Spain, Prussia, Austria, and other European countries.	

DATES & SOME KEY EVENTS IN HUGO'S LIFE	HUGO'S WORKS, FOLLOWED BY SOME FRENCH HISTORICAL EVENTS	*LES MISÉRABLES* ACTIONS, WITH REFERENCES TO CHAPTERS
1809: Victor's father becomes a Napoleonic general in Spain. After spending time with Léopold in Italy, the brothers and their mother return to Paris and live at the home known as *Les Feuillantines*.		Jean Valjean makes a fourth escape attempt. (I, 2,6)
1810		Marius is born in Paris. He will live with his royalist grandfather, M. Gillenormand, who despises Marius's father for supporting the Emperor Napoleon. (III, 3, 4)
1811		Fantine arrives in Paris, an innocent from the countryside, and falls in love with a university student named Félix Tholomyès. (I, 3, 2)
1812: Victor returns to Paris from Spain with Sophie and Eugène. Abel stays in Spain with Léopold and prepares for a military career, although he also becomes a writer, as well.	Napoleon's Russian campaign ends in a disastrous French retreat. He had crossed Russia's western border with an army of 650,000 but returned with fewer than 30,000.	
1814: Sophie seeks to separate officially from Léopold, and he files for divorce.	Napoleon abdicates after the European allies enter Paris and is exiled on the island of Elba. Louis XVIII returns to the throne, and the Restoration (of the Bourbon monarchy) begins.	
1815: Victor writes his first poems.	Napoleon returns from exile and seizes power, a period called "the Hundred Days." After his army is defeated at Waterloo on June 18, Napoleon abdicates again and is exiled to the remote island of St. Helena. Louis XVIII returns to power, and the Second Restoration begins.	Jean Valjean is released from prison and, passing through Digne, is invited into Bishop Myriel's home. (I, 2, 1) At the Battle of Waterloo, Thénardier robs Colonel Pontmercy, who believes that Thénardier has saved his life. (II, 1, 19) Cosette and Éponine are born. (I, 4, 1) Arriving in Montreuil-sur-Mer, Valjean saves two children from a fire, and no one thinks to ask for his "ex-convict" passport. (I, 5, 1)
1816: Victor and Eugène enter the collège royal Louis-le-Grand, studying philosophy and math.		Under the name M. Madeleine, Valjean reinvents the Montreuil glass bead industry, raising the townspeople's standard of living and becoming wealthy himself. (I, 5, 1)

APPENDIX A

DATES & SOME KEY EVENTS IN HUGO'S LIFE	HUGO'S WORKS, FOLLOWED BY SOME FRENCH HISTORICAL EVENTS	*LES MISÉRABLES* ACTIONS, WITH REFERENCES TO CHAPTERS
1817: Victor wins an honorable mention from the Académie Française for his poem on the subject "The Happiness Which Study Brings to All Life's Situations."	First public gaslights in Paris.	Tholomyès abandons Fantine in Paris, leaving her as an unwed mother with Cosette. (I, 3, 5)
1818: Victor's parents legally separate. Victor's friend and teacher Félix Biscarrat shares his concern about Eugène's mental health. Victor enrolls in law school in Paris.	*Odes* (P) After the Aix-la-Chapelle Congress, allied troops leave France on November 21.	Leaving Paris to find work, Fantine entrusts Cosette to the Thénardiers, now innkeepers and swindlers in Montfermeil. (I, 4, 1)
1819: Victor wins the "Lys d'or" prize in the *Jeux floraux de Toulouse* poetry competition in March. He and Adèle Foucher declare their love to each other. Victor, Abel, and Eugène found the critical literary journal, *Le Conservateur littéraire*, in December.		
1820: After Victor publishes his ode on the death of the duc de Berry, King Louis XVIII gives him a grant of 500 francs. Victor's mother discovers that Victor and Adèle Foucher (whom his brother Eugène also loves) have been secretly courting. Victor decides to embark on the literary career that he has been yearning for, rather than pursue the law.	*Bug-Jargal*, Victor's short story celebrating a Haitian slave revolt led by the black hero, Bug-Jargal, is published in *Le Conservateur littéraire*. The duc de Berry (the king's great-nephew) is assassinated. The Restoration government begins a campaign of censorship against the French press.	Upon his fellow citizens' insistence, Madeleine accepts the office of Mayor of Montreuil. (I, 5, 2)
1821: Hugo's mother dies on June 27. Léopold Hugo marries his mistress, Catherine Thomas, on September 6.	Napoleon dies on St. Helena. The Greek war for independence from the Turks begins.	Madeleine goes into mourning for Bishop Myriel. (I, 5, 4) As Inspector Javert watches, Madeleine saves one of his few enemies—an old man named Fauchelevent—from being crushed beneath an overturned cart. (I, 5, 7) Fantine is dismissed from her job at the glass bead factory. (I, 5, 8)
1822: Victor marries Adèle Foucher on October 12. That evening, Eugène becomes delirious and has to be restrained.	*Odes et poésies diverses* (P) The Restoration government enacts additional repressive laws against the press.	Fantine descends into poverty and, failing to find honest work, despairingly turns to prostitution. (I, 5, 10)
1823: Victor grows closer to his father. In June, Eugène is permanently institutionalized in the Charenton asylum for the insane. The Hugos' first-born son, named Léopold after Victor's father, dies at age three months on October 9.	*Han d'Islande* (N)	Bamatabois attacks Fantine on the street, and she scratches him. Javert arrests her. (I, 5, 12) Madeleine, testifying that Bamatabois was the aggressor and Fantine the victim, takes Fantine to the hospital. (I, 5, 13)

DATES & SOME KEY EVENTS IN HUGO'S LIFE	HUGO'S WORKS, FOLLOWED BY SOME FRENCH HISTORICAL EVENTS	LES MISÉRABLES ACTIONS, WITH REFERENCES TO CHAPTERS
		In February, Madeleine declares his true identity at the trial of Champmathieu in Arras. (I, 6, 2) Back in Montreuil, as Javert attempts to arrest Valjean, Fantine dies. (I, 8, 2) Arrested and reimprisoned, Valjean makes a daring escape. (II, 2, 1-3) December 24: Jean Valjean finds Cosette in the forest near Montfermeil. (II, 3, 5) December 25: Jean Valjean saves Cosette from the Thénardiers after acceding to their demands for more money. (II, 3, 11)
1824: The Hugos' first daughter, Léopoldine, is born on August 28.	*Nouvelles Odes* (P) Louis XVIII dies. Charles X ascends to the throne and abolishes all censorship.	In January, Jean Valjean and Cosette move into the miserable Gorbeau house in Paris. (II, 4, 2) A month or two later, Cosette and Jean Valjean escape Javert's pursuit by climbing into the Petit-Picpus convent garden. (II, 4, 4)
1825: With Adèle, Hugo travels through various French regions. In late May, he is invited to Charles X's coronation in Reims and is named a *Chevalier de la Légion d'honneur* (regarded as the highest possible civilian or military honor).	Charles X begins a series of measures designed to restore the authority of the Catholic Church and the king, such as declaring sacrilege a capital offense.	
1826: The Hugos' son Charles is born on November 3. Juliette Drouet's daughter, Claire (from her liaison with sculptor James Pradier) is born on November 12. Literary critic and poet Charles Augustin Sainte-Beuve praises Hugo's *Odes et Ballades*.	*Bug-Jargal* (N; expanded into a novella and published as such) *Odes et Ballades* (P)	
1827: Hugo develops a close friendship with Charles Augustin Sainte-Beuve. Hugo's "Ode à la colonne de la place Vendôme" is a sign of his growing liberalism. Hugo's preface to his very long play *Cromwell* quickly becomes the manifesto for French Romanticism, and the Hugos' home becomes the leading salon of Romantics.	*Cromwell* (T) Charles X, finding himself more and more attacked by journalists, begins again suppressing the freedom of the press. Greek hostilities come to an end.	At seventeen, Marius learns that his father is ill but arrives at his home in Vernon too late to see him alive. (III, 3, 4) Back at his grandfather's home in Paris, Marius discovers his father's admirable career as a colonel for the Empire and becomes filled with enthusiasm for his father and for Napoleon I. (III, 3, 5)

DATES & SOME KEY EVENTS IN HUGO'S LIFE	HUGO'S WORKS, FOLLOWED BY SOME FRENCH HISTORICAL EVENTS	LES MISÉRABLES ACTIONS, WITH REFERENCES TO CHAPTERS
1828: Hugo's father, Léopold Hugo, dies. The Hugos' second son, Victor, is born on October 21. He will take the name François-Victor to distinguish himself from his father.	*Amy Robsart* (T) is performed and then banned from theaters. *Odes et Ballades* (P) is published in its definitive form. The first French railway, drawn by horses, opens.	Marius and M. Gillenormand quarrel over Marius's new-found respect for his father. M. Gillenormand disinherits Marius, who leaves their home. (III, 3, 8) Still studying the law but deep in poverty (III, 5, 1-2), Marius meets the young activists who call themselves the Friends of the ABC (a pun emphasizing their support of the downtrodden, *les abaissés*). (III, 4, 3)
1829: Hugo refuses a new royal pension from King Charles X after *Marion Delorme* is received at the Théâtre-Français (today the Comédie-Française) and then barred from the stage by the censors.	*Les Orientales* (P) *Le Dernier Jour d'un condamné* (novella) *Marion Delorme* (T) Gas lighting comes to the streets of Paris.	After Fauchelevent dies, Jean Valjean leaves the convent with Cosette and buys three houses in Paris: one in Rue Plumet, one in Rue de l'Ouest, and one in Rue de l'Homme-Armé. (IV, 3, 1)
1830: Charles-Augustin Sainte-Beuve and Adèle Foucher become intimately involved, and Victor begins to suspect their relationship. The Hugos' second daughter, Adèle (their last child), is born on August 28. Beginning on September 1, Hugo writes *Notre-Dame de Paris* in less than five months, writing sixteen hours a day, about nine days out of ten, in order to meet his publisher's final deadline.	The February 25 premiere of *Hernani* (T) causes a scandal because of its literary audacity, which sparks a debate over art and ushers in Romantic theater. *Hernani* also solidifies Hugo's reputation as the leader of the Romantic movement. The Revolution of the Three Glorious Days (*les Trois Glorieuses*) takes place from July 27-29, changing France's government. Louis-Philippe Ier becomes king under a constitutional monarchy. Belgium becomes independent. France begins a conquest of Algeria.	In the Jardin du Luxembourg, Marius regularly encounters a man with white hair and a girl of about fifteen, whom he finds rather unattractive. (III, 6, 1)
1831: Hugo continues to fight for the abolition of censorship.	*Notre-Dame de Paris* (N) *Les Feuilles d'automne* (P) Riots in Paris and Lyon. Insurrections in Italy.	Cosette and Marius fall in love. (III, 6, 3) Marius loses track of M. Leblanc and Mlle Lanoire after his attention to the young girl makes the old man suspicious. (III, 8, 1) In October, Jean Valjean and Cosette see a column of chained convicts pass by. (IV, 3, 8)

DATES & SOME KEY EVENTS IN HUGO'S LIFE	HUGO'S WORKS, FOLLOWED BY SOME FRENCH HISTORICAL EVENTS	LES MISÉRABLES ACTIONS, WITH REFERENCES TO CHAPTERS
1832: The Hugo family moves to the Place Royale (today known as the Place des Vosges). Hugo loses his court battle against royal censorship of *Le Roi s'amuse*, but his oratorical skills during the trial are praised. June 5: Riots break out in Paris around the funeral of General Lamarque, who was a republican hero. Hugo, heading home to the Place des Vosges after working at the Tuileries, saw some of the twenty-seven barricades go up in the Les Halles neighborhood. The fighting trapped him in the passage du Saumon for at least a quarter hour, as he later described in *Les Misérables*.	*Le Roi s'amuse* (T) is suspended after the premiere. Adapted by the Italian composer Verdi and librettist Piave, Hugo's play becomes the highly successful opera *Rigoletto*. Cholera epidemic. Insurrections take place across France, including a June republican riot during General Lamarque's funeral (the event that ignited the insurrection depicted in the *Les Misérables* barricades scenes).	In early February, living in the Gorbeau house, Marius meets Éponine, who lives next door with her family, the Jondrettes (alias for the Thénardiers). (III, 8, 2) Shortly afterwards, M. Leblanc is ambushed by the Jondrettes and their criminal associates, but he escapes soon after Javert arrives. Javert arrests the Thénardiers and their gang. (III, 8, 21) In early April, Marius kisses Cosette for the first time. (IV, 5, 2) June 4: Marius asks his grandfather's permission to marry Cosette and angrily leaves when M. Gillenormand suggests that he take Cosette as his mistress. (IV, 8, 7) June 5: Riots breaking out at the funeral of General Lamarque turn into an insurrection. Barricades appear in Paris, including the one manned by the Friends of the ABC. (IV, 10, 3) Éponine is shot there protecting Marius and dies in his arms. IV, 14, 6) Jean Valjean, learning that Cosette and Marius love each other, heads to the barricade to find Marius. (IV, 15, 3) June 6: Gavroche dies on the barricade. (V, 1, 15) The barricade is taken by storm. (V, 1, 21-23) June 6: In the Jardin du Luxembourg, Gavroche's abandoned brothers forage for food. (V, 1, 16) Jean Valjean spares Javert's life. (V, 1, 19) Before nightfall, he carries the wounded Marius through the sewers. (V, 3, 1-8) In the evening, Jean Valjean, accompanied by Javert, takes Marius to his grandfather's house. (V, 3, 10) That night, Javert commits suicide. (V, 4)

DATES & SOME KEY EVENTS IN HUGO'S LIFE	HUGO'S WORKS, FOLLOWED BY SOME FRENCH HISTORICAL EVENTS	LES MISÉRABLES ACTIONS, WITH REFERENCES TO CHAPTERS
1833: Hugo is attracted to actress/model Juliette Drouet when she has a small role in his *Lucrèce Borgia*. They famously spend their first night together on February 16-17. Juliette stars in *Marie Tudor* in the early performances, but she loses her role after the audience boos her performance.	*Lucrèce Borgia* (T) *Marie Tudor* (T) The Guizot Law makes primary education the state's responsibility.	On February 16, Marius and Cosette are married. (V, 6, 1) On the morning of February 17, Jean Valjean reveals his true identity to Marius, who is shocked and no longer welcoming. (V, 7, 1) Living alone, Jean Valjean grows weaker and weaker. (V, 9, 2-3) When Thénardier tries to blackmail Marius, he unwittingly reveals that Jean Valjean had saved Marius's life. (V, 9, 4) Jean Valjean dies soon after he tells Cosette and Marius about Fantine. (V, 9, 5)
1834: In August, Victor and Juliette begin traveling together incognito, spending three weeks in Brittany.	*Littérature et philosophie mêlées* (E) *Claude Gueux* (a story inspired by the life and death of Claude Gueux, who, like Jean Valjean in *Les Misérables*, was imprisoned for stealing a loaf of bread) Republican riots in Paris and Lyon are severely repressed.	
1835: Charles Sainte-Beuve and Adèle Hugo continue to meet in secret, as do Victor and Juliette. *Angelo, tyran de Padoue* is a theatrical success.	*Angelo, tyran de Padoue* (T) *Les Chants du crépuscule* (P) Assassination attempt on King Louis-Philippe.	
1836: Early and late in the year, Hugo fails at his first two attempts to be elected to the Académie Française.	*Esmeralda*, based on *Notre-Dame de Paris* with music by Louise Bertin and libretto by Hugo, premieres at the Opera without great success. On October 3, Louis-Napoleon Bonaparte, nephew of the former Emperor Napoleon, fails in his attempt to overthrow the monarchy.	
1837: Hugo is received by King Louis-Phillipe at Versailles, and he is friends with the Duc d'Orléans, heir to the throne. His brother Eugène dies.	*Les Voix intérieures* (P)	
1838: Hugo writes perhaps his greatest Romantic play in verse, *Ruy Blas*, in about five weeks.	*Ruy Blas* (T) Death of French statesman and diplomat Talleyrand, who held high office during the French Revolution, under Napoleon, at the restoration of the Bourbon monarchy, and under King Louis-Philippe.	

DATES & SOME KEY EVENTS IN HUGO'S LIFE	HUGO'S WORKS, FOLLOWED BY SOME FRENCH HISTORICAL EVENTS	LES MISÉRABLES ACTIONS, WITH REFERENCES TO CHAPTERS
1839: On May 12, Hugo observed the insurrection, gathering details he used for the *Les Misérables* barricades. Hugo plays a role in obtaining the pardon of Armand Barbès. Hugo travels in the Haut-Rhine, Switzerland, and Provence with Juliette.	Republican and socialist insurrection led by Armand Barbès and Louis-Auguste Blanqui in Paris.	
1840: Hugo fails for the third time to be elected to the Académie Française. He travels in the lower Rhine with Juliette.	*Les Rayons et les Ombres* (P) Louis-Napoleon Bonaparte fails in his attempt to take over Boulogne. The Emperor Napoleon's ashes are returned to Paris and interred at Les Invalides.	
1841: Hugo is elected to the Académie Française on January 7. Two days later, he testified in support of a prostitute attacked by a "gentleman." He wins his civil suit against the publisher and translator of Donizetti's opera for plagiarism of his play *Lucrèce Borgia*.	France begins a serious effort to take total control of Algeria, a former colony.	
1842: Hugo is asked to express the official condolences of the Institut de France on the death of the duc d'Orléans.	*Le Rhin* (E) Death by accident on July 13 of the duc d'Orléans, the eldest son of the King Louis-Philippe.	
1843: Léopoldine marries Charles Vacquerie on February 14-15. On September 4, both drown in a boating accident on the Seine near their Villequier home. Hugo learns of her death in a newspaper article.	*Les Burgraves* (T)	
1844: Grieving, Hugo writes little and does not publish.	Charles Nodier, the leader of the Romantic movement before Hugo, dies on January 27.	
1845: Soon after being named a peer of France, Hugo is caught *in flagrante delicto* in an adulterous affair with Léonie d'Aunet Biard on or around July 5. She is imprisoned but his peer status protects him. He begins drafting the future *Les Misérables* on November 17.	*Le Rhin* (E; new, expanded edition)	

DATES & SOME KEY EVENTS IN HUGO'S LIFE	HUGO'S WORKS, FOLLOWED BY SOME FRENCH HISTORICAL EVENTS	LES MISÉRABLES ACTIONS, WITH REFERENCES TO CHAPTERS
1846: On February 21, Hugo records having seen a man arrested for stealing bread. Hugo gives numerous speeches in the Chamber of Peers. Claire Pradier dies on June 21.	Louis-Napoleon Bonaparte escapes from prison.	
1847: On June 14, Hugo successfully pleads in the Chamber of Peers for the pardon of Jérôme Bonaparte (the Emperor's brother), arguing on behalf of all exiles.	Economic crises and riots over hunger. Various scandals threaten the government.	
1848: Elected to the Constitutional Assembly, Hugo sits on the right but argues and votes for liberal policies. He supports Louis-Napoleon Bonaparte over the right-wing General Cavaignac in the December presidential election but is soon disappointed by his candidate. The Hugo family leaves the Place Royale, moving first to the rue d'Isly, in July, and then to the rue de la Tour-d'Auvergne, in October.	The Revolution of February 22-24 leads to Louis-Philippe's abdication and the proclamation of the Second Republic. With poet Lamartine as minister, the legislature votes for such republican values as universal suffrage, abolition of slavery, abolition of the death penalty for political offences, and complete freedom of the press. General Cavaignac's troops viciously repress a Parisian workers' strike in June. Louis-Napoleon Bonaparte is elected president on December 11.	
1849: Elected to the Legislative Assembly, Hugo speaks in favor of eliminating poverty, explicitly breaking with the conservatives. Hugo is elected president of the first Paris Peace Congress, where on August 21 he gives the opening speech, talking about the United States of Europe.	Leftist protests in France are repressed, as are revolutionary movements in several European countries.	
1850: On January 15, Hugo gives what becomes a famous speech for free, required, universal education, a speech against the Loi Falloux (which put Catholic clerics in charge of state education).		
1851: With some other legislators, Hugo unsuccessfully tries to organize Parisian resistance to the December 2 coup d'état. Sought by the police and hidden by Juliette and her friends, he flees to Belgium on December 11. Adèle remains in Paris to sell their belongings and prepare for exile. Juliette follows Victor to Brussels with his trunk of manuscripts.	In July, Charles Hugo is condemned to the Conciergerie prison for having written an article against the death penalty. In November his brother and friends Paul Meurice and August Vacquerie join him because of their journalistic stances. With an overnight coup d'état, Louis-Napoleon Bonaparte takes over the government on December 2 and institutes a severe repression. In a December 20 referendum, a majority of the French approves of the coup d'état.	

DATES & SOME KEY EVENTS IN HUGO'S LIFE	HUGO'S WORKS, FOLLOWED BY SOME FRENCH HISTORICAL EVENTS	LES MISÉRABLES ACTIONS, WITH REFERENCES TO CHAPTERS
1852: Along with sixty-five other legislative deputies, Hugo is officially exiled from France. Leaving Brussels before he is expelled because of *Napoléon le petit*, Hugo and his family settle into Marine-Terrace on Jersey.	*Histoire d'un crime* (history of the coup d'état) is drafted. *Napoléon le petit* (polemical pamphlet against Louis-Napoleon Bonaparte and his government) The Empire is reestablished and Bonaparte is proclaimed Napoleon III. Extremely repressive legislation against the press and the theater is passed.	
1853: Hugo and his family begin experimenting with séances, hoping to communicate with Léopoldine.	*Châtiments* (P) Napoleon III marries Eugénie de Montijo.	
1854: Hugo argues against the execution of convicted murderer Charles Tapner on Guernsey and then writes a controversial letter to British Lord Palmerston after Tapner is executed.	The Crimean War is declared.	
1855: The séances end. Hugo begins *Dieu*. Expelled from Jersey for supporting criticism of Napoleon III and Queen Victoria's rapprochement, Hugo and his family move to Guernsey. Hugo's brother Abel dies.	The French-English allies declare victory in the Crimea.	
1856: Hugo buys Hauteville House in St. Peter Port, Guernsey, and the family moves in on October 17.	*Les Contemplations* (P)	
1857: Juliette moves to La Fallue, a house from which she can see Victor's bedroom window.		
1858: Adèle Hugo and daughter Adèle leave Guernsey to travel in England and Europe from January into May. From June into October, Hugo suffers from a bacterial infection that puts his life in danger.	Emperor Napoleon III and the Empress Eugénie escape from Orsini's assassination attempt, which kills eight and wounds 150. More repressive laws follow.	
1859: On August 18, Hugo publicly refuses the amnesty granted to those who opposed the 1851 coup d'état, saying that he will return to France only when liberty returns. On December 2, he writes to the U.S. government to protest the execution of abolitionist John Brown and his colleagues.	*La Légende des siècles*, Première série (P) France declares war on Austria and begins to colonize Indochina.	

DATES & SOME KEY EVENTS IN HUGO'S LIFE	HUGO'S WORKS, FOLLOWED BY SOME FRENCH HISTORICAL EVENTS	LES MISÉRABLES ACTIONS, WITH REFERENCES TO CHAPTERS
1860: On April 25, Hugo takes his manuscript of Les Misérables out of his trunk and spends the rest of the year rereading and thinking about it.	Italian general, nationalist, and republican Giuseppe Garibaldi, whom Hugo admires, leads the Expedition of the Thousand (i Mille / the Redshirts) to conquer Sicily as part of his effort to unify Italy.	
1861: Hugo finishes Les Misérables on June 30 at the battlefield of Waterloo, Belgium, having traveled there with Juliette and his son Charles.	The war against Mexico, designed to defend French interests there, begins.	
1862: On July 28, Hugo leaves with Juliette to travel in Brussels, Luxembourg, Germany, and the Rhine valley, travels they will continue in future years. On September 16, he attends a celebratory banquet in his honor organized by the publishers of Les Misérables.	Les Misérables (N) The Second Empire begins to become more liberal.	
1863: Victor Hugo raconté par un témoin de sa vie (written by Hugo's wife, Adèle, but edited by family members and close friends) is published anonymously. On June 18, while her mother is away in Paris, the Hugos' daughter Adèle secretly travels to Canada, falsely believing that she will marry Lieutenant Pinson, whom she loves. This trip signals the beginning of her mental instability, and she will be away from home for nearly ten years.	France conquers Mexico, but guerilla fighting continues.	
1864: Juliette moves from La Fallue to Hauteville II (sometimes called "Hauteville Fairy"), which is very near to Hauteville House.	William Shakespeare (E) The French win the right to strike.	
1865: François-Victor's fiancée dies on January 14. Tired of exile, Hugo's wife and sons spend most of their time in England and Europe. Charles marries Alice Lehaene in Brussels on October 17.	Les Chansons des rues et des bois (P) The first transatlantic cable is laid.	
1866 : Hugo works on plays that will become part of his Théâtre en liberté and begins the novel L'Homme qui rit.	Les Travailleurs de la mer (N) As Prussia gains in strength, hostilities grow between Prussia and Napoleon III.	

DATES & SOME KEY EVENTS IN HUGO'S LIFE	HUGO'S WORKS, FOLLOWED BY SOME FRENCH HISTORICAL EVENTS	*LES MISÉRABLES* ACTIONS, WITH REFERENCES TO CHAPTERS
1867: Adèle Hugo pays a courtesy call on Juliette Drouet for the first time. The Hugos' first grandchild, Georges (Charles and Alice's son) is born on March 31 but dies at age one.	*Paris* (E) *Hernani* (T) opens in a revival at the *Théâtre-Français*. French troops leave Mexico. The Universal Exposition takes place in Paris.	
1868: Charles and Alice's second son, born on August 16, is also named Georges. Hugo's wife, Adèle, dies suddenly of apoplexy on August 27 in Brussels.	Laws concerning the press and public meetings become relatively liberal.	
1869: In Paris, Hugo's sons and friends found the republican journal *Le Rappel*. Charles and Alice's daughter, Jeanne, is born on September 29.	*L'Homme qui rit* (N) The republican party gains strength in France. Hugo presides at the Lausanne Peace Conference.	
1870: Hugo returns to Paris on September 5, after the declaration of the Third Republic. He and his family remain in Paris throughout the Prussian siege of the city.	A French plebiscite approves liberal reforms. France declares war on Prussia on July 19. By September 2, the French army is defeated at Sedan, and Napoleon III is taken prisoner. The Third Republic is declared on September 4. The Prussians begin a siege of Paris on September 19 that lasts until Paris surrenders on January 28, 1871. Parisians endure many privations, including eating vermin and zoo animals.	
1871: Hugo is elected Parisian deputy to the National Assembly in Bordeaux. His son Charles dies suddenly of apoplexy in Bordeaux on March 13. He is buried in Père-Lachaise cemetery in Paris on the day the Commune begins, March 18. In Brussels in May to settle Charles' estate, Hugo offers asylum to the Communards even though he had not supported their insurrection.	As part of the treaty with Prussia, France loses Alsace-Lorraine. With Thiers as President of the Republic, the National Assembly moves from Bordeaux to Versailles. The Paris Commune insurgency (which begins when the government attempts to disarm the Paris National Guard on March 18 and aims to set up an independent Parisian government) is repressed through violent bloodshed ("*la Semaine sanglante*," May 21-28).	

DATES & SOME KEY EVENTS IN HUGO'S LIFE	HUGO'S WORKS, FOLLOWED BY SOME FRENCH HISTORICAL EVENTS	*LES MISÉRABLES* ACTIONS, WITH REFERENCES TO CHAPTERS
1872: Hugo loses in a National Assembly election. His daughter Adèle, who was found wandering the streets of Barbados, is brought to Paris on February 12. Diagnosed as mentally ill, she is institutionalized in the Saint-Mandé asylum in eastern Paris. With Juliette Drouet, his daughter-in-law, Alice, and his grandchildren, Hugo goes in August to Guernsey. There he begins an affair with Juliette's maid, Blanche Lanvin.	*L'Année terrible* (P) *Ruy Blas*, in a successful revival at the Théâtre de l'Odéon, stars the famous Sarah Bernhardt.	
1873: Hugo and his family return to Paris on July 31. His son, François-Victor, dies on December 26.	Napoleon III dies on January 7. Mac-Mahon becomes President and establishes "l'Ordre moral" as political strategists envision a new restoration of the monarchy. The Sacré-Coeur Basilica in Montmartre is consecrated.	
1874: On April 29, Hugo and his family move into the fourth floor at 21 rue de Clichy, Paris, and Juliette moves into the third floor.	*Quatre-vingt-treize* (N) *Mes fils* (E) Censorship gains in power.	
1875: Hugo spends April 19-27 at Hauteville House on Guernsey.	*Actes et Paroles I et II* (S) The Assembly votes for constitutional laws that recognize the republican nature of the government.	
1876: Hugo is elected to the French Senate on January 30. On May 22, he gives his first speech in favor of amnesty for the Communards.	*Actes et paroles III* (S) The Republicans gain a majority in the legislative elections.	
1877: Charles Hugo's widow, Alice, marries Edmond Lockroy on April 3.	*La Légende des Siècles, Deuxième série* (P) *L'Art d'être grand-père* (P) *Histoire d'un crime* (S) Mac-Mahon dissolves the Republican chamber in May, but the Republicans win in the October elections.	
1878: On June 28, Hugo experiences what seems to have been a mini-stroke. On July 4, he travels with his family and Juliette to Guernsey to convalesce, returning to Paris on November 9, when he and Juliette move to 130 rue d'Eylau. The Lockroys live at 132.	*Le Pape* (P)	

DATES & SOME KEY EVENTS IN HUGO'S LIFE	HUGO'S WORKS, FOLLOWED BY SOME FRENCH HISTORICAL EVENTS	LES *MISÉRABLES* ACTIONS, WITH REFERENCES TO CHAPTERS
1879: On February 28, Hugo offers his second Senate speech for amnesty for the Communards.	*La Pitié Suprême* (P) Mac-Mahon resigns and is replaced by Grévy, a moderate Republican. The Communards are granted partial amnesty.	
1880: On July 3, Hugo offers his third Senate speech for amnesty for the Communards.	*Religions et religion* (P) *L'Âne* (P) The Communards are granted full amnesty. The Jules Ferry laws on public education passed this year reflect Hugo's views from the 1840s.	
1881: Large public festivities celebrate Hugo's entering his eightieth year on February 26, and a section of the Avenue d'Eylau is renamed the Avenue Victor Hugo.	*Les Quatre Vents de l'esprit* (P) Laws relating to the press and public gatherings become more liberal. Laws establish free primary education.	
1882:	*Torquemada* (T) Laws make primary education secular and obligatory.	
1883: Juliette Drouet dies of stomach cancer on May 11, leaving Hugo deeply stricken and unable to attend her burial.	*La Légende des Siècles, Dernière série* (P) *L'Archipel de la manche* (E)	
1885: May 22, at 1:27 p.m., Hugo dies of heart congestion at age eighty-three. His body lies in state under the Arc de Triomphe on May 31. Between one and two million people attend his national funeral on June 1.	On March 28, Minister Jules Ferry succeeds in getting passed his law for free, required, universal education (which echoes 1850 Hugo's speech). The Panthéon (formerly the Sainte-Geneviève Church) is deconsecrated so that Hugo can be entombed there.	

Posthumous Publications: 1886: *La Fin de Satan* (P); *Le Théâtre en liberté* (T). 1887 & 1900: *Choses vues* (journal). 1888: *Toute la lyre* (P). 1889: *Actes et paroles IV* (S). 1890: *Alpes et Pyrénées* (E). 1891: *Dieu* (P). 1892: *France et Belgique* (E). 1898: *Les Années funestes* (P). 1901: *Préface de mes œuvres et post-scriptum de ma vie* (E). 1902: *Dernière Gerbe* (P). 1942: *Océan vers* (P) and *Océan prose* (mostly writing notes).

APPENDIX B
Titles of Hugo's Works in French and English

Designed to help you follow the references to Hugo's works, this appendix contains Hugo's major works listed alphabetically by French title. Where standard English titles exist, those are given; otherwise, the English titles are a reasonable translation of the French. In parentheses, you will find a note of the genre of the publication, with an indication of those works Hugo left to be published after his death.

Actes et paroles	*Deeds and Words* (collected essays and speeches)
Alpes et Pyrénées	*The Alps and the Pyrenees* (travel writings published posthumously)
Amy Robsart	*Amy Robsart* (play)
Les Années funestes	*The Fateful Years* (posthumous poetry collection)
L'Année terrible	*The Terrible Year* (poetry collection)
Angelo, tyran de Padoue	*Angelo, Tyrant of Padua* (play)
L'Art d'être grand-père	*The Art of Being a Grandfather* (poetry collection)
Bug-Jargal	*Bug-Jargal* (novel)
Les Burgraves	*The Burgraves* (play: title is German for governor)
Les Chansons des rues et des bois	*Songs of the Streets and the Woods* (poetry collection)
Les Chants du crépuscule	*Songs at Dusk* (poetry collection)
Les Châtiments	*Punishments / Chastisements* (poetry collection) [translated by some as *The Empire in the Pillory*]
Choses vues	*Things Seen* (journal entries and notes)
Claude Gueux	*Claude Gueux* (novella)
Les Contemplations	*Contemplations* or *Reflections* (poetry collection)
Cromwell	*Cromwell* (preface and play)
Dernière Gerbe	*Final Sheaf* or *The Last Gleaning* (posthumous poetry collection)
Le Dernier Jour d'un condamné	*The Last Day of a Condemned Man* (novella)

Dieu	*God* (narrative poem published posthumously)
Les Feuilles d'automne	*Autumn Leaves* (poetry collection)
La Fin de Satan	*The End of Satan* (narrative poem published posthumously)
France et Belgique	*France and Belgium* (travel writings published posthumously)
Han d'Islande	*Han of Iceland* (novel)
Hernani	*Hernani* (play)
L'Homme qui rit	*The Man Who Laughs* or *The Laughing Man* (novel)
Journal de ce que j'apprends chaque jour	*Journal of What I Learn Every Day* (journal entries)
La Légende des siècles	*The Legend of the Centuries* (poetry collection in several volumes)
Littérature et philosophie mêlées	*Literature and Philosophy Combined* (essays)
Lucrèce Borgia	*Lucrezia Borgia* (play)
Marie Tudor	*Marie Tudor* (play)
Marion de Lorme	*Marion Delorme* (play)
Les Misérables	*Les Misérables* (literally, "the wretched [ones]")
Napoléon le petit	*Napoleon the Small* (political pamphlet)
Notre-Dame de Paris, 1482	*The Hunchback of Notre-Dame* (novel)
Océan prose	*Ocean Prose* (writing notes published posthumously)
Océan vers	*Ocean Verses* (poetry notes published posthumously)
Odes	*Odes* (poetry collection)
Odes et Ballades	*Odes and Ballads* (poetry collection)
Les Orientales	*Orientals* or *Orientalia* (poetry collection)
Le Pape	*The Pope* (narrative poem)
Paris	*Paris* (political essay; introduction to *Paris-Guide*)
Préface de mes œuvres et post-scriptum de ma vie	*Preface to My Works and Postscript to My Life* (philosophical essay published posthumously)

Promontorium somnii	*The Promontory of Dreams* (philosophical essay)
Les Quatre Vents de l'esprit	*The Four Winds of the Spirit* (poetry collection)
Quatrevingt-treize	*Ninety-Three* (novel)
Les Rayons et les ombres	*Light and Shadow* (poetry collection)
Religions et religion	*Religions and Religion* (narrative poem)
Le Rhin	*The Rhine* (travel writings)
Le Roi s'amuse	*The King's Revels* or *The King Takes His Amusement* (play)
Ruy Blas	*Ruy Blas* (play)
Le Théâtre en liberté	*Theater in Liberty* (collection of plays)
Torquemada	*Torquemada* (play)
Toute la lyre	*The Whole Lyre* (posthumous poetry collection)
Les Travailleurs de la mer	*Toilers of the Sea* (novel)
Les Voix intérieures	*Inner Voices* (poetry collection)
William Shakespeare	*William Shakespeare* (book-length essay)

APPENDIX C

Further Resources

This alphabetical list includes both sources that have contributed to my general knowledge and understanding of Victor Hugo and *Les Misérables* and resources not in the bibliography. Most sites are in French (as "fr" indicates), but, where possible, I have listed the English-language versions of sites (also, web browsers normally offer English translations of web pages).

Hugo's life and works, on scholarly and French institutional sites:

Bicentennial of Hugo's birth (2002):

- French National Library (Bibliothèque Nationale de France); catalogue at https://www.bnf.fr/en/bibliotheque-nationale-de-france-catalogue-general
- French Senate: http://www.senat.fr/evenement/archives/D24/hugo.html
- Unfortunately, the Ministry of Culture site (Victor Hugo: Conscience et Combats, 1802-2002, http://www.victorhugo.culture.fr/) can now be consulted only from the French National Library reading rooms.

Groupe Hugo at the Université de Paris 7 (Jussieu):

- Main page: http://groupugo.div.jussieu.fr/
- Chronologie Victor Hugo: A searchable database of Hugo's contemporaries, letters, works, and so on: http://groupugo.div.jussieu.fr/Default _Chronologie.htm
- To search through Hugo scholars' talks, critical texts, and other documents: http://groupugo.div.jussieu.fr/Default_Recherches.htm

Juliette Drouet's letters to Victor Hugo, with details of her life: http://www.juliettedrouet.org

Hugo's works in English translation:

Les Misérables, with the translations I most recommend listed first:

Christine Donougher, translator. London & New York: Penguin Books, 2015. An engaging, modern translation. Includes detailed historical, cultural, and literary notes.

Lee Fahnestock and Norman MacAfee, translators. New York: Signet Classics / Penguin Random House, 2013. A classic translation based on Wilbour's 1862 translation and in print since 1987. No informational notes.

Julie Rose, translator. New York: Modern Library, 2009. A lively translation that sometimes rewrites Hugo. Includes detailed historical, cultural, and literary notes.

Norman Denny, translator. London & New York: Penguin Classics, 1982. An appealing, somewhat abridged translation (some sentences are shortened or

simplified and Hugo's book on slang (IV, 7, 1-4) appears in an appendix). No
informational notes.

Charles Wilbour, translator. London: Everyman's Library, 1998. Also published
in an abridged edition by New York: Barnes & Noble Books, 1996; 2003. The
original American 1862 translation, generally considered quite faithful to the
original but sounding dated in ways that Hugo's original does not. No informational notes.

Isabel Hapgood, translator. A translation from 1887 that is published in various
formats. Dated in style, Hapgood's translation is the least nearly accurate of those
included here. No informational notes.

*Poetry (in alphabetical order by title; some include Hugo's original verse alongside the
translation):*

The Essential Victor Hugo. Trans. by E.H. Blackmore and A.M. Blackmore. Chicago:
University of Chicago Press, 2004. Includes some prose excerpts, as well as
poems.

God and the End of Satan / Dieu et la Fin de Satan. Trans. & edited by R. G. Skinner.
Chicago: Swan Isle Press, 2013.

Satan and His Daughter, the Angel Liberty. Trans. & edited by R. G. Skinner. Chicago: Swan Isle Press, 2019.

Selected Poems of Victor Hugo: A Bilingual Edition. Trans. by E.H. Blackmore and
A.M. Blackmore. Chicago: University of Chicago Press, 2004.

Victor Hugo: Selected Poems. Trans. by Brooks Haxton. New York: Penguin Books,
2002.

Victor Hugo: Selected Poetry in French and English. Trans. by Steven Monte. New
York: Routledge, 2002.

Other Hugo titles:

Project Gutenberg offers a selection of works free of copyright but also, by definition, dated in their translation style: http://www.gutenberg
.org/ebooks/search/?query=victor-hugo

Hugo's works in French online:

Most of Hugo's works, individually listed, at Wikisource online:
http://fr.wikisource.org/wiki/Victor_Hugo

The first posthumous French set of complete works (known as the "Imprimerie
Nationale" edition) online from the University of Toronto via Wikisource
(missing one volume): https://fr.wikisource.org/wiki/Discussion:%C5%92uvres
_compl%C3%A8tes_de_Victor_Hugo,_%C3%A9dition_dite_de
_l%E2%80%99Imprimerie_nationale

Project Gutenberg site with many of Hugo's works in French, English, and other
languages: http://www.gutenberg.org/browse/authors/h#a85

APPENDIX C

Hugo museums and societies in alphabetical order:

Casa de Victor Hugo in Pasaja, Spain: Site in English: http://www
.oarsoaldeaturismoa.eus/en/explore-oarsoaldea/our-museums/
victor-hugo-house.html

Casa Victor Hugo in Havana, Cuba: Summary in English: http://www.lahabana
.com/guide/casa-victor-hugo/. 2014 video tour: https://www.youtube.com/
watch?v=VsUhP4F1PhE

Hauteville House, St. Peter Port, Guernsey (the Hugos' residence 1856-70, where
Hugo designed much of the interior): http://www.maisonsvictorhugo.paris.fr/
fr/musee-collections/visite-de-hauteville-house-guernesey
Site in English: http://www.maisonsvictorhugo.paris.fr/en/
museum-collections/house-visit-guernsey

Maison de Victor Hugo, Place des Vosges, Paris (the Hugos' residence 1832-48):
http://www.maisonsvictorhugo.paris.fr/fr/
musee-collections/visite-de-lappartement
Site in English: http://www.maisonsvictorhugo.paris.fr/en/museum-collections/
place-des-vosges-apartment-visit

Maison de Victor Hugo, Musée littéraire Victor Hugo, Vianden, Luxembourg:
http://www.victor-hugo.lu/

Maison Littéraire de Victor Hugo, Bièvres (in the Bertin family's Château des
Roches, where the Hugos sometimes vacationed in the 1830s): http://www
.maisonlitterairedevictorhugo.net/sitefrancais.htm
Site in English: http://www.maisonlitterairedevictorhugo.net/siteanglais.htm

Maison Natale de Victor Hugo in Besançon (where Hugo was born and lived the
first six weeks of his life): http://www.besancon.fr/hugo

Musée Victor Hugo – Maison Vacquerie, Villequier (where Léopoldine lived with
her husband Charles Vacquerie): http://www.museevictorhugo.fr/fr/home/
Site in English: http://www.museevictorhugo.fr/en/permanent-course/.

Société des Amis de Victor Hugo / Society of the Friends of Victor Hugo (at the
time of this book's publication, the English site had not been completed): http://
victor-hugo.org/fr/

Victor Hugo in Guernsey Society: https://www.victorhugoinguernsey.gg/

Other sites devoted to Victor Hugo:

The France of Victor Hugo, a site created in 1999 by students in Professor Robert
Schwartz's HIS 255 course: https://www.mtholyoke.edu/courses/rschwart/
hist255/jkr/hugo.html

Hauteville House (a collection of photos, floor plans, and descriptions): http://www
.hautevillehouse.com

Victor Hugo Central, a site which also includes research data on Hugo and his
works: http://gavroche.org/vhugo/

The musical *Les Misérables* official site: https://www.lesmis.com/.

NOTES

Introduction

1   "After an ill-fated love affair": Adèle Hugo's story of frustrated love and encroaching insanity is movingly and memorably told the 1975 film, *The Story of Adèle H.*, directed by François Truffaut.

2   "Never was a book devoured so furiously": Grossiord, *Victor Hugo*, 432.

3   "Published in several cities," and finances related to *Les Misérables* publication: Grossman, *Conversion*, 10, 14.

4   Gustave Simon's story of 48,000 copies: Marseille and Gomez, *Les Années Hugo*, 151.

5   Adèle Hugo to Victor Hugo: Letter dated May 11, 1862. CFL XII, 1169. Original French: "Mon grand homme, . . . à distance, il ne se rend pas bien compte de l'effet des *Misérables* qui produisent dans toutes les classes une émotion sans pareille. Le livre est dans toutes les mains; les personnages devenus types déjà sont cités à toute occasion et à tout propos. Les images de ces personnages sont à toutes les vitrines des marchands d'estampes; des affiches monstres annonçant les *Misérables* sont placardées à tous les coins de rue. L'ouvrage et le nom de Victor Hugo sont des projectiles qui agitent et remuent Paris."

6   Sand, Rimbaud, Dostoevsky, and Tolstoy on *Les Misérables*: Grossman, *Conversion*, 18. Tolstoy's admiration of Hugo and prediction of long-term success: Karp, "Victor Hugo in Russia," 322.

7   Dickens, Swinburne, and Sinclair on Hugo: Dickens described Hugo in a letter to Lady Blessington: https://libwww.freelibrary.org/diglib/SearchItem .cfm?searchKey=3866891944&ItemID=cdc276101. As presented by the Victor Hugo museum in Paris: http://maisonsvictorhugo.paris.fr/en/ node/1061. Swinburne on Hugo: Brombert, *Victor Hugo*, 2. Sinclair on *Les Misérables*: Sinclair, *Cry for Justice*, 182.

8   Contemporary reactions to Hugo's novel: The comments from Flaubert and Baudelaire are cited by Robert Legg, in "Beyond the Barricade: Adolescents Rehearsing and Performing Masculinities in Music Theatre," in "Les Cultures ado: consommation et production," Heather Braun, Elisabeth Lamothe, and Delphine Letort (eds.), *Publije: e-Revue de critique littéraire*, no. 1 (2018), n.p. http://revues.univ-lemans.fr/index.php/publije/article/view/45/54.

9   *Les Misérables* banned by the Vatican: *Modern History Sourcebook: Index librorum prohibitorum, 1557-1966 [Index of Prohibited Books]*, Fordham University. On the contemporary reception of *Les Misérables*, see Grossman, *Conversion*, 14-15; Maladain, "La réception des *Misérables*," 1071.

10   Translations of *Les Misérables*: Grossman, *Conversion*, p. 10.

11   First U.S. translation: Moore, "Some Translations," 240.

12 Called themselves "Lee's Miserables": Stiles, *Four Years*, 252; Masur, "In Camp," n.p.

13 Read *Les Misérables* around the campfire: Pickett, *Pickett and His Men*, 358. Renamed themselves as the members of the barricade defenders: Blémont, ed., *Le Livre d'or*, 210.

14 "dozens of animated movies, television series, and radio broadcasts": For the figure "at least sixty filmmakers," see Arnaud Laster, "A New Creation: *Histoire de Gavroche* in Words and Song," p. 175 in Grossman and Stephens, eds., *Les Misérables and its Afterlives*. For a list of film, television, radio, and manga adaptations, see https://en.wikipedia.org/wiki/Adaptations_of_Les_Mis%C3%A9rables#Film. For more details on the early reception of Hugo's novel and its adaptations, see Kathryn M. Grossman, "The Making of a Classic: *Les Misérables* Takes the States," in Grossman and Stephens, eds., *Les Misérables and Its Afterlives*, 113-28.

15 "One of the most celebrated books" in India: Grossman, *Conversion*, 19.

16 Hugo Chávez's "You want to meet Jean Valjean?": Denis, "Chávez Loved *Les Misérables.*"

17 For information about the 1980 Palais des sports production, see Vermette, *Musical World*, 22-23; Cox, *Stage by Stage*.

18 Popularity of the musical *Les Mis*: https://www.lesmis.com/us-tour/about.

19 Hugh Jackman on playing Valjean: Hugh Jackman, email message to author, December 12, 2012.

20 "Open up, I am here for you": Letter to G. Daëlli dated October 18, 1862. CFL XII, 1195-96. Original French: "Vous avez raison, monsieur, quand vous me dites que le livre *Les Misérables* est écrit pour tous les peuples. Je ne sais s'il sera lu par tous, mais je l'ai écrit pour tous. . . . Les plaies du genre humain, ces larges plaies qui couvrent le globe, ne s'arrêtent point aux lignes bleues ou rouges tracées sur la mappemonde. Partout où l'homme ignore et désespère, partout où la femme se vend pour du pain, partout où l'enfant souffre faute d'un livre qui l'enseigne et d'un foyer qui le réchauffe, le livre *Les Misérables* frappe à porte et dit: Ouvrez-moi, je viens pour vous."

21 Kretzmer's comment on *Les Misérables* around the world: Kretzmer, "Interview," 6.

22 "books like this one cannot be useless" / epigraph for *Les Misérables*: Original French: "Tant qu'il existera, par le fait des lois et des mœurs, une damnation sociale créant artificiellement, en pleine civilisation, des enfers, et compliquant d'une fatalité humaine la destinée qui est divine; tant que les trois problèmes du siècle, la dégradation de l'homme par le prolétariat, la déchéance de la femme par la faim, l'atrophie de l'enfant par la nuit, ne seront pas résolus; tant que, dans de certaines régions, l'asphyxie sociale sera possible; en d'autres termes, et à un point de vue plus étendu encore, tant qu'il y aura sur la terre ignorance et misère, des livres de la nature de celui-ci pourront ne pas être inutiles."

23 Sartre on Hugo: Brombert, *Victor Hugo*, 3-4.

Chapter 1 | Seeing Others

24 Epigraph: A note from probably 1840, from "Philosophie prose," in Laffont, *Océan*, 99. Original French: "Devant la conscience, être capable, c'est être coupable."

25 Hugo's February 22, 1846, journal entry: From Hugo, *Choses vues*, v. I, 333-34. Original French: "Hier, 22 février, j'allais à la Chambre des pairs. Il faisait beau et très froid, malgré le soleil et midi. Je vis venir rue de Tournon un homme que deux soldats emmenaient. Cet homme était blond, pâle, maigre, hagard; trente ans à peu près, un pantalon de grosse toile, les pieds nus et écorchés dans des sabots avec des linges sanglants roulés autour des chevilles pour tenir lieu de bas; une blouse courte et souillée de boue derrière le dos, ce qui indiquait qu'il couchait habituellement sur le pavé, la tête nue et hérissée. Il avait sous le bras un pain. Le peuple disait autour de lui qu'il avait volé ce pain et que c'était à cause de cela qu'on l'emmenait.... / Cette femme ne voyait pas l'homme terrible qui la regardait. / Je demeurai pensif. / Cet homme n'était plus pour moi un homme, c'était le spectre de la misère, c'était l'apparition brusque, difforme, lugubre, en plein jour, en plein soleil, d'une révolution encore plongée dans les ténèbres mais qui vient.... Du moment où cet homme s'aperçoit que cette femme existe tandis que cette femme ne s'aperçoit pas que cet homme est là, la catastrophe est inévitable."

26 "But Hugo's upcoming meeting did not stop him from *seeing* what was in front of him": For more on Hugo's attention to seeing and observing, see Gomis, *Hugo devant l'objectif*, 15-24.

27 "the drama of conscience, the epic of the soul": Hugo used this phrase in a letter to his publisher Albert Lacroix about *Les Misérables* on May 14, 1862. Original French: "Le drame de la conscience, l'épopée de l'âme."

28 "notes about its people and events": Hugo's notes about people and events that eventually appear in *Les Misérables* began as early as 1829, when he was thinking about the economical black-jet imitations that M. Madeleine developed. In 1840, he laid out the plan of his book: "Story of a saint / Story of a man / Story of a woman / Story of a doll" ("Histoire d'un saint / Histoire d'un homme / Histoire d'une femme / Histoire d'une poupée"). Cited by Tersen, "Chronologie des *Misérables*," 206-07. The text of Hugo's 1845-48 draft of the novel he once entitled *Les Misères* is available online in Rosa's "édition critique et génétique." See Chapter 2 for more details of Hugo's preliminary ideas about his epic.

29 "the soul of our life and our home": Hugo's words come from a September 10, 1843, letter to his friend, artist Louis Boulanger, quoted in Hovasse, *Victor Hugo* I, 910, and in CFL VI, 1241. Original French: "l'âme de notre vie et de notre maison."

30 "This distressing happiness of marrying off one's daughter": CFL VI, 1393. Original French: "Ce bonheur désolant de marier sa fille."

31 "Kisses over and over. V.": Hugo's letter to Léopoldine on July 18, 1843. Hovasse, *Victor Hugo* I, 890. Original French: "Cette journée passée au Havre est un rayon dans ma pensée; je ne l'oublierai de ma vie... Je suis partie avec

un serrement de cœur, et le matin, en passant près du bassin, j'ai regardé les fenêtres de ma pauvre chère Didine endormie. Je t'ai bénie et j'ai appelé Dieu sur toi du plus profond de mon cœur. Sois heureuse, ma fille, toujours heureuse, et je serai heureux. Dans deux mois je t'embrasserai. En attendant, écris-moi, ta mère te dira où. Je t'embrasse encore et encore. V."

32 Hugo learns of Léopoldine's death: Hovasse, *Victor Hugo* I, 907-13. I am indebted to Hugo scholar and biographer Jean-Marc Hovasse for his lively, well-researched recounting of Léopoldine's death and Hugo's learning of it.

33 Newspaper story of Léopoldine's death: Hovasse, *Victor Hugo* I, 907-08. Original French: "Un affreux événement qui va porter le deuil dans une famille chère à la France littéraire est venu, ce matin, affliger de son bruit sinistre notre population qui, parmi les victimes, compte des concitoyens... Le filet ramena le corps inanimé de l'infortunée jeune femme, qui fut transportée à terre et déposée sur un lit." Hugo's exclamation: "Voilà qui est horrible!"

34 Juliette Drouet's comments: Hovasse, *Victor Hugo* I, 909. Original French: "Le courage et la résignation de Victor Hugo sont plus poignants à voir que la douleur la plus bruyante."

35 Hugo's letter to Louise Bertin: CFL, 1241-42. Original French: "10 septembre 1843. Saumur / Chère mademoiselle Louise, je souffre, j'ai le cœur brisé; vous le voyez, c'est mon tour. J'ai besoin de vous écrire, à vous qui l'aimiez comme une autre mère; elle vous aimait bien aussi, vous le savez. / Hier, je venais de faire une grande course à pied au soleil dans les marais; j'étais las, j'avais soif, j'arrive à un village qu'on appelle, je crois, Subise, et j'entre dans un café. On m'apporte de la bière et un journal, le Siècle. / J'ai lu. C'est ainsi que j'ai appris que la moitié de ma vie et de mon cœur était morte. / J'aimais cette pauvre enfant plus que les mots ne peuvent le dire. Vous vous rappelez comme elle était charmante. C'était la plus douce et la plus gracieuse femme. / Oh! mon Dieu, que vous ai-je fait? Elle était trop heureuse, elle avait tout, la beauté, l'esprit, la jeunesse, l'amour. Ce bonheur complet me faisait trembler; j'acceptais l'éloignement où j'étais d'elle afin qu'il lui manquât quelque chose. Il faut toujours un nuage. Celui-là n'a pas suffi. Dieu ne veut pas qu'on ait le paradis sur la terre. Il l'a reprise. Oh! mon pauvre ange, dire que je ne la verrai plus! / Pardonnez-moi, je vous écris dans le désespoir. Mais cela me soulage. Vous êtes si bonne, vous avez l'âme si haute, vous me comprendrez, n'est-ce pas? Moi, je vous aime du fond du cœur et, quand je souffre, je vais à vous. / J'arriverai à Paris presque en même temps que cette lettre. Ma pauvre femme et mes pauvres enfants ont bien besoin de moi. / Je mets tous mes respects à vos pieds. / VICTOR HUGO. / Mes amitiés à mon bon Armand. Que Dieu le préserve et qu'il ne souffre jamais ce que je souffre."

36 he "cried bitterly for three days" and "wanted to break his head on the pavement": From "Oh! Je fus comme fou . . ." ("Oh! It was like I was mad . . ."), *Les Contemplations* IV, iv. Original French: "Hélas! et je pleurais trois jours amèrement, . . . Je voulais me briser le front sur le pavé."

37 "angelic sacred unity": Original French: "une unité angélique et sacrée" (IV, 5, 4). Hugo expressed his belief in Léonie's and Léopoldine's connection to

God by emphasizing the power of their prayers, as in this letter to Léonie, quoted in Hovasse, *Victor Hugo* I, 933: "Pray for us, my beloved, my Léonie, you must be heard on high because you come from there! Because you still speak that language! Everything that you say could be said by angels; all that you think could be thought by heaven." (Original French: "Prie pour nous, ma bien aimée, ma Léonie, tu dois être écoutée là-haut, car tu en viens! Car tu en parles encore la langue! Tout ce que tu dis pourrait être dit par les anges; tout ce que tu penses pourrait être pensé par le ciel.") [Sunday 2:00, no. 12]. Hugo seeks Léopoldine's prayers, too, in for example, "La Prière pour tous" ("Prayer for Everyone"), *Les Feuilles d'automne* XXXVII, for example.

38 Victor's letters to Léonie: Quoted in Hovasse, *Victor Hugo* I, 933, from Hugo, *Lettres de Victor Hugo à Léonie Biard*, no. 97 and 76. Original French: "Je te baise à te faire toute rose de la tête aux pieds." (Draft letter, "Tuesday, 9:00 in the morning") and "Que j'ai été heureux dans tes bras aujourd'hui! Quelle extase mêlée à cette volupté! L'amour, ô ma bien aimée, c'est la rencontre du ciel et de la terre. À un certain moment, l'union des âmes et l'union des corps ne fait plus qu'un seul bonheur, à la fois idéal et réel." (Draft letter, "Saturday night").

39 *Voyage d'une femme à Spitzberg*: Published in 1854, Biard's book has not been translated into English but might have been entitled *A Woman's Trip to Spitsbergen*.

40 "And I loved her": A note dated 1854, published in Laffont, *Océan*, 305. Original French: "J'avais trente-neuf ans quand je vis cette femme. / De son regard plein d'ombre il sortit une flamme. / Et je l'aimai."

41 "his drawings related to her always took the form of a rebus": Hovasse, *Victor Hugo* I, 929.

42 "*in flagrante delicto*": I am grateful to Jean-Marc Hovasse for putting together these pieces of the puzzle around Hugo's actions during this period, and for suggesting connections to Hugo's writing of *Les Misérables* in his *Victor Hugo* I, 964-74, and in email messages to the author in 2014. Details of these July-September, 1845, events come from his *Victor Hugo* I, 957-63. Tradition says that Victor and Léonie were discovered in the morning hours of July 5, 1845, while scholars argue that they were surprised in the passage Saint-Roch on the evening of July 3.

43 "affairs typical of the times": Jean-Marc Hovasse confirmed the normality of Hugo's affairs in an email message to the author, November 8, 2014.

44 "Abuse that I foresee": Dated December 20, 1847. Laffont, *Chantiers*, 731, quoted in Hovasse, *Victor Hugo* I, 973. Original French: "Injures que je prévois après la publication des *Misères*: l'auteur aurait pu nous peindre les Misères d'un Pair de France et d'une femme pris en flagrant délit d'adultère."

Chapter 2 | Why Forgive?

45 Epigraph: From "Fraternité," *L'Art d'être grand-père*, XVIII, 4. Original French: "Je rêve l'équité, la vérité profonde, / L'amour qui veut, l'espoir qui luit, la foi qui fonde, / Et le peuple éclairé plutôt que châtié. / Je rêve la douceur, la bonté, la pitié, / Et le vaste pardon. De là ma solitude."

46 Families of murder victims who forgive: Von Drehle, "How Do You Forgive a Murder?"

47 Benefits of forgiveness: Worthington, "New Science of Forgiveness."

48 Jackman on nineteenth-century prisons: Jackman, "Great Performances: Historic Acts." Hugo puts it this way: "The peculiarity of punishment of this kind, in which the pitiless—that is to say, brutalizing—part predominates, is to transform gradually by a slow numbing process a man into an animal, sometimes into a ferocious beast." Original French: "Le propre des peines de cette nature, dans lesquelles domine ce qui est impitoyable, c'est-à-dire ce qui est abrutissant, c'est de transformer peu à peu, par une sorte de trans-figuration stupide, un homme en une bête fauve, quelquefois en une bête féroce" (I, 2, 7).

49 Jackman on the prisoner transport scene: Hugh Jackman, email message to author, March 18, 2013.

50 "A sort of modern Job": Hugo wrote the phrase "une sorte de Job du monde moderne" on an envelope dated June 11, 1860, apparently as part of his proposed preface or epigraph for the novel.

51 "Jean Tréjean": Jean-Marc Hovasse noted this first use of "Jean Tréjean" in his lecture "Victor Hugo méditerranéen." The trip journal reference to "Jean Tréjean" appears in CFL VI, 719. Hugo recounts this visit in *Alpes et Pyrénées*, "Voyage de 1839 – Alpes: Toulon," which appears in Laffont, *Voyages*, 702-705.

52 Grace: Definition from *The Merriam-Webster Dictionary* online.

53 Hugo's calls for clemency for Brown and Maximilian: Hugo's December 2, 1859, letter arguing for clemency for John Brown: Laffont, *Politique: Actes et paroles*, II, Pendant l'exil, 1859, II "John Brown," 512-14. Hugo's June 20, 1867, letter arguing for clemency for Emperor Maximilian: Laffont, *Politique: Actes et paroles*, II, Pendant l'exil, 1867, III, "L'empereur Maximilien. À Juarez," 586-88. Brown was executed by hanging on December 2 in Charles Town, as were several of his co-conspirators on December 16. President Juarez's government executed Maximilian in 1867.

54 "The Civil War in France": Karl Marx published his pamphlet "The Civil War in France" in London in June 1871.

55 "toppled the Vendôme Column": On May 16, 1871, the Communards pulled down the Vendôme Column in Paris. Originally erected by Emperor Napoléon I to commemorate his victory at Austerlitz and topped with the emperor's statue, the monument represented for the Communards brute force and false glory, a constant reminder of conquerers' power over the conquered (see https://fr.wikipedia.org/wiki/Colonne_Vend%C3%B4me#Histoire _de_la_colonne).

56 "le Mur des Fédérés": On the Commune, see, for example, Alistair Horne, *The Terrible Year: The Paris Commune 1871* (New York: Viking Press, 1971) and Littlewood, *Timeline History*, 244-47.

57 Hugo's letter to *L'Indépendance belge*: Laffont, *Politique: Actes et paroles*, III, Depuis l'exil, 1870-1876, I (Bruxelles) V. "L'Incident belge," 1, 796-98. The

full text, together with details of Hugo's fight for the Communards, is available at the French Senate's site: http://www.senat.fr/histoire/victor_hugo_et _lamnistie_des_communards/hugo_hugo_et_la_commune.html. Hugo's original French for excerpts from his May 26, 1871, letter: "Leurs violences m'ont indigné comme m'indigneraient aujourd'hui les violences du parti contraire. . . . / Attendons pour juger. . . . Premièrement, pour tous les hommes civilisés, la peine de mort est abominable; deuxièmement, l'exécution sans jugement est infâme . . . . Si vous tuez sans jugement, vous assassinez. . . . / Si l'on vient chez moi prendre un fugitif de la Commune, on me prendra. . . . Et, pour la défense du droit, on verra, à côté de l'homme de la Commune, qui est le vaincu de l'Assemblée de Versailles, l'homme de la République, qui a été le proscrit de Bonaparte. / Je ferai mon devoir. Avant tout les principes. . . . Dans tous les cas, j'aurai ma conscience."

58 "Hugo's open letter was published": Laffont, *Politique: Actes et paroles* III, Depuis l'exil, 1870-1876, I (Bruxelles) V, "L'Incident belge," 2, 798-800.

59 "minister's son had orchestrated the attack": Fillipetti, *Victor Hugo*, 275.

60 Tutu on the power of forgiveness for the future: Tutu, "Let South Africa Show," speech, 2000.

61 Hugo's May 22, 1876, Senate speech arguing for amnesty for the Communards: Laffont, *Politique: Actes et paroles* III, Depuis l'exil, 1870-1876, 1: XXXII "L'Amnistie au Sénat—séance du 22 mai 1876," 917-25. Original French: "La clémence n'est autre chose que la justice, plus juste. La justice ne voit que la faute, la clémence voit le coupable. À la justice, la faute apparaît dans une sorte d'isolement inexorable; à la clémence, le coupable apparaît entouré d'innocents; il a un père, une mère, une femme, des enfants, qui sont condamnés avec lui et qui subissent sa peine. Lui, il a le bagne ou l'exil; eux, ils ont la misère. Ont-ils mérité le châtiment? Non. L'endurent-ils? Oui. Alors la clémence trouve la justice injuste. Elle s'interpose et elle fait grâce. La grâce, c'est la rectification sublime que fait à la justice d'en bas la justice d'en haut."

62 "but in order not to allow it to imprison us": Tutu, "Foreword," *Commission on Truth and Reconciliation Report*, 178. About South Africa's Truth and Reconciliation Committee, see https://www.britannica.com/topic/ Truth-and-Reconciliation-Commission-South-Africa.

63 "ruthless forgiveness . . . advocated politically and personally": Hugo explained the paradoxical concept of ruthless forgiveness ("*la clémence implacable*") in a letter about his *Les Châtiments*, his scathing poetry collection indicting Louis-Napoleon Bonaparte for crimes that broke both moral and judicial laws. Noting that Old Testament prophets and Jesus Christ were violent, Hugo defended the intensity of his poetry: "I want one day to have the right to end reprisals, to block the path of vengeance, to stop blood from flowing if it can be done, and to save every head, even Louis Bonaparte's. . . . Keep in mind my current goal: implacable clemency." From a letter to his publisher Hetzel, February 6, 1853 (CFL VIII, 1044). Original French: "Je veux avoir un jour le droit d'arrêter les représailles, de me mettre en travers des vengeances, d'empêcher s'il se peut le sang de couler, et de sauver toutes les

têtes, même celle de Louis Bonaparte. . . . Ayez mon but présent à l'esprit: *clémence implacable*" [Hugo's italics].

Chapter 3 | Love Is Action

64 Epigraph: Hugo wrote these words on May 19, 1885, three days before he died. The manuscript is preserved at the Maison Littéraire de Victor Hugo in Bièvres, France, in the Château de Roches, where Hugo and his family spent many summer vacations. This manuscript has been declared an historical monument (see http://www.maisonlitterairedevictorhugo.net/cdtexte.htm). Original French: "Aimer, c'est agir."

65 "Whoever loves his fellow man is closer to God on earth": Original French: "Qui aime son prochain est plus près de Dieu sur la terre," from http://www .frmusique.ru/texts/m/miserables/finalcestpourdemain.htm.

66 Juliette's lovers and debts: Pouchain and Sabourin, *Juliette Drouet*, 40-41.

67 "give myself to you completely": Juliette's undated note is assumed to have been written on February 16, 1833. CFL IV, 1137. "Mme K." refers to Juliette's friend Laure Kraft (or Krafft) (http://www.juliettedrouet.org/ lettres/spip.php?page=article&id_article=558#.W8x1QmhKjD4). Original French: "Monsieur Victor, / Viens me chercher soir chez Mme K. / Je t'aimerai jusque-là pour prendre patience. / A ce soir. Oh! ce soir ce sera tout! / Je me donnerai à toi tout entière."

68 Juliette's letters: Scholarly editions of the approximately 22,000 letters that Juliette wrote to Victor are being published and annotated at http://www .juliettedrouet.org/. As of this writing, Juliette's letters are available mostly only in the original French. A few English translations, many inaccurate, were published in the early twentieth century. For a good selection of Drouet's letters in English, see Larson, *My Beloved Toto*.

69 "We've suffered a great deal": Dated May 20, 1839. CFL V, 1252-53. Original French: "Nous avons beaucoup souffert, nous avons beaucoup travaillé, nous avons fait beaucoup d'efforts pour racheter aux yeux du bon Dieu ce qu'il y avait d'irrégulier dans notre bonheur par ce qu'il y avait de saint dans notre amour."

70 "People in need turned to Juliette": I am indebted to Drouet biographer and Hugo scholar Gérard Pouchain for this information about Juliette's transmission of requests to Victor Hugo (personal conversation with the author, January 9, 2019).

71 "50,000 francs": Hugo's will and testament, written on August 2, 1883, stated, "I give fifty thousands francs to the poor. I want to be carried to the cemetery in their hearse. I refuse the funeral oration of any church; I ask for a prayer from all souls. I believe in God." Original French: "Je donne cinquante mille francs aux pauvres. Je désire être porté au cimetière dans leur corbillard. Je refuse l'oraison de toutes les églises, je demande une prière à toutes les âmes. Je crois en Dieu."

72 Hugo's lunches for poor children: For details about the Hugos' midday dinners, I am indebted to Hugo scholars Jean-Marc Hovasse, *Victor Hugo:*

Pendant l'exil I, 691-94, and Florence Naugrette, "Victor Hugo et la question sociale de l'enfance."

73 "the sacred democratic formula: Liberty, Equality, Fraternity": Hugo's October 5, 1862, letter to his publisher, Castel, appears in Laffont, *Politique: Actes et paroles* II, Pendant l'exil (1852-1870): 539-40. Cited by Naugrette, "Victor Hugo et la question sociale," 5. Original French: "Cette pénétration des familles indigentes dans les nôtres nous profite comme à eux: elle . . . fait marcher pour ainsi dire devant nous la sainte formule démocratique: Liberté, Égalité, Fraternité."

74 "Alms should be secret—brotherhood should not": Cited by Hovasse, *Victor Hugo: Pendant l'exil* I, 693. Original French: "L'aumône doit se cacher, la fraternité non."

75 "to truly help the poor we must abolish poverty": Laffont, *Politique: Actes et Paroles* II, Pendant l'exil, 1852-1870, 1869, VIII: 636-37. Cited by Naugrette, "Victor Hugo et la question sociale," 6. Original French: "Le vrai secours aux misérables, c'est l'abolition de la misère."

76 Tim Costello: "Rev Tim Costello AO is recognised as one of Australia's leading voices on social justice, leadership and ethics. . . . Most recently with World Vision Australia, Tim has been instrumental in ensuring that the issues surrounding global poverty are placed on the national agenda," from https://thefatheringproject.org/people/rev-tom-costello-ao/.

77 "Story of a saint": Cited by Tersen, "Chronologie des *Misérables*," 206-07, and by Laforgue, "La symbolisation." Original French: "Histoire d'un saint / Histoire d'un homme / Histoire d'une femme / Histoire d'une poupée."

78 "God has only one face . . .": From *Dieu*, "L'Océan d'en haut," VIII. Original French: "Dieu n'a qu'un front: Lumière! et n'a qu'un nom: Amour!"

79 From Adèle Hugo's journal of May 1-2, 1855: Adèle Hugo, *Le Journal d'Adèle Hugo*, 169. Original French: "Mon père parle des révélations par les Tables, puis il arrive enfin à sa propre religion, qui se résume dans ce grand mot *Amour* [Adèle's emphasis]."

80 Denby, Lane, and Hooper's response: Denby, "There's Still Hope." Lane, "Love Hurts." Hooper's response appears in Fish, "'Les Misérables' and Irony."

81 "Over one-fifth of American children live in poverty": Data from the National Center for Children in Poverty: http://www.nccp.org/topics/childpoverty.html.

Chapter 4 | Seeking—and Finding—God

82 Epigraph: Dated 1859, the year before Hugo began revising and finishing *Les Misérables*, and published in Laffont, *Océan*, 275. Original French: "— Solitude! Océan! Cette sombre nature m'attire souverainement et m'entraîne vers les ombres éblouissantes de l'infini. Je passe quelquefois des nuits entières à rêver sur mon toit en présence de l'abîme, je me sens comme accablé de Dieu, et j'en arrive à ne plus que m'écrier: des astres! des astres! des astres!"

83 "One in ten Millenials identify with non-Christian faiths": Pew Research Center, "In U.S., Decline." Also of interest is Lipka, "10 facts about religion."

84 "how do we want to live?": Ravitz, "Indian Awakening." Krista Tippett's site is https://onbeing.org/.
85 "Atheism 2.0.": de Botton, "Atheism 2.0." For connections between the beliefs of various religions, see https://en.wikipedia.org/wiki/List_of_religions _and_spiritual_traditions.
86 "I believe in God.": From "Moi prose" in Laffont, *Océan*, 295. Dated around 1870. Original French: "Je crois en Dieu. / Je me sens, âme immortelle, en présence du Dieu éternel. / Je le supplie de m'admettre, avec ceux que j'aime et ceux qui m'aiment, dans la vie meilleure. / Toutes les religions sont vraies et fausses; vraies par Dieu, fausses par le dogme. Chacune veut être la seule; de là, les mensonges. J'espère que Dieu ne les exceptera pas de l'immense pardon qu'il accordera. / Je n'accepte pas les oraisons des églises, je demande leur prière à toutes les âmes. / Je supplie le Dieu éternel."
87 "Pictures everywhere! what happiness! what ecstasy!": From *Les Contemplations* V, x. Original French: "Des estampes partout! quel bonheur! quel délire!" The poem's title, "At the Feuillantines," refers to Hugo's beloved childhood home secluded in a Paris garden.
88 "Hugo was never Catholic": Winock, *Victor Hugo*, 15.
89 "the divine reality and its unity": I am grateful to Jean Baptiste Hugo for our conversations about Victor Hugo's understanding of the Supreme Being, for his knowledge of Hinduism, and, especially, for his insightful email of November 2, 2019.
90 "We must destroy all religions in order to rebuild God": Letter to republican journalist Auguste Nefftzer, December 6, 1860. Original French: "Il faut détruire toutes les religions afin de reconstruire Dieu. J'entends: le reconstruire dans l'homme."
91 "The author . . . does not belong to any of today's prevailing religions." When Hugo drafted this essay in spring 1860, he called it "Philosophie: Commencement d'un livre" ("Philosophy: Beginning of a Book"). It was published posthumously under the title "Préface philosophique" ("Philosophical Preface"). CFL XII, 13-14. Original French: "Le livre qu'on va lire est un livre religieux … L'auteur de ce livre, il le dit ici du droit de la liberté de conscience, est étranger à toutes les religions actuellement régnantes."
92 "There's no religion that doesn't blaspheme a little": *Religions et religion* I, ii; cited in Laffont, *Poésie* III, 972. Original French: "Pas de religion qui ne blasphème un peu." *Religions et religion* was mostly written from 1856-58, a few years before Hugo returned to *Les Misérables* and completed it. In 1870, he more or less finalized this poetic argument that spirituality goes beyond established religion, and he published it in 1880. *Religions et religion*, together with *Dieu* and *La Fin de Satan*, are the core of what is considered to be Hugo's philosophical will and testament (note by Jean-Claude Fizaine, in Laffont, *Poésie* III, 1469).
93 "Pope Francis . . . Bishop Myriel": Mulholland, "Pope Francis and 'Les Mis,'" analyzes parallels between Pope Francis and Bishop Myriel. One of Hugo's

most scathing works was his satiric poem *Le Pape*, written in 1874 and 1875, published in 1878. There he recounts an unnamed pope's generous help for the needy, and we might think that Hugo had grown to appreciate the pope. At the end, however, we learn that the pope had dreamed of doing all these good works. Horrified at what he has done, he exclaims upon awakening, "What a ghastly nightmare I had!" ["Quel rêve affreux je viens de faire!"]

94 Monseigneur de Miollis: For more details of Monseigneur de Miollis's life, see Benoît-Lévy, *Les Misérables de Victor Hugo*, 33-47.

95 "the sharpest satire of today's priests": Hugo's adult daughter Adèle recorded this conversation in her journal when the family lived at their Jersey home, Marine-Terrace, in the early 1850s. Recounted by Leulliot, "Philosophie(s)," 61. Original French: "Cette pure et haute figure du vrai prêtre était la plus sanglante satire dirigée contre le prêtre actuel."

96 "Valjean's story is fundamentally a New Testament Christian tale": Vermette, *Musical World*, 131-32.

97 "free-thinker": For more details about how the Miollis family reacted to the character of Bishop Myriel, see Hovasse, "L' évêque des *Misérables*," 63-65.

98 "I would miss the ocean": Victor Hugo to Noël Parfait, June 27, 1861, while he was revising *Les Misérables*. CFL XII, 1120. Original French: "Je suis un oiseau de tempête. Je commence à sentir le besoin de nuées, d'écume et d'ouragan. Il me serait difficile à présent d'habiter tout à fait les villes. J'aurais la nostalgie de l'océan."

99 "I live in a splendid solitude": Dated "Guernesey – avril 1856," in Laffont, *Océan*, 73. Original French: "Je vis dans une solitude splendide, comme perché à la pointe d'un rocher, ayant toutes les vastes écumes des vagues et toutes les grandes nuées du ciel sous ma fenêtre; j'habite dans cet immense rêve de l'océan, je deviens peu à peu un somnambule de la mer. C'est de cette éternelle contemplation que je m'éveille de temps en temps pour écrire. Il y a toujours sur ma strophe ou sur ma page un peu de l'ombre du nuage et de la salive de la mer; ma pensée flotte et va et vient, comme dénouée par toute cette gigantesque oscillation de l'infini. / Ce qui ne flotte pas, ce qui ne vacille pas, c'est l'âme devant l'éternité, c'est la conscience devant la vérité."

100 "Clearing Sky": "Éclaircie": *Les Contemplations*, VI, x, written July 4, 1855.

101 "Yes, I'm the dreamer": "Oui, je suis le rêveur ... ," *Les Contemplations* I, xxvii, written on October 15, 1854. Original French: "En mai, quand de parfums les branches sont gonflées, / J'ai des conversations avec les giroflées; / Je reçois des conseils du lierre et du bleuet. / L'être mystérieux, que vous croyez muet, / Sur moi se penche, et vient avec ma plume écrire." And "Ne vous étonnez pas de tout ce que me dit / La nature aux soupirs ineffables. Je cause / Avec toutes les voix de la métempsycose."

102 "Hinduism": Venkatesh, *Victor Hugo et la philosophie indienne*, explores the numerous appearances of Hindu philosophy in Hugo's work, especially in his visionary poetry.

103 "Hauteville House library": The list of sacred books which Hugo collected and consulted in his personal library while in exile on Guernsey is at http://groupugo.div.jussieu.fr/Biblioth%C3%A8que_Hugo/Les_livres_de_Hauteville-House/00-Sommaire.htm.

104 Séances: For this summary of the séances I am indebted to Boivin, ed., *Le Livre des tables*, which also includes carefully edited transcriptions of the Hugos' séances (see, especially, pp. 20-25). For excerpts of séance messages in English, see Chambers, *Conversations with Eternity*.

105 "And I saw above my head a black speck": Hugo lays out these investigations in Part II, "The Ocean of the Heights." Original French:" Et je vis au-dessus de ma tête un point noir.........."

106 "Blind man who thinks he reads": From Part VIII, "The Light," the penultimate section of *Dieu*. Original French:"Aveugle qui croit lire et fou qui croit savoir!"

107 Adèle Hugo's journal notes,"the brink of the infinite" and"without ever arriving": Adèle Hugo, *Le Journal d'Adele Hugo*, 169, May 1-2, 1855. Original French:"Ce poème termine par des points suspensifs, c'est-à-dire qu'il ne se termine que devant l'infini. Il était deux heures et demi quand mon père a terminé son poème, ce poème à 1946 vers, ce dénombrement des religions qui ont cherché à trouver Dieu sans jamais y arriver." Cited by Skinner, *God*, n. 17, 456-57.

108 "formidable dark infinite": From near the end of Hugo's 1864 manuscript *Les Choses de l'infini (Things of the Infinite)*, CFL XII, 108. Original French: "Au delà du visible l'invisible, au delà de l'invisible l'inconnu. / Partout, toujours, au zénith, au nadir, en avant, en arrière, au-dessus, au-dessous, en haut, en bas, le formidable infini noir."

109 "I remove Christ from Christianity.": Hugo's letter to Michelet, May 9, 1856. CFL X, 1249. Original French:"Je décloue le Christ du christianisme." Hugo's choice of verb is telling, as *déclouer* means literally"to pull nail(s) (*clou[s]*) out of." On Hugo's relationship with Christianity and the Catholic Church, see Winock, *Le Monde selon Victor Hugo*, 287-303.

110 "the Jefferson Bible": By physically cutting away all references to miracles and reorganizing the remaining Gospel excerpts in chronological order, Jefferson created in 1820 a chronological edition—his personal copy—of Jesus's life, parables, and moral teachings. *The Jefferson Bible*, Smithsonian Edition, 11.

111 *Qur'an*; Hinduism; Dalai Lama: "Two Hundred Verses about Compassionate Living in the Quran," https://themuslimtimes.info/2013/10/29/three-hundred-verses-about-compassionate-living-in-the-quran/; "Healing Through Compassion," http://www.hinduwebsite.com/divinelife/compassion.asp; "Compassion and the Individual," https://www.dalailama.com/messages/compassion-and-human-values/compassion. I am indebted to Aiden Carroll (UVA Class of 2020) for sharing these sources. See, also, Neusner and Chilton, *Altruism in World Religions*.

112 Ecclesiastes 3:21: Quotation from the Latin Vulgate Bible, the edition Hugo most likely knew:"Quis novit si spiritus filiorum Adam ascendat sursum, et si

spiritus jumentorum descendat deorsum." Cited at http://www.drbo
.org/x/d?b=lvb&bk=23&ch=3&l=21#x.

113 Distinctions are illusory: Flood, *An Introduction to Hinduism*, 242.

Chapter 5 | Is Change Possible?

114 Epigraph: Hugo wrote this statement about how he understood God in
a May 2, 1862, letter to his friend and famous French abolitionist Victor
Schoelcher. CFL XII, 1663. Original French: "Croire à la vertu, à la liberté,
au progrès, à la lumière, c'est croire à Dieu. Dieu, c'est la concrétion vivante de
cette clarté sublime qui est votre âme même."

115 Poverty rate: Fessler, Pam. "U.S. Census Bureau."

116 *rédemption* meaning: *Trésor de la langue française informatisé*: http://atilf
.atilf.fr/.

117 consciousness/conscience connection: For a thoughtful analyis of Hugo's
connecting consciousness and conscience, see Guy Rosa's notes to his edition
of *Les Misérables* 2: 1969-70.

118 "Anybody can have a transformation . . . to happen": Senghor, Bio Video,
http://www.shakasenghor.com/.

119 "compassion for the men around me": Senghor, *Writing My Wrongs*, 191-92.

120 Senghor's son's letter and his response: Senghor, *Writing My Wrongs*, 197-99.

121 "Real change comes": Senghor, *Writing My Wrongs*, 16.

122 "a timeline we can't predict": Senghor, "About Me," http://www.shakasenghor
.com/.

123 "Our worst deeds don't define who we are": Senghor, Bio, http://www
.shakasenghor.com/?page_id=134.

124 "transfiguration" meaning: The first meaning is from *The Merriam-Webster
Dictionary* online and the second from *The Oxford English Dictionary* online.

125 "Since he is at the seaside": Laffont, *Politique: Actes et paroles* II, Pendant
l'exil, 1852-1870, "Ce que c'est que l'exil," ("What Exile Is") V, 402. Original
French: "Puisqu'il est au bord de la mer, qu'il en profite. Que cette mobilité
sous l'infini lui donne la sagesse. Qu'il médite sur l'émeute éternelle des flots
contre le rivage et des impostures contre la vérité."

126 "poem of universal fate and hope": Pierre Albouy cites this manuscript
note dated October 1-13, 1854, in his edition of *Les Contemplations*
(n. 2, p. 409). Original French: "ce poème de la fatalité universelle et de
l'espérance universelle." "Ce que dit la bouche d'ombre" is poem xxvi in Book
VI of *Les Contemplations*. Other *Les Contemplations* poems that articulate
Hugo's cosmology include "Saturne" ("Saturn") (III, iii), written on April
30, 1839, and "Explication" ("Explanation") (III, xii), written on October 5,
1854. Hugo published another poem about his cosmology, "Cæruleum
Mare" ("Sea of Azure"), written on March 25, 1839, in *Les Rayons et les
ombres*, XL.

127 "after visiting Léopoldine's grave in Villequier for the first time": I am grateful
to Jean-Marc Hovasse for sharing with me his insight into the redemptive
aspects of "À Villequier" (email message to author, December 7, 2015).

128 "not to *you*": "À Villequier," *Les Contemplations* IV, xv. Original French: "Je sais . . . / qu'un enfant qui meurt, désespoir de sa mère, / Ne vous fait rien, à vous!"

Chapter 6 | Listening to Our Best Selves

129 Epigraph: From Hugo's *Post-scriptum de ma vie* (*Postscript to My Life*), the section "Rêveries sur Dieu" ("Thoughts on God"), likely written sometime in the 1850s. Original French: "La conscience, c'est le spectre solaire moral intérieur. / Le soleil éclaire le corps. Dieu éclaire l'esprit. / Au fond de tout cerveau humain il y a comme une lune de Dieu."

130 "didn't touch the man": Recounted by Hugo in Laffont, *Voyages*, 1214-15. I am indebted to Jean-Marc Hovasse for his lively retelling of this adventure in *Victor Hugo* I, 827-28.

131 "contemporary ethical questions along the way": For University of Virginia students' op-eds about contemporary ethical issues connected to *Les Misérables*, see http://www.marvabarnett.com/teaching2/student-op-eds -connecting-les-mis-to-today/.

132 Quotations on conscience: Sources of quotations: Gandhi, *The Gandhi Reader*, 194. King, "Remaining Awake," in *The Essential Writings*, 268. Snowden, "Biography: Snowden's Leaks." For a thoughtful analysis of the pros and cons of whistleblowing—and potential conflicts between self-interest and the public good, see Vines, "On whistleblowing," *South China Morning Post*, August 24, 2016.

133 "M. Madeleine": Guy Rosa notes connections between M. Madeleine's name and that of Mary Magdalene (*Les Misérables*, vol. 1, p. 88, n. 2). Mary Magdalene (Mary of Magdala) is also called Marie Madeleine. During Hugo's lifetime, the Catholic Church still promoted the story of Mary Magdalene as a persuasive model of repentance and reform, although scholars today note the complexity of understanding her role (see, for instance, James Carroll, "Who Was Mary Magdalene?," *Smithsonian Magazine*, June 2006, https://www .smithsonianmag.com/history/who-was-mary-magdalene-119565482/).

134 "sacrifice on the cross": "A Storm Inside a Mind" (I, 7, 3) ends with a comparison between Jean Valjean's anguish and Jesus Christ's agony in the Garden of Gethsemane, after the Last Supper: "In this way, his [Valjean's] unhappy soul struggled with its anguish. Eighteen hundred years before this ill-fated man, the mysterious being in whom are concentrated all the saintliness and all the sufferings of humanity had also refused for a long time the terrible chalice, streaming with darkness and brimming with shadow, that appeared to him in the star-filled depths while the olive trees shook in the fierce blast of the infinite." Jesus ("in whom are concentrated all the saintliness and all the sufferings of humanity"), in Gethsemane, at the foot of the Mount of Olives, knows his future (see, for example, Matthew 26:31-46; Luke 22:39-54). Jesus withdraws a "stone's throw" from his disciples: "And he went a little farther, and fell on his face, and prayed, saying, "O my Father, if it be possible, let this cup pass from me: nevertheless not as I will, but as thou wilt" (Matthew

29:39). We learn Jesus's state of mind from Luke 22:44: "And being in agony he prayed more earnestly: and his sweat was as it were great drops of blood falling down to the ground." Both Jesus and Jean accept their self-sacrifices with intensely human emotions. But while in Christian theology Jesus Christ is a man who is also divine, Hugo shows how Jean Valjean is a man moving closer to divinity through love and grace (see Guy Rosa's note "Jean Valjean Christ" in his edition of *Les Misérables* 2: 1959).

135　"His conscience, or God": Here Hugo continues the watching-eye metaphor that we saw in the Petit-Gervais scene (see Chapter 5). Hugo often described conscience as a physical presence, as he did in his poem "Conscience" (*La Légende des siècles, première série*, I, 2, 1859), which retells Cain's flight from Jehovah after having killed his brother, Abel (Genesis 4). Hugo wrote "Conscience" in 1853, not in conjunction with *Les Misérables* but rather as a possible poem for *Les Châtiments*, his poetry collection denouncing what he saw as Louis-Napoleon Bonaparte's immoral actions. Still, the parallels are striking, since, in "Conscience," an unblinking eye sees Cain wherever he hides, watching him through night's darkness. The eye still watches from the horizon after Cain flees for thirty days and nights to the seashore. Cain sees it from underneath his tent, from behind a bronze wall, and from under granite towers. In desperation, Cain has himself buried. When he is all alone in the tomb, sealed up, at the end of the poem, "the eye was in the tomb and was watching Cain."

136　Tom Hooper's "genius idea": Karger, "Interview with Hugh Jackman," "The Frontrunners," December 20, 2012.

137　"magic notes": Vermette, *Musical World*, p. 130 explains the "magic notes." An actor sings them at https://www.broadway.com/videos/155339/video-talking-magic-notes-talking-french-with-the-new-cast-of-les-miserables/.

138　"Obeying my conscience is a rule": Laffont, *Politique: Actes et paroles* I, Avant l'exil, "Le Droit et la loi, II," 68. Hugo wrote "La Droit et la loi" ("Right and Law") in 1875 to introduce his collection of speeches and public statements, *Actes et paroles*. Original French: "Obéir à sa conscience est sa règle; règle qui n'admet pas d'exception."

139　"*The Extinction of Poverty*": Bonaparte, *Extinction du paupérisme*.

140　"What! Because we had Napoleon the Great": Hugo's National Assembly speech on July 17, 1851. In Laffont, *Politique: Actes et paroles* I, Avant l'exil, Assemblée législative – 1849-1851, "Révision de la constitution," 290. Original French: "Quoi! parce que nous avons eu Napoléon le Grand, il faut que nous ayons Napoléon le Petit!"

141　"One more step": Laffont, *Politique: Actes et paroles* I, Avant l'exil, "Le 2 décembre 1851: Proclamation à l'armée," 331-32. Original French: "Soldats! un pas de plus dans l'attentat, un jour de plus avec Louis Bonaparte, et vous êtes perdus devant la conscience universelle."

142　Victor's and Juliette's actions December 2-11, 1851: Hovasse, *Victor Hugo* I, 1133-59, includes elements from Hugo's eyewitness account entitled *Histoire d'un crime* and Juliette Drouet's summary of the events. Details of Victor's,

Juliette's, and Adèle's activities during this period also come from Juliette Drouet's diary of the events (Pouchain, *Juliette Drouet: Souvenirs*, 177-252).

143 "25,000 francs": 25,000 francs would be between $120,000 and $300,000 in today's dollars, calculated via https://ask.metafilter.com/275442/Historical-Value-of-French-Franc-in-comparison-to-US-dollar and https://www.measuringworth.com/uscompare/.

144 "That brings happiness": December 14, 1852, letter: CFL VIII, 949. Original French: "Pendant douze jours, j'ai été entre la vie et la mort, mais je n'ai pas eu un moment de trouble. J'ai été content de moi. Et puis je sais que j'ai fait mon devoir et que je l'ai fait tout entier. Cela rend content."

145 Hugo's August 18th declaration: Laffont, *Politique: Actes et paroles* II, Pendant l'exil, 1852-1870, "L'Amnistie, Déclaration," 511. Original French: "Personne n'attendra de moi que j'accorde, en ce qui me concerne, un moment d'attention à la chose appelée amnistie. / Dans la situation où est la France, protestation absolue, inflexible, éternelle, voilà pour moi le devoir. / Fidèle à l'engagement que j'ai pris vis-à-vis de ma conscience, je partagerai jusqu'au bout l'exil de la liberté. / Quand la liberté rentrera, je rentrerai. / VICTOR HUGO. / Hauteville-House, 18 août 1859."

146 "Ultima Verba": *Les Châtiments* VII, xvii. Written on December 14, 1852, and attributed to the first anniversary of the coup d'état, December 2, 1852. Original French: "La conscience humaine est morte; dans l'orgie, / sur elle il s'accroupit. . . . / Et s'il n'en reste qu'un, je serai celui-là!"

147 "Return with the happiness": Victor Hugo to Dr. Terrier, August 30, 1859, cited by Hovasse, *Victor Hugo* II, 557. Original French: "Rentrez-y avec le bonheur de la conscience sereine, avec nos bénédictions, nos souvenirs, notre estime tendre et profonde, et vos huit années d'exil fièrement portées."

148 "longer sojourns away from Guernsey": Fillipetti, *Victor Hugo*, 220.

149 "Deepest indignation": Mandela, "No Easy Walk." Elected ANC (Transvaal) President earlier that year, Mandela had been subsequently served with a banning order, so that his address had to be read on his behalf. For biographies of Nelson Mandela, see, for instance, https://www.nelsonmandela.org/content/page/biography and https://en.wikipedia.org/wiki/Nelson_Mandela.

150 "I am prepared to die": From Mandela's statement from the dock at the opening of the defense case in the Rivonia Trial, April 20, 1964. Quoted at the Nelson Mandela Foundation site: https://www.nelsonmandela.org/news/entry/i-am-prepared-to-die.

151 "It has not been easy": From Mandela's defense of himself at the Rivonia Trial. Cited by Mandela, *Long Walk to Freedom*, 289.

152 "What it is to be an exile": Laffont, *Politique: Actes et paroles* II, Pendant l'exil, 1852-1870, "Ce que c'est que l'exil" ("What Exile Is"), II, 398. Original French: "Un homme tellement ruiné qu'il n'a plus que son honneur, tellement dépouillé qu'il n'a plus que sa conscience, tellement isolé qu'il n'a plus près de lui que l'équité, tellement renié qu'il n'a plus avec lui que la vérité, tellement jeté aux ténèbres qu'il ne lui reste plus que le soleil, voilà ce que c'est qu'un proscrit."

153 "I would say that the whole life of any thinking African": Mandela, *Long Walk to Freedom*, 288.

154 "The exile's power": Laffont, *Politique: Actes et paroles* II, Pendant l'exil, 1852-1870, "Ce que c'est que l'exil" ("What Exile Is"), XIII, 415. Original French: "La puissance du proscrit se compose de deux éléments; l'un qui est l'injustice de sa destinée, l'autre qui est la justice de sa cause. Ces deux forces contradictoires s'appuient l'une sur l'autre; situation formidable et qui peut se résumer en deux mots: / Hors la loi, dans le droit."

Chapter 7 | Either Valjean or Javert !

155 Epigraph: Hugo wrote this statement about his years as a legislator in his essay "Rights and the Law." Laffont, *Politique: Actes et paroles* I, Avant l'exil, "Le Droit et la loi, II," 68. Original French: "Sa conscience lui a imposé . . . une confrontation permanente et perpétuelle de la loi que les hommes font avec le droit qui fait les hommes."

156 "complete disregard of a former criminal's reformation": Innocent people take plea bargains: Yoffe, "Innocence Is Irrelevant." People are wrongly convicted: Gould and Leo, "One Hundred Years Later;" and a recent case in California, for example: https://www.nytimes.com/2017/11/23/us/jerry-brown-pardon -murder.html?emc=edit_th_20171125&nl=todaysheadlines&nlid=76373914 &_r=0. Reformed convicts cannot get parole: Nicolais, "Rene Lima-Marin."

157 "The United States faces": See, for example, Dewan and Hulse, "Republicans and Democrats."

158 "starting a deadly fire by accident?": America has world's highest incarceration rate: Tsai and Scommegna, "U.S. Has World's Highest Incarceration Rate," and Gibson, "Color and Incarceration." See also http://factmyth.com/ factoids/the-us-has-the-highest-incarceration-rate-in-the-world/ and https://en.wikipedia.org/wiki/United_States_incarceration_rate. American prisons hold twenty-five percent of the world's prisoners: Pfaff, *Locked In*, 1. Selling marijuana a violent felony in Virginia: Hausman, "Life Without Parole." Where marijuana is legal in the U.S. (as of June 2019): Berke and Gould, "Illinois just became the first state." Trina Garnett was imprisoned for life at age fourteen after she illegally entered a house to see friends and the matches she lit started a deadly fire: Stevenson, *Just Mercy*, 148-51.

159 "EJI": https://eji.org/. Stories of people helped are at https://eji.org/just -mercy/stories. *Just Mercy* was made into a film by Warner Bros. Studios in 2019: https://en.wikipedia.org/wiki/Just_Mercy. I focus here on Stevenson's work with the Equal Justice Initiative, but many other organizations work toward a more just criminal justice system in the U.S., including these: The Innocence Project exonerates the wrongly convicted through DNA testing and reforms the criminal justice system to prevent future injustice (https:// www.innocenceproject.org/). Witness to Innocence "empowers the exoner- ated to end the death penalty" (https://www.witnesstoinnocence.org/). The Death Penalty Information Center provides "analysis and information on issues concerning capital punishment" (https://deathpenaltyinfo.org). The

National Coalition to Abolish the Death Penalty works "to abolish the death penalty in the United States and supports efforts to abolish the death penalty worldwide" (http://www.ncadp.org/). The Safety and Justice Challenge tackles the misuse and overuse of jails (http://www.safetyandjusticechallenge .org/). The Prison Policy Initiative "produces cutting edge research to expose the broader harm of mass criminalization, and then sparks advocacy campaigns to create a more just society" (https://www.prisonpolicy.org/). The Justice Policy Institute (JPI) "works to enhance the public dialog on incarceration through accessible research, public education, and communications advocacy with the goal of ending society's reliance on incarceration" (http://www.justicepolicy.org).

160 "the incarcerated, and the condemned": Quotations from Stevenson, *Just Mercy*, 313, 314, 18.

161 "duties of the strong": Laffont, *Politique: Actes et paroles* I, Avant l'exil, "Le Droit et la loi, XII," 87. Original French: "C'est du droit de tous les faibles que se compose le devoir de tous les forts."

162 "human being with a soul": In Victor Hugo's focus on each person's humanity, I see parallels with how *New York Times* columnist David Brooks understands human equality on the basis of souls: "What Makes Us All Radically Equal."

163 "often had this feeling": Stevenson, *Just Mercy*, 312.

164 *Trésor de la langue française* definiton of "droit": Original French: "Fondement des règles régissant les rapports des hommes en société, et impliquant une répartition équitable des biens, des prérogatives et des libertés."

165 "*Pro jure contra legem*": Laffont, *Politique: Actes et paroles* I, Avant l'exil, "Le Droit et la loi, II," 68. Original French: "une des formules de sa vie publique a été: *Pro jure contra legem.*"

166 "The sacredness of human life": Laffont, *Politique: Actes et paroles* I, Avant l'exil, "Le Droit et la loi, II," 67. Original French: "L'inviolabilité de la vie humaine, la liberté, la paix, rien d'indissoluble, rien d'irrévocable, rien d' irréparable; tel est le droit. / L'échafaud, le glaive et le sceptre, la guerre, toutes les variétés de joug, depuis le mariage sans le divorce dans la famille jusqu'à l'état de siège dans la cité; telle est la loi. . . . / La chose jugée, c'est la loi; la justice, c'est le droit. / Mesurez l'intervalle. / La loi a la crue, la mobilité, l'envahissement et l'anarchie de l'eau, souvent trouble; mais le droit est insubmersible."

167 "In order for everything to be saved": Laffont, *Politique: Actes et paroles* I, Avant l'exil, "Le Droit et la loi, II," 67. Original French: "Pour que tout soit sauvé, il suffit que le droit surnage dans une conscience. On n'engloutit pas Dieu."

168 "toward the superb future": From Hugo's third Senate speech arguing for amnesty for the Communards (July 3, 1880), in Laffont, *Politique: Actes et paroles*, IV, Depuis l'exil, 1880, "Troisième discours pour l'amnistie, Séance du Sénat du 3 juillet," 1018. Original French: "Quand on comprendra, pour employer les mots dans leur sens absolu, que toute action humaine est une

action divine, alors tout sera dit, le monde n'aura plus qu'à marcher dans le progrès tranquille vers l'avenir superbe."

169 "the highest expression of what is right": Laffont, *Politique: Actes et paroles* I, Avant l'exil, "Le Droit et la loi, III," 68. Original French: "la plus haute expression du droit, c'est la liberté."

170 "a crucified, dismembered corpse, still bloody": Hugo's childhood experiences are detailed in Hovasse, *Victor Hugo* I, 109. For a chronology of Hugo's encounters with executions and writings against the death penalty, see Rosa, "Commentaires," 272-80.

171 "People are supposed to die on God's schedule.": Stevenson, *Just Mercy*, 313, 312.

172 "the irrevocable, the irreparable, the indissoluble": Hugo's speech against the death penalty to the Constituent Assembly, September 15, 1848: Laffont, *Politique: Actes et paroles* I, Avant l'exil, Assemblée Constituante 1848, IV, "La Peine de mort," 180-81. Original French: "Je vote l'abolition pure, simple et définitive de la peine de mort." And "Vous écrivez en tête du préambule de votre constitution: 'En présence de Dieu,' et vous commenceriez par lui dérober, à ce Dieu, ce droit qui n'appartient qu'à lui, le droit de vie et de mort. Messieurs, il y a trois choses qui sont à Dieu et qui n'appartiennent pas à l'homme: l'irrévocable, l'irréparable, l'indissoluble."

173 "the poet's unambiguous stance": French Minister of Justice Robert Badinter is credited with prompting the abolition of the death penalty in France in 1981: Badinter, "Victor Hugo contre la peine de mort," 1981. See also "Badinter Outlines Victor Hugo's Opposition," a summary of Badinter's talk about Hugo's views and work against the death penalty.

174 "Montcharmont's head under the blade": For the story of Charles Hugo's article and the trial, I am indebted to Jean-Marc Hovasse, *Victor Hugo* I, 1117-18, and to Graham Robb, *Victor Hugo*, 291-92. Charles's article was published in *L'Événement* on May 16, 1851. Hugo's courtroom speech, "Pour Charles Hugo: La Peine de mort," appears in Laffont, *Politique: Actes et paroles* I, Avant l'exil, 309-16.

175 Beccaria and Franklin: For more details on Benjamin Franklin's antagonism toward the death penalty and references to the work of Cesare Beccaria, the Italian Enlightenment jurist who first put forward modern arguments against the death penalty , see John Bessler, "Op-Ed: Actually, the Founders Rejected the Death Penalty," *The National Law Journal*, October 27, 2014: https://www.law.com/nationallawjournal/almID/1202674529812/?slreturn=20171019125309.

176 "this law before which human conscience recoils with an anxiety that grows deeper every day—the death penalty": From "Pour Charles Hugo," Laffont, *Politique: Actes et paroles* I, Avant l'exil, 310. Original French: "Cette loi devant laquelle la conscience humaine recule avec une anxiété chaque jour plus profonde, c'est la peine de mort."

177 "more cynicism and abomination": From "Pour Charles Hugo, La Peine de mort," Laffont, *Politique: Actes et paroles* I, Avant l'exil, 315. Original French: "Un frémissement sort de toutes les consciences. Jamais le meurtre légal n'avait apparu avec plus de cynisme et d'abomination."

178 "What! Is that what we've come to?": "Pour Charles Hugo," Laffont, *Politique: Actes et paroles* I, Avant l'exil, 311-12. Original French: "Quoi! est-ce donc là que nous en sommes? Quoi! à force d'empiétements sur le bon sens, sur la raison, sur la liberté de pensée, sur le droit naturel, nous en serions là, . . . qu'on viendrait nous demander . . . le respect moral, pour ces pénalités qui ouvrent des abîmes dans les consciences, qui font pâlir quiconque pense, que la religion abhorre . . . ! Non! non! non! nous n'en sommes pas là! non!" Ces pénalités "font douter de l'humanité quand elles frappent le coupable, et qui font douter de Dieu quand elles frappent l'innocent!"

179 "knows that he must move forward": I am indebted to Ruth Long and Maria Lee (UVA Class of 2016) for noting these two occurrences of "owl" imagery. Hugo implies an ironic contrasting parallel between the two men when he writes that Javert's new awareness makes him feel that his "skull" ("*crâne*") is about to burst, reminding us of Valjean's successful triumph over the storm inside his mind, in the chapter Hugo entitled "Une Tempête sous un crâne" ("A Storm Inside a Mind") (I, 7, 3) (see Chapter 6).

180 "two distinctively different ways of living": Bradley Stephens discusses Javert as the "flip side" of Valjean in "*Les Misérables*: Page to Stage to Screen." Film director Tom Hooper notes Hugo's awareness of patterns and symmetry, for example, how the names Jean Valjean and Javert are contained within each other (Fernandez, "The Spoils"). Independently, Robert F. Cook (UVA Professor Emeritus) and Patricia Jerjian (UVA Class of 2014) noted that, juxtaposed, "Javert" and "Valjean" form a sort of chiasmus, in which the last syllables ("Ja" and "jean") reflect each other, as do the "vert" and "Val," emphasizing the parallels between the characters. For an analysis of how Valjean's and Javert's musical themes interact, see Whitfield, *Boublil and Schönberg's Les Misérables*, 20-21.

181 "a protest against the inexorable and nothing else": From late 1861. CFL vol. XI, 1002. Original French: "Tant que l'homme se croira le droit d'introduire l'indissoluble dans ses mœurs et l'irréparable dans ses lois, des livres de la nature de celui-ci pourront ne pas être inutiles. Ce livre n'est pas autre chose qu'une protestation contre l'inexorable."

182 "The closer we get to mass incarceration": Stevenson, *Just Mercy*, 18.

Chapter 8 | Finding Strength to Carry On

183 Epigraph: *Les Travailleurs de la mer* (II, 2, 4). Original French (with Hugo's Latin): "Presque tout le secret des grands cœurs est dans ce mot: *Perseverando*."

184 "the doctors recommend you not visit her": The 1975 film, *The Story of Adèle H.*, directed by François Truffaut, realistically portrays Adèle Hugo's sudden

departure from Guernsey for Nova Scotia in pursuit of Lt. Albert Pinson and her eventual return to Paris from Barbados, where she was discovered wandering in the streets. We will likely never know precisely what Adèle was thinking.

185 "have a reason to endure it" / Viktor Frankl quotations: Quotations from Frankl, *Man's Search for Meaning*: "Everything can be taken from a man …": 86; "a task waiting for them to fulfill": 126; "A man who becomes conscious …": 101. On page 126, Frankl quotes Nietzsche, whose original formulation—"He who has a *why?* to live for can bear almost any *how?*"—comes from the "Maxims and Arrows" section of Nietzsche's introduction to his philosophy entitled *Twilight of the Idols, or, How to Philosophize with a Hammer* (in German: *Götzen-Dämmerung, oder, Wie man mit dem Hammer philosophirt*), published in 1889. See http://www.thenietzschechannel.com/quotes/popular-quotes.htm.

186 "what she calls 'bounce forward'" / Sandberg and Yousafzai: Sandberg and Grant, *Option B*, 78-93. Yousafzai, *I Am Malala*, 294.

187 "promote more resilience" / McGonigal, Seligman, Hanson: McGonigal, *The Upside of Stress*, quoted at https://ggsc.berkeley.edu/what_we_do/event/how_compassion_creates_resilience). Seligman, *Learned Optimism*, cited by Sandberg and Grant, *Option B*, 16. Hanson, *Resilient*, summarized at https://ggsc.berkeley.edu/what_we_do/event/the_science_and_practice_of_resilience.

188 "actualizes himself": Frankl, *Man's Search for Meaning*, 133.

189 "(it wasn't removed until 1846)": Beauhaire, Béjanin and Naudeix, *L'Éléphant de Napoléon*, 13.

190 "things could be worse": Sandberg and Grant, *Option B*, 13, 25.

191 "God, grant me the serenity … I cannot change": Shapiro, "Who Wrote the Serenity Prayer?"

192 *Perseverando*: I am indebted to Jean-Marc Hovasse for summarizing Hugo's ongoing attention to perseverance and for offering insights about the importance of this concept in his *Victor Hugo: Pendant l'exil I*, 563-64. Also for his insights about the relationship between Hugo and Sainte-Beuve (*Victor Hugo* I, 338-41). Hugo accurately identified "Perseverando" as the motto of the Ducies, an aristocratic British family, in "À mon ami S.-B.," *Odes et Ballades* IV, xvii, (in Laffont *Poésie* I, 248-49; see https://en.wikipedia.org/wiki/Earl_of_Ducie). Hugo could have discovered the family's motto while doing research for *Cromwell* (CFL III, 459, n. 2). This motto was also attributed to the Baron Ducie by Amicus (pseud.), in *A Translation, in Verse, of the Mottos of the English Nobility and Sixteen Peers of Scotland, in the Year 1800*. (London: Printed for the author, and sold by Robert Triphook, 1822): https://books.google.com/books?id=UF0BAAAAQAAJ&pg=PA73&lpg=PA73&dq=ducie+perseverandosource=bl&ots=idS5qezCWu&sig=jZ3bz1rvuiwrWVd-yMB6vmCUhrM&hl=en&sa=X&ved=0ahUKEwif46i_mJ7ZAhWCTd8KHYOrBbAQ6AEIMzAB#v=onepage&q=ducie%20perseverando&f=false.

193 "it's this: *perseverando*": Dated January 16, 1833. CFL IV, 1092. Original French: "Travaillez. Vous avez ce qu'il faut pour réussir; travaillez. Ne vous découragez et ne vous lassez pas. Savez-vous le secret de tout succès dans ce monde quand on est fort, le voici: *perseverando*."

194 "You know my motto: *perseverando*": Dated April 14, 1852. CFL VIII, 995. Original French: "Maintenant, prends-moi ton idée à deux mains, et ne la lâche pas. Tu sais ma devise: *perseverando*."

195 "life's experiences and ordeals": From Charles Hugo, *Chez Victor Hugo*. CFL XII, 1577-78. Cited by Brière, "Hauteville House," 2. Original French: "Victor Hugo a semé dans sa maison les maximes qui résument l'expérience et les épreuves de sa vie."

196 "on my apartment door": From Hugo's Guernsey Agenda note dated August 29, 1859. Cited by Hovasse, *Victor Hugo: Pendant l'exil I*, 563 and in CFL X, 1490. Original French: "J'ai tracé et Mauger a doré sur la porte de mon appartement l'inscription PERGE — SURGE." Striking photos of Hauteville House by Jean Baptiste Hugo are in *Hauteville House: Victor Hugo décorateur*, and other photos are available at http://www.hautevillehouse.com/.

197 "AD AUGUSTA PER ANGUSTA": This inscription was carved by Mauger in 1859 (Grossiord, *Hauteville House*, 24). See also Brière, "Hauteville House," 5. "AD AUGUSTA PER ANGUSTA" is also the password in Hugo's first theatrical hit, the play that ushered in French Romanticism, *Hernani* (IV, 3).

198 "A superb flame . . . we achieve suffering—and triumph": From *Les Travailleurs de la mer* (II, 2, 4). Original French: "Flamme superbe, la volonté visible. L'œil de l'homme est ainsi fait qu'on y aperçoit sa vertu. Notre prunelle dit quelle quantité d'homme il y a en nous. . . . Les petites consciences clignent de l'œil, les grandes jettent des éclairs. Si rien ne brille sous la paupière, c'est que rien ne pense dans le cerveau, c'est que rien n'aime dans le cœur. Celui qui aime veut, et celui qui veut éclaire et éclate. La résolution met le feu au regard; feu admirable qui se compose de la combustion des pensées timides. / Les opiniâtres sont les sublimes. . . . Presque tout le secret des grands cœurs est dans ce mot: *Perseverando*. La persévérance est au courage ce que la roue est au levier; c'est le renouvellement perpétuel du point d'appui. Que le but soit sur la terre ou au ciel, aller au but, tout est là; . . . Ne pas laisser discuter sa conscience ni désarmer sa volonté, c'est ainsi qu'on obtient la souffrance, et le triomphe."

199 "human life cannot be complete": Frankl, *Man's Search for Meaning*, 88.

200 "form part of the collective unconscious": Oxford English Dictionary definition of the Jungian concept of "archetypes."

201 "it makes the unfortunate hope too much": Lamartine, "Considérations d'un chef-d'œuvre." CFL XII, 1621. Mario Vargas Llosa deeply explores Lamartine's and Hugo's notions in *The Temptation of the Impossible*.

202 "everyone's right to be educated and vote": I am indebted to Janet Horne for details of nineteenth-century French radicalism (personal email, March 6, 2010)

203 "progress as its summit": Letter to Alphonse de Lamartine, June 24, 1862: CFL, XII, 1180. Original French: "Oui, je suis radical. . . . Oui, une société

qui admit la misère, oui, une religion qui admet l'enfer, oui, une humanité
qui admet la guerre, me semblent une société, une religion et une humanité
inférieures, et c'est vers la société d'en haut, vers l'humanité d'en haut et vers
la religion d'en haut que je tends: société sans roi, humanité sans frontières,
religion sans livre. . . . Le but est éloigné. Est-ce une raison pour ne pas
y marcher? . . . Oui, autant qu'il est permis à l'homme de vouloir, je veux
détruire la fatalité humaine; je condamne l'esclavage, je chasse la misère,
j'enseigne l'ignorance, je traite la maladie, j'éclaire la nuit, je hais la haine. /
Voilà ce que je suis, et voilà pourquoi j'ai fait *les Misérables*. / Dans ma pensée,
les Misérables ne sont autre chose qu'un livre ayant la fraternité pour base et le
progrès pour cime."

**Appendix A | Time Line of Hugo's Life, Works, French History, and *Les
Misérables* Events**

204 This time line draws on these sources: the "Chronologie" of the Groupe
Hugo: http://groupugo.div.jussieu.fr/Default_Chronologie.htm; Marseille
and Gomez, *Les Années Hugo*; Fillipetti, *Victor Hugo*; Littlewood, *Timeline
History of France*; Barnett, ed., *Victor Hugo on Things That Matter*; Hugo's
works at Wikisource online: http://fr.wikisource.org/wiki/Victor_Hugo;
Encyclopaedia Britannica: https://www.britannica.com; Montel, ed., *Les
Misérables*. I am grateful to Robert F. Cook for his help in creating this
document. Any errors here are, of course, mine.

BIBLIOGRAPHY

References to Victor Hugo's works come primarily from the two latest editions of his complete works. Here are the abbreviations you will see and the reasons for using each of those editions:

"Laffont" refers to this edition:

Hugo, Victor. *Oeuvres complètes*. Edited by Jacques Seebacher and Guy Rosa. 15 volumes. Paris: Éditions Robert Laffont, collection "Bouquins," 1985-90; 2002.

Since the Laffont edition is the more recent and more nearly accurate edition of Victor Hugo's complete works, I cite from it, rather than the Club Français du Livre (CFL) edition, except when the cited text appears only in the CFL edition. Hugo scholars commonly refer to this as the "Laffont" or "Bouquin" edition. The volumes in this edition are identified by name rather than by volume number. So, for example, the citation "Laffont, *Océan*, 275" refers to page 275 of the volume entitled "*Océan*." And "Laffont, *Poésie* III, 369" refers to page 369 of the third volume of the four volumes of poetry in the series.

"CFL" refers to this edition:

Hugo, Victor. *Oeuvres complètes*. Edition chronologique sous la direction de Jean Massin. 18 volumes. Paris: Club Français de Livre, 1967-70.

This edition, the most complete, includes in chronological order all Hugo's literary and political works (including unpublished material and drafts), many of his letters and important letters to him, and black-and-white samples of his artwork. Organized chronologically and including a highly detailed time line in each volume, this edition is helpful in placing Hugo's work in personal and historical context. It includes extensive, detailed notes by Hugo scholars but, unfortunately, also a significant number of errors. The volumes in this edition are identified by number. So, for example, the citation "CFL XIII: 6, n. 1" refers to note number one on page six of the thirteenth volume (which covers the dates 1865-1867).

Albouy, Pierre, ed. Notes for Victor Hugo, *Les Contemplations*. Paris: Gallimard, 1967, 1973.

Badinter, Robert. "Badinter Outlines Victor Hugo's Opposition to the Death Penalty," *The Hoya*. Lecture at "Victor Hugo and the Death Penalty," Georgetown University, Washington, DC, September 20, 2002. http://www.thehoya.com/badinter-outlines-victor-hugos-opposition-to-the-death-penalty/.

———. "Victor Hugo contre la peine de mort." Oral statement excerpted from "Victor Hugo, écriture et politique," SCÉRÉN/CNDP, 1981. Video and audio available at https://www.reseau-canope.fr/tdc/tous-les-numeros/

crime-et-chatiment/videos/article/victor-hugo-contre-la-peine-de-mort
-par-robert-badinter.html.

Barnett, Marva, ed. *Victor Hugo on Things That Matter*. New Haven, CT:
Yale University Press, 2010.

Beauhaire, Matthieu, Mathilde Béjanin and Hubert Naudeix. *L'Éléphant de Napoléon*. Arles: Éditions Honoré Clair, 2014.

Behr, Edward. *The Complete Book of* Les Misérables. New York: Arcade, 1989.
Republished with slight changes as Les Misérables: *History in the Making*.
New York: Arcade, 1996.

Bénichou, Paul. *Les Mages romantiques*. In *Romantismes français* II, pp. 988-1474.
Paris: Gallimard, 2004.

———. *Le Sacre de l'écrivain, 1750-1830*. In *Romantismes français* I, pp. 19-441.
Paris: Gallimard, 2004.

Benoît-Lévy, Edmond. Les Misérables *de Victor Hugo*. Paris: Edgar Malfère, 1929.

Berke, Jeremy and Skye Gould. "Illinois just became the first state to legalize
marijuana sales through the legislature — here are all the states where
marijuana is legal." *Business Insider*, June 25, 2019. https://www.businessinsider.
com/legal-marijuana-states-2018-1.

Blémont, Émile, ed. *Le Livre d'or de Victor Hugo*. Paris: Librairie artistique,
H. Launette, 1883. https://books.google.com/books?id=7vm_
wSUZXXcC&pg=PA210&lpg=PA210&dq=%C3%A9dition-des
-volontaires+les-mis%C3%A9rables&source=bl&ots=mp9iFAQyCx&sig
=EZdx3inkZm7FHHWvAaO6SsmduXM&hl=en&sa=X&ved
=0ahUKEwjD7Nf2odnKAhXKJB4KHU2kAiwQ6AEIHDAA#v
=onepage&q=%C3%A9dition-des-volontaires%20les-mis%C3%A9rables
&f=false.

Boivin, Patrice, ed. *Le Livre des tables. Les séances spirites de Jersey*. Paris: Gallimard,
2014.

Bonaparte, Napoléon-Louis. *Extinction du paupérisme*. Paris: Pagnerre, 1844. http://
gallica.bnf.fr/ark:/12148/bpt6k9628969d/f1.image.

Brière, Chantal. "Hauteville House ou 'le goût des inscriptions.'" *L'œil de Victor Hugo*.
Actes du colloque, 19-21 septembre 2002. Paris: Éditions des Cendres /
Musée d'Orsay, 2004. http://groupugo.div.jussieu.fr/Groupugo/Textes_et
_documents/Briere_Hauteville%20House.pdf.

Brombert, Victor. *Victor Hugo and the Visionary Novel*. Cambridge, MA: Harvard
University Press, 1984.

Brooks, David. "What Makes Us All Radically Equal." *The New York Times*, October
10, 2019. https://www.nytimes.com/2019/10/10/opinion/frederick
-douglass-detroit.html?searchResultPosition=3.

Chambers, John. *Conversations with Eternity: The Forgotten Masterpiece of Victor Hugo*. Boca Raton, FL: New Paradigm Books, 1998.

Charles, Corinne. *Victor Hugo, visions d'intérieurs, du meuble au décor / Interior Visions, from Furniture to Decoration*. Translations by John Zeimbekis. Paris:
Paris Musées, 2003.

Cox, Martin. *Stage by Stage: The Making of* Les Mis. Telstart Independent
 Programmes, 1988. VHS. Also available on the DVD *Les Misérables,*
 10th Anniversary Concert, reissued by the BBC in 2012.

d'Aunet, Léonie. *Voyage d'une femme à Spitzberg.* Paris: Hachette, 1875. http://
 books.google.fr/books?id=-GZKAAAAYAAJ&printsec=frontcover&dq
 =L%C3%A9onie+d%27Aunet&source=bl&ots=zmBLvRiik7&sig
 =lqzqdM2Hy6mbGiRgXuBQa7uEns&hl=fr&sa=X&ei
 =2nMLUN3kFaTk0QGttO3zAw&ved=0CDgQ6AEwAA#v=onepage
 &q=L%C3%A9onie%20d%27Aunet&f=false

de Botton, Alain. "Atheism 2.0." TEDGlobal talk, July 2011. https://www.ted.com/
 talks/alain_de_botton_atheism_2_0.

Denby, David. "There's Still Hope For People Who Love 'Les Mis.'" *The New Yorker,*
 January 3, 2013. http://www.newyorker.com/culture/culture-desk/theres
 -still-hope-for-people-who-love-les-mis.

Denis, Daphnée. "Why Hugo Chávez Loved *Les Misérables.*" https://slate.com/,
 March 6, 2013. http://www.slate.com/blogs/browbeat/2013/03/06/hugo
 _ch_vez_loved_les_mis_rables_why.html.

Dewan, Shaila and Carl Hulse. "Republicans and Democrats Cannot Agree
 on Absolutely Anything. Except This." *The New York Times,* November 14,
 2018. https://www.nytimes.com/2018/11/14/us/prison-reform-bill
 -republicans-democrats.html

Drouet, Juliette. *Juliette Drouet: Souvenirs 1843-1854.* Edited by Gérard Pouchain.
 Paris: Des femmes-Antoinette Fouque, 2006.

Drouet, Juliette; translated by Victoria Tietze Larson. *My Beloved Toto: Letters from*
 Juliette Drouet to Victor Hugo, 1833-1882. French edition edited and annotated
 by Evelyn Blewer, with a preface by Jean Gaudon. Albany, NY: State University
 of New York Press, 2005.

Druckerman, Pamela. *Lust in Translation: The Rules of Infidelity from Tokyo to*
 Tennessee. New York: Penguin, 2007.

Fernandez, Jay A. "The Spoils: 'Les Miserables' Director Tom Hooper Answers His
 Critics." *IndieWire,* December 26, 2012. http://www.indiewire.com/article/
 les-miserables-director-tom-hooper-the-one-q-a-you-have-to-read?page=1
 #articleHeaderPanel.

Fessler, Pam. "U.S. Census Bureau Reports Poverty Rate Down, But Millions
 Still Poor." NPR, September 10, 2019. https://www.npr.org/2019/09/10/
 759512938/u-s-census-bureau-reports-poverty-rate-down-but-millions
 -still-poor

Fillipetti, Sandrine. *Victor Hugo.* Paris: Éditions Gallimard, 2011.

Fish, Stanley. "'Les Misérables' and Irony." *The New York Times,* Opinionator section,
 January 28, 2013. http://opinionator.blogs.nytimes.com/2013/01/28/
 les-miserables-and-irony/?_r=0.

Fizaine, Jean-Claude. "L'Intertexte biblique dans quelques romans de Victor Hugo."
 Lecture, colloquium "L'intertexte biblique dans le roman du XIXe siècle,"
 Toulouse, France, January 14-15, 2010. http://groupugo.div.jussieu.fr/

Groupugo/Textes_et_documents/Fizaine_L'intertexte%20biblique %20dansles%20romans%20de%20Hugo.pdf.

Flood, Gavin. *An Introduction to Hinduism*. Cambridge: Cambridge University Press, 1996.

Frankl, Viktor. *Man's Search for Meaning*. New York: Washington Square Press, 1985. (First Austrian publication, 1946. First English publication, Boston, MA: Beacon Press, 1959.)

Gandhi, Mahatma. *The Gandhi Reader: A Sourcebook of His Life and Writings*. Edited by Homer A. Jack. Revised ed. New York: Grove Press, 1994.

Georgel, Pierre, ed. *La Gloire de Victor Hugo*. Paris: Éditions de la Réunion des musées nationaux, 1985. Published in conjunction with the exhibition "La gloire de Victor Hugo" shown at the Galéries nationales du Grand Palais, Paris, October 1, 1985-January 6, 1986.

Gibson, Lydialyle. "Color and Incarceration." *Harvard Magazine*, September-October 2019. https://www.harvardmagazine.com/2019/09/elizabeth-hinton.

Gille, Vincent. "Victor Hugo and *Les Misérables*: The Political and Social Setting." In *Victor Hugo: Les Misérables—from Page to Stage*, ed. Tim Fisher and Anaïs Lellouche, 38-50. Melbourne: State Library of Victoria, 2014.

Godo, Emmanuel. *Victor Hugo et Dieu: Bibliographie d'une âme*. Paris: Éditions du Cerf, 2001.

Gomis, Jean-Marc. *Victor Hugo devant l'objectif*. Paris: L'Harmattan, 2018.

Gould, Jon B., and Richard A. Leo. "One Hundred Years Later: Wrongful Convictions After a Century of Research." *The Journal of Criminal Law and Criminology* 100, no. 3 [Centennial Symposium: A Century of Criminal Justice] (Summer 2010): 825-868.

Grossiord, Sophie. *Hauteville House: General Guide*. Paris: Paris Musées, 1994.
———. *Victor Hugo: "Et s'il n'en reste qu'un . . .".* Paris: Gallimard/Paris Musées, 1998.

Grossman, Kathryn M. *Les Miserables: Conversion, Revolution, Redemption*. Twayne's Masterwork Series No. 160. New York: Twayne, 1996.
———, and Bradley Stephens, eds. Les Misérables *and Its Afterlives: Between Page, Stage, and Screen*. Surrey, England: Ashgate Publishing Ltd., 2015.

Hanson, Rick, with Forrest Hanson. *Resilient: How to Grow an Unshakable Core of Calm, Strength, and Happiness*. New York: Harmony Books, 2018.

Hausman, Sandy. "Life Without Parole: A Five-Part Series," WVTF, May 2, 2016. http://wvtf.org/post/life-without-parole-five-part-series.

Heilbrun, Françoise and Danielle Molinari, eds. *En collaboration avec le soleil: Victor Hugo, photographies de l'exil*. Paris: Paris Musées, 1998. Published in conjunction with the exhibition "En collaboration avec le soleil: Victor Hugo, photographies de l'exil" shown at the Musée d'Orsay and the Maison de Victor Hugo, October 27, 1998-January 24, 1999.

Hervé-Montel, Caroline, ed. Les Misérables *de Victor Hugo*. Paris: Petits Classiques Larousse, 2004.

Hovasse, Jean-Marc. "L'évêque des *Misérables*, 9 juin 1862." In *Autour de Victor Hugo: Donation Norbert Ducrot-Granderye*, 63-65. Edited by Jean-Marc Hovasse.

Besançon: Maison Victor Hugo, 2015. Published in conjunction with the exhibition "Autour de Victor Hugo: Donation Norbert Ducrot-Granderye" shown at the Musée du Temps and Maison Victor Hugo, Besançon, France, September 20, 2014-January 4, 2015.

———. *Victor Hugo I: Avant l'exil (1802-1851)*. Paris: Fayard, 2001.

———. *Victor Hugo II: Pendant l'exil I (1851-1864)*. Paris: Fayard, 2008.

———. "Victor Hugo méditerranéen." Invited lecture at the Centre Universitaire Méditerranéen (CUM), Nice, June 2, 2015.

Hugo, Adèle. *Le Journal d'Adèle Hugo, 1852-55*. Edited with notes by Frances Vernor Guille (Vol. 4 co-edited by Jean-Marc Hovasse). 4 vols. Paris: Lettres Modernes Minard, 1968-2002.

[Hugo, Charles]. *Chez Victor Hugo, par un passant*. Paris: Cadart & Luquet, Paris, 1864. The full text of this booklet, which was published anonymously, appears in CFL XII: 1573-88.

Hugo, Marie, Jean Baptiste Hugo, and Laura Hugo. *Hauteville House: Victor Hugo décorateur*. Paris: Paris Musées, 2016.

Hugo, Victor. *Choses vues: Souvenirs, journaux, cahiers*. Edited by Hubert Juin. 4 vols. Paris: Gallimard, 1972.

———. *Les Contemplations*. Edited by Pierre Albouy. Preface by Léon-Paul Fargue. Paris: Gallimard, 1967, 1973.

———. *Journal de ce que j'apprends chaque jour (juillet 1846-février 1848)*. Edited by René Journet and Guy Robert. Paris: Flammarion, 1965.

———. *Lettres de Victor Hugo à Léonie Biard*. Edited by Jean Gaudon. [Paris]: Mille et une nuits, département de la Libraire Arthème Fayard, 2007.

———. *Oeuvres complètes*. Edited by Jacques Seebacher and Guy Rosa. 15 vols. Paris: Robert Laffont, collection "Bouquins," 1985-90. Cited in this book as "Laffont."

———. *Oeuvres complètes: Édition chronologique*. Edited by Jean Massin. 18 vols. Paris: Club Français de Livre, 1967-70. Cited in this book as "CFL."

Jackman, Hugh. Interview. "Great Performances: Historic Acts," *Time*, February 18, 2013: 53.

———. "Interview with Hugh Jackman." By Dave Karger. Fandango's *The Front-runners*, December 20, 2012. https://www.youtube.com/watch?v=TKf7OF4vpUg.

Jefferson, Thomas. *The Jefferson Bible: The Life and Morals of Jesus of Nazareth Extracted Textually from the Gospels in Greek, Latin, French & English*. Smithsonian Edition, with essays by Harry R. Rubenstein, Barbara Clark Smith and Janice Stagnitto Ellis. Washington, DC: Smithsonian Books, 2011.

Karp, Carole. "Victor Hugo in Russia." *Comparative Literature Studies* 14, no. 4 (December, 1977): 321-327.

King, Jr., Martin Luther. "Remaining Awake through a Great Revolution" (Sermon delivered on Passion Sunday, March 31, 1968). In *The Essential Writings and Speeches of Martin Luther King, Jr*. Cited at https://harpers.org/blog/2008/01/king-on-the-importance-of-conscience-in-action/).

Kretzmer, Herbert. "Interview with Lyricist Herbert Kretzmer." By Al Sheahen. *The Barricade*, 1998: 3-7.

Kristof, Nicholas. "Three TVs and No Food: Growing up Poor in America."
    The New York Times, October 10, 2016. http://www.nytimes.com/2016/
    10/30/opinion/sunday/3-tvs-and-no-food-growing-up-poor-in-america
    .html?emc=edit_th_20161030&nl=todaysheadlines&nlid=76373914&_r=0.
Laforgue, Pierre. "La symbolisation de l'histoire chez Hugo, l'exemple de Cosette et
    de Gavroche." Talk given to the Groupe Hugo, Paris, France, November 18,
    1989. http://groupugo.div.jussieu.fr/Groupugo/89-11-18laforgue.htm.
Laiter, Joël. *Victor Hugo, l'exil: L'Archipel de la Manche*. Paris: Hazan, 2001.
Lamartine, Alphonse de. "Considérations d'un chef-d'œuvre, ou le danger du génie:
    Les Misérables de Victor Hugo." Cours familier de littérature, entretiens 83, 84,
    85, 86 et 87. In CFL XII: 1607-21.
Lane, Anthony. "Love Hurts: 'Les Misérables,' 'Django Unchained,' and 'Amour.'"
    The New Yorker, January 7, 2013. http://www.newyorker.com/magazine/
    2013/01/07/love-hurts-2.
Laster, Arnaud. *Pleins feux sur Victor Hugo*. Paris: Comédie-Française, 1981.
Laurent, Franck. "Victor Hugo, la République et la Commune." In *". . . Avoir pour
    patrie le monde et pour nation l'humanité": Actualité[s] de Victor Hugo*, 207-36.
    Edited by Frank Wilhelm. Paris: Maisonneuve et Larose, 2005.
Leuilliot, Bernard. "Philosophie(s): commencement d'un livre." In *Lire* les Misérables,
    59-75. Edited by Anne Ubersfeld and Guy Rosa. Paris: José Corti, 1985.
Lipka, Michael. "10 facts about religion in America." *Fact Tank*, Pew Research
    Center, May 12, 2015. http://www.pewresearch.org/fact-tank/2015/08/27/
    10-facts-about-religion-in-america/.
Littlewood, Ian. *The Timeline History of France*. New York: Barnes and Noble,
    2002, 2005.
Maladain, Pierre. "La réception des *Misérables* ou 'Un lieu où des convictions sont en
    train de se former.'" *Revue d'histoire littéraire de la France* 86, no. 6, Victor Hugo
    (November-December 1986): 1065-1079.
Mandela, Nelson. *Long Walk to Freedom: The Autobiography of Nelson Mandela*.
    New York: Little, Brown, 1994.
———. "No Easy Walk to Freedom." Presidential address to the ANC [African
    National Congress] (Transvaal division) Conference, September 21, 1953.
    http://www.columbia.edu/itc/history/mann/w3005/mandela01.html.
Marseille, Jacques, in collaboration with Françoise Gomez. *Les Années Hugo*. Paris:
    Larousse/VUEF, 2002.
Marx, Karl. "The Civil War in France: Address of the General Council of the
    International Working-Men's Association." London, 1871.
Masur, Louis. "In Camp, Reading 'Les Miserables,'" *The New York Times*, February 9,
    2013, "The Opinion Pages." https://opinionator.blogs.nytimes.com/2013/02/
    09/in-camp-reading-les-miserables/.
McGonigal, Kelly. *The Upside of Stress: Why Stress Is Good for You, and How to Get
    Good at It*. New York: Avery, 2015.
Merriam-Webster Dictionary Online. https://www.merriam-webster.com/.
"*Les Misérables*: Page to Stage to Screen." Screentalk organized by the Society of
    Friends of Victor Hugo (*Société des amis de Victor Hugo*) in conjunction with

Ciné Lumière as part of the international "Victor Hugo et Égaux" Festival 2013. January 26, 2013. With William Nicholson, Hadley Fraser, and Bradley Stephens; moderated by Dave Calhoun. http://www.youtube.com/watch?v=rEtTaSgs2F4.

Modern History Sourcebook: Index librorum prohibitorum, 1557-1966. Fordham University. http://www.fordham.edu/halsall/mod/indexlibrorum.asp.

Moore, Olin H. "Some Translations of *Les Misérables.*" *Modern Language Notes* 74, no. 3 (March 1959): 240-46.

Mulholland, Edward. "Pope Francis and 'Les Mis': Fiction Meets Fact." *National Catholic Register*, March 26, 2013. http://www.ncregister.com/blog/edward-mulholland/pope-francis-and-les-mis-fiction-meets-fact.

Naugrette, Florence. "Victor Hugo et la question sociale de l'enfance." *Normandie impressionniste, Magazine éphémère* n° 2 (May 2013): 2-6.

Neusner, Jacob, and Bruce Chilton, eds. *Altruism in World* Religions. Washington, DC: Georgetown University Press, 2005.

Nicolais, Mario. "Rene Lima-Marin is Colorado's own Jean Valjean." *The Denver Post*, May 18, 2017. http://www.denverpost.com/2017/05/18/rene-lima-marin -colorados-own-jean-valjean/.

Nightingale, Benedict. "Stage View: In London, a Musical 'Miserables.'" *The New York Times*, October 27, 1985, late city final edition, section 2, Arts and Leisure Desk. https://www.nytimes.com/1985/10/27/theater/stage-view-in-london-a -musical-miserables.html.

———, and Martyn Palmer. *Les Misérables: From Stage to Screen.* Milwaukee, WI: Applause Theatre & Cinema Books, 2013.

Oxford Encyclopedic English Dictionary, 3rd ed. New York: Oxford University Press, 1996. Online: http://www.oed.com/.

Pew Research Center, Religion and Public Life Report. "In U.S., Decline of Christianity Continues at Rapid Pace," October 17, 2019. https://www.pewforum.org/2019/10/17/in-u-s-decline-of-christianity-continues-at-rapid-pace/.

Pfaff, John F. *Locked In: The True Causes of Mass Incarceration—and How to Achieve Real Reform.* New York: Basic Books, 2017.

Pickett, La Salle Corbell. *Pickett and His Men.* 2nd ed. Atlanta: Foote & Davies, 1900.

Pouchain, Gérard. *Promenades dans l'Archipel de la Manche avec un guide nommé Victor Hugo.* Condé-sur-Noireau, France: Éditions Charles Corlet, 1985.

———, and Robert Sabourin. *Juliette Drouet, ou la dépaysée.* Paris: Fayard, 1992.

Raser, Timothy. "Victor Hugo." In *Dictionary of Literary Biography: Nineteenth-Century French Fiction Writers: Romanticism and Realism, 1800-1860.* Edited by Catherine Savage Brosman: 119: 164-92. Detroit, London: Gale Research Inc., 1992.

Ravitz, Jessica. "Indian Awakenings: How a Holy Place and Its People Helped a Western Woman Find Wholeness." CNN, June 2014. http://www.cnn.com/interactive/2014/06/world/rishikesh/.

Rosa, Guy. "Commentaires." In Victor Hugo, *Le Dernier Jour d'un condamné suivi de Claude Gueux et de l'Affaire Tapner.* Paris: Librairie Générale Française, 1989.

211

———, ed. *Les Misérables: édition critique et génétique*. Paris: Université Paris-Diderot and Guy Rosa, n.d. http://groupugo.div.jussieu.fr/Miserables/Default.htm

———, ed. Préface and notes for Victor Hugo, *Les Misérables*. 2 vols. Paris: Librairie Générale Française, Livre de poche, 1998.

Sandberg, Sheryl, and Adam Grant. *Option B: Facing Adversity, Building Resilience, and Finding Joy*. New York: Knopf, 2017.

Saurat, Denis. *La Religion de Victor Hugo*. Paris: Librairie Hachette, 1929.

Seligman, Martin E. P. *Learned Optimism: How to Change Your Mind and Your Life*. New York: Pocket Books, 1991.

Senghor, Shaka. *Writing My Wrongs: Life, Death, and Redemption in an American Prison*. New York: Convergent Books, 2016. http://www.shakasenghor.com/.

Shapiro, Fred R. "Who Wrote the Serenity Prayer?" *The Chronicle Review*, April 28, 2014. https://www.chronicle.com/article/Who-Wrote-the-Serenity -Prayer-/146159.

Sinclair, Upton, ed. *The Cry for Justice: An Anthology of the Literature of Social Protest*. Philadelphia: John C. Winston Co., [1915].

Skinner, R. G., ed. and trans. *God and the The End of Satan / Dieu et la Fin de Satan by Victor Hugo. Selections in a Bilingual Edition*. Chicago: Swan Isle Press, 2014.

Snowden, Edward. "Biography: Snowden's Leaks." https://www.biography.com/ people/edward-snowden-21262897.

Stephens, Bradley. *Victor Hugo*. London: Reaktion Books, 2019.

Sternfeld, Jessica. *The Megamusical*. Bloomington and Indianapolis: Indiana University Press, 2006.

Stevenson, Bryan. *Just Mercy: A Story of Justice and Redemption*. New York: Spiegel & Grau, 2014.

Stiles, Robert. *Four Years Under Marse Robert*. 3rd ed. New York & Washington: Neale Publishing Co., 1904.

The Story of Adele H. VHS tape. Directed by François Truffaut. Les Films Du Carrosse, 1975; MGM/UA Home Video, 1991. https://en.wikipedia.org/ wiki/The_Story_of_Adele_H.

Tersen, Émile. "Chronologie des *Misérables*," *Europe* (février-mars 1962) (40e Année), no. 394-395: 206-09.

Trésor de la langue française dictionary. http://atilf.atilf.fr.

Tsai, Tyjen, and Paola Scommegna. "U.S. Has World's Highest Incarceration Rate." Population Reference Bureau, August 10, 2012. http://www.prb.org/ Publications/Articles/2012/us-incarceration.aspx.

Tutu, Desmond. "Foreword," *Commission on Truth and Reconciliation Report*," October 29, 1998. Excerpts published in "Documents on Democracy," *Journal of Democracy* 10, no. 1 (1999): 177-181. https://muse.jhu.edu/login?auth =0&type=summary&url=/journals/journal_of_democracy/v010/10.1docs _on_democracy.html.

———. "Let South Africa Show the World How to Forgive," *Knowledge of Reality*, Issue 19. http://www.sol.com.au/kor/19_03.htm.

Ubersfeld, Anne, and Guy Rosa, eds. *Lire* les Misérables. Paris: Libraire José Corti, 1985.

212

Vance, J. D. *Hillbilly Elegy: A Memoir of a Family and Culture in Crisis*. New York: HarperCollins, 2016.

Vargas Llosa, Mario. *The Temptation of the Impossible: Victor Hugo and Les Misérables*. Translated by John King. Princeton and Oxford: Princeton University Press, 2007.

Venkatesh, Suman. *Victor Hugo et la philosophie indienne: Influences et ressemblances*. Paris: Éditions Banyan, 2020.

Vermette, Margaret. *The Musical World of Boublil and Schönberg: The Creators of Les Misérables, Miss Saigon, Martin Guerre, and The Pirate Queen*. New York: Applause Theatre and Cinema Books, 2006.

Vines, Stephen. "On whistleblowing, should you let your conscience be your guide?" In "The View," *South China Morning Post*, August 24, 2016. http://www.scmp .com/business/article/2008204/whistleblowing-should-you-let-your -your-conscience-be-your-guide.

Von Drehle, David, with Ja Newton-Small and Maya Rhodan. "How Do You Forgive a Murder?" *Time*, November 23, 2015: 42-68. http://time.com/ time-magazine-charleston-shooting-cover-story/.

Whitfield, Sarah. *Boublil and Schönberg's Les Misérables*. London and New York: Routledge, 2019.

Winock, Michel. *Le Monde selon Victor Hugo: Pensées, combats, confidences, opinions de l'homme-siècle*. Paris: Éditions Tallandier, 2018.

———. *Victor Hugo dans l'arène politique*. Paris: Bayard, 2005.

———. *Les Voix de la liberté: les écrivains engagés au XIXe siècle*. Paris: Éditions du Seuil, 2001.

Worthington, Jr., Everett L. "The New Science of Forgiveness," *Greater Good Magazine*, "Education," September 1, 2004. https://greatergood.berkeley.edu/ article/item/the_new_science_of_forgiveness.

Yoffe, Emily. "Innocence Is Irrelevant," *The Atlantic Monthly*, September 2017. https://www.theatlantic.com/magazine/archive/2017/09/innocence-is-irrelevant/534171/.

Yousafzai, Malala, with Christina Lamb. *I Am Malala: The Girl Who Stood up for Education and Was Shot by the Taliban*. New York: Little, Brown & Co., 2013.

Swan Isle Press is a not-for-profit literary and
academic publisher of fiction, nonfiction, and poetry.

For information on books of related interest
or for a catalog of new publications contact:
https://www.press.uchicago.edu/ucp/books/
publisher/pu3430685_3430697.html

To Love Is to Act
Designed by Marianne Jankowski
Typeset in Adobe Jenson Pro
Printed on 55# Natural Offset Antique